W9-AKT-567

Stories of the Hindus

STORIES OF THE HINDUS

AN INTRODUCTION
THROUGH TEXTS AND
INTERPRETATION

by JAMES A. KIRK

The Macmillan Company • *New York, New York*

Collier-Macmillan Limited • *London*

TO LOIS, ROBERT, ALETHA AND ANN

The Macmillan Company
866 Third Avenue, New York, N.Y. 10022
Collier-Macmillan Canada Ltd., Toronto, Ontario

Library of Congress Catalog Card Number: 72-77651

First Macmillan Paperbacks Edition 1972

Printed in the United States of America

Bharatiya Vidya Bhavan, Bombay, for *Stories from Indian Classics,* translated by P. Sankaranarayanan (pp. 93-99; 135-139); and for *The Ramayana,* by C. Rajagopalachari (pp. 15-16).

Sankar Bhattacharya, Punthi Pustak, Calcutta, for various selections from their 1961 reprint of *The Viṣṇu Purāṇa,* by H. H. Wilson.

University of Chicago Press, Chicago, for "The City of Gold," from *Tales of Ancient India,* translated by J. A. B. van Buitenen, 1959 (pp. 79-101); and for "The Lion Makers," from *The Panchatantra,* translated by Arthur W. Ryder, 1925 (pp. 442-444).

The Clarendon Press, Oxford, for *The Tiruvaçagam,* by G. U. Pope (pp. 111-113, 118, 141-145; Appendix, pp. xxxviii-xlvi).

Thomas Y. Crowell Co., New York, for adaptations from *Asiatic Mythology,* article by H. de Wilman-Grabowska (pp. 125-129).

E. P. Dutton Company, New York, for quotations from *The Ramayana: Condensed into English Verse,* by Romesh C. Dutt, 1911.

Macmillan and Company, London and Basingstoke, for "Snatched from Death," from *Sacred Tales of India,* by Dwijendra Nath Neogi, 1919 (pp. 14-21).

V. K. Ramanujachari, Kumbakonam, Madras, for quotations and adaptations from *Sribhagavatam: Parts I to IX and XII,* 1933; and *Sribhagavatam: Part X,* 1934.

CONTENTS

PART III   STORIES OF THE GODS

PREFACE

THIS BOOK IS the product of a curious irony and a fond hope. The irony arises with the awareness that the serious study of other men's religion (or of one's own, for that matter) is never really an easy process. Understanding religion demands a combination of critical, philosophical subtlety and an outreaching empathy and openmindedness which are hard to balance. It demands that we become familiar with things obscure and remote, and that we re-examine the familiar to find concealed inner meanings. Hinduism fits all the requirements for a very difficult religion. In the light of this it is remarkable that in India even slightly educated villagers have so little trouble practicing what learned scholars have such difficulty explaining. Of course, part of the irony grows from the fact that the religious practice of the villager is only a small part of what the scholar seeks to comprehend, but the point remains that if we would introduce the study of religion in simpler forms, there might be more success in understanding it. We would then be prepared to move beyond the village level, to the *ashramas* of holy men, the discussions of priests and pundits, the conversation of highly literate and well-trained laymen and teachers of the faith. One way to start with simpler forms has been to start with the earlier forms, but in India this is just not so. Early Hinduism or Brahmanism is at least as difficult to understand as the later religion. This book grows from the hope that

vii

in following the ways people naturally learn we may find an effective strategy for an introduction to Hinduism. This is a book for adults who want to undertake a serious study of Hinduism and offers them a way to begin.

With respect to Indian culture, all of us, as beginners, are like children. We can grow into Hinduism rather easily and delightfully if we start where children start. That is what this book is intended to make possible. There is little here that will not be well known to the expert, but there are samples of the variety, the humor, the pride and enthusiasm which is the heart of Indian literature and the fun of any story. The philosophy and more mature lessons are in these stories too, as assumptions, implications, background, illustrations and underlying purposes. The commentary is designed to lift up part of this, but the reader has been left much of the joy of such discovery for himself.

There are many who have made this task possible, fun or better. I would wish especially to mention Professor and Mrs. T. K. Venkateswaran (then of Madras, South India) for their gracious help and hospitality, Professor T. M. P. Mahadevan, Director of the Center for the Advanced Study of Philosophy, University of Madras, for his assistance and profound teaching, and Dr. and Mrs. G. K. Khandige for their warm friendship and thoughtfulness. Many American friends in India helped induct us into their appreciation of the culture surrounding us, and we would especially thank Dr. and Mrs. John B. Carman and family, Dr. and Mrs. Victor Nuovo and sons and Mr. and Mrs. Walter Neevel. One always owes much to students and colleagues, but I would especially mention my appreciation for encouragement and helpful suggestions by Professor Francis Brush of Denver University and to Dr. Robert Lester and Mrs. Susan Tripp, who helped me find some important ideas. There are also those more distant colleagues one meets anew at annual meetings, who say or ask something significant and thus make thoughts move in new and better ways, people like Donald Swearer, Franklin Jocelyn, H. Daniel Smith and Charles Kennedy. Finally, there is a very special appreciation for those who made life and study in India possible, Professor Kenneth Morgan, the Fund for the Study of the Great

Religions, the Society for Religion in Higher Education, and the University of Denver.

My wife, Lois, is a librarian for children, and our children came home from India with a rich collection of the children's literature of Hindu culture. These were often the books which effectively illustrated the issues for my college classes and inducted my students, as they have inducted Hindus for generations, into the thought and life-world of that remarkable religion. Thus from her came the initial possibility and now the final proof-reading of this book. The book, and the memories and hopes which go with it, are dedicated to her and to Robert, Aletha and Ann, who first wanted to know the stories of the Hindus.

None of the people or institutions who have helped me are in any way responsible for the particular views expressed, but if there is anything useful here it is surely due to them and to unnamed others like them.

INTRODUCTION

THE MOST NATURAL WAY to understand Hinduism would be to grow up in an appropriate family in India. Religion in India is a bewildering array of values, views, practices, traditions, associations, attitudes and loyalties, but for the most part the growing child is unaware of all that. He has come a long way in the life and thought of his religion before he realizes that he has one, or that it has any kind of ideological structure. It is when the differentiation of one's ways of life and thought from those of others becomes important that the possibility arises that one already believes an ideology. When that occasion for comparison and contrast does arise, it often seems relatively easy to describe concisely the ideologies of others, but one's own views require much more elaborate descriptions and qualifications. It is natural for those outside the Hindu traditions to want a simple, straightforward and brief statement of the ideology of Hinduism. Understanding the authentic religion, however, requires a subtle kind of sensitivity and sympathy, deeper and more pervasive than ideology alone.

To the modern European or American the religious life of India is likely to be an alien spiritual universe. He does not share its tacit assumptions and values. He has not been reared to adulthood on its traditions. He is not familiar with Hinduism's innumerable variations in form and content. He has not properly celebrated the holidays, shared the joys and sorrows, dramatized the stories, participated in the rituals of home and temple, or observed the ways of the world from the standpoint of these attitudes and traditions. The alien spiritual universe, that is, any very different faith and culture, can only with some difficulty become one's familiar spiritual home, just as a foreign language can seldom fully replace one's mother tongue. This does not mean, however, that sympathetic understanding of the spiritual worlds of others is unimportant or impossible. It is possible to speak a foreign language well rather than badly. It does mean that the task of entering an alien spiritual universe requires a sympathetic exercise of imagination and outreaching interest. The stories expressive of Indian imagination may provide a useful and enchanting door into the spiritual universe of Hinduism.

THE HISTORICAL APPROACH

For the past couple of centuries the religions of Asia have been both studied and taught by Western scholars primarily according to historical methods, which have proved so fruitful in understanding our own heritage. These historical methods have made possible also comparative methods whereby one can compare various epochs, processes or interpretations. It has long been recognized, perhaps especially by the best historians of India, that historical methods encounter enormous difficulties when dealing with the heritage of India. Few documents in the Indian tradition have any adequate internal or external evidence concerning their historical circumstances or dates. Few ancient individuals can be identified clearly or separated from the everpresent shadows of myth and legend. Few ancient Indians were concerned to preserve the historical accounts which would have provided a framework for interpretation of their artifacts and literature. Immensely complex historical methods derived from philology, art criticism, cultural anthropology and archeology have had to be developed and employed. It is a testimony to the enormous devotion and skill of the early historians and their successors, both Western and Indian, that despite such difficulties a reconstruction of Indian social, political, literary and religious history has been possible, though it still is at some points rather sketchy and incomplete.

The results of this approach form the outline of many courses and texts concerned with Hinduism. In following this pattern one begins with pre-Vedic, pre-Aryan India, traces the Aryan immigrations from the north and the succeeding movements in politics and literature, especially the early *Vedas*. One then discusses the Aryan/Dravidian settlement in India and the emerging significance of the Brahmins (priests) and their literature, the *Brāhmaṇas,* followed by the turn toward reflective monism and the increasing significance of the noble, Kshatriya, class as shown in the *Upanishads* and in the great reform movements of Buddhism and Jainism. The succeeding Hindu renaissance would be developed and illustrated by the reading of the *Bhagavadgītā.* Purānic literature and popular Hinduism might be introduced, either followed or preceded by the "Six Orthodox Systems" and the major classical Hindu philosophers. In practical terms this kind of comprehensive study is available only in specialized graduate schools. The introduction to Hinduism for the American undergraduate is likely to be an abbreviation of the same basic pattern.

In terms of research and comprehensive study we must be deeply grateful for the alternative which the historical approach has offered to the sectarian and polemical styles of the Hindu groups and their missionary competitors. Our clearest and most comprehensive understanding of Hinduism has been brought to us by persons who have used one or another of the historical approaches. Our objective here, however, is somewhat different. We do not wish to propose a new research method or a variation of an old one, but to find appropriate ways to induct the interested, modern, Western inquirer into the alien spiritual universe of Hindu thought, values and sensitivities. Learning to think in Hindu ways, to see as Hindus see, to know what Hindus know is graceful and natural for the Hindu (though not always easy). For us, it is often more difficult because we start with the finished product instead of growing up into it. Our introduction is the advanced lesson of the Hindu. As a way of learning and appreciating, particularly for beginners, the historical method may create as well as solve problems. One problem is that the history of Hinduism begins with the most remote, uncertain and difficult pre-Vedic and early Vedic materials which require a very sophisticated knowledge of the culture to appreciate. Understanding the principal *Vedas* themselves is not easy. The *Upanishads* which follow are perhaps the most obscure philosophical documents which ever became a widespread religious literature. Even when their reflections are apparently simple, the more important Hindu interpretations are impossible to imagine without the personal help of a devoted and informal traditional teacher who has been convinced that you are a worthy and serious student.

A second objection arises from the fact that the historical method is essentially foreign to the material it must interpret. Hindu self-understanding does not naturally take the form of historical categories or values. The *Vedas*, the most important parts of which are expressed in the books now available, are an eternal wisdom. The fact that they have to be written at all is evidence of our degenerate condition. It is believed that they have always taught whatever interpretation is most convincing to the current interpreter, and that if there are apparent inconsistencies in the teachings this is not a fault of the text or even of interpretation, but an indication of the different ways in which the same truth may be grasped. The assumption that this is only one of myriads of worlds of past, present and future reduces the sense of the importance of our particular history with its peculiarities and incidents. Many thoughtful Hindus regard the historical method as essentially alien and largely irrelevant for the true understanding of their teachings. This view, of course, does not mean that the historical method is unable to provide a fair and judicious understanding of Hindu religion. Many groups believe that their views are not "merely historical" but are inspired by "eternal truth." Our purpose is not to judge among such claims, but to find an appropriate way in which we can begin to induct persons into the spiritual universe of Hinduism, a way which is as far as possible itself an expression of Hindu style, imagination, attitudes and interests.

THE PERSONAL-DEVELOPMENTAL MODEL

As a person grows up in India he is told stories, participates in events, sees other people and finds himself seen in terms of a specific sense of values, a Hindu point of view. Hindu children soon come to know what is expected of them and why. They learn how to live each day in the direction of the ultimate destiny which they believe is building in and through their specific acts and choices. But all of this is so natural, so matter-of-fact, that they may be unaware either that there is or that they have a "Hindu" point of view. Our approach is to seek to know some of these stories and lived events, especially the imaginary ones which contain ideals of character and heroic models, which serve as lures in the shaping of attitudes and interests, to recapitulate in a selective way the basic process of growing up in Hinduism. This is what we mean by the personal-developmental model. *Stories of the Hindus* seeks to follow in some respects the natural life processes by which Hindus come into possession of their own traditions, values and convictions. Unfortunately it is not possible to follow this model in many ways. The full complexity of Hindu life is rich with values which cannot be put into books—attitudes, emotions, celebrations, traditions, music, art, food, dress, etc. Despite these limitations, however, it is possible to combine various available materials—readings, recordings, photographs, motion pictures, art objects, etc., in order to develop a reasonably fair-minded understanding of some of the significant views, attitudes and values of the Hindu spiritual universe.

This procedure for interpretation begins with a collection of Indian literary materials. These stories contain, transmit and form the texture of tradition for India. They are not primarily important religious texts, certainly not scripture, but implicitly they employ many of the assumptions, attitudes and unsophisticated forms of the Hindu religion. One cannot treat them as serious religious arguments or objects of literal belief any more than one would verify a theological point by a quotation from Mother Goose or use a fairy tale as evidence for current Christian thinking. The stories themselves do not usually tempt one to make such ludicrous errors. Most of them have a rather ob-

vious lesson to teach even while they entertain. Generally the
stories speak for themselves, and why they are here will show
in what they have to say. Their literary history is often very
obscure and for the most part is irrelevant for our current purposes. They have been arranged here with topical interests in
view.

The available supply of stories which might induct one into
the spiritual universe of Hinduism is virtually boundless. No
serious attempt will be made to defend the present selections.
They are Indian stories available in English. They presuppose,
describe and illustrate significant Hindu themes, ideas, ideals,
traditions, values, attitudes. They have been reasonably well
known (at least regionally) in India. They are usually interesting in and of themselves to Western students. Although some of
these stories contain elements which would be offensive to contemporary Hindu opinion, they are, on the whole, representative of significant forms of Hindu reflection. They suit the purposes of the present collection by building toward an understanding of certain fundamental assumptions and views of
Hinduism.

In this anthology, Part I contains stories which portray the
assumptions and ideals of the Hindu culture in rather general
terms. The first three of these, particularly "The City of Gold,"
have been left, as nearly as the English language permits, the
way the Indian storyteller tells them—slightly archaic, filled
with digressions, rich with opportunity for the reader to use his
own imagination. For the most part the following stories have
been edited to abbreviate them and make them move toward
their main point more directly, though this diminishes their
original complexity and diversity. The stories in Part II have a
more specifically religious content, though it takes various
forms. The meditations are all popular and devotional rather
than truly philosophic or yogic. The legends and stories are
intended to show both the respect for the sincere holy man and
also the absurdity of the pseudo-holy man which are felt in Indian culture. Western students can scarcely appreciate the intensity of devotion which characterizes the Hindu saint.
Though none of these stories may be taken literally, some of

them do suggest that incredible intensity which consumes the whole being of a true and complete devotee. The stories in Part III are much more heavily edited and retold so as to get at the heart of the material. These are stories of the principal gods, Shiva and Vishnu. They include the ten main *avatāras* or descents of Vishnu, including a condensation of the *Rāmāyaṇa* and of the cycle of Krishna stories. These accounts are known in essence and sometimes in great detail by almost every Hindu, even those who cannot read. They are sung, danced, dramatized, played in movies, interpreted in the daily newspaper, depicted in sculpture and painting, and recited all over India. They ought to be read so that one sees through the story, even through the god being depicted, to that ultimate divine structure of all reality which the stories of the gods illuminate. These stories of Vishnu along with the most familiar of the Shiva stories serve as a fitting climax to a collection of the imaginative literature, and they lead naturally into the more exalted "religious" literature of India such as the *Bhagavadgītā, Upanishads* and *Vedas*.

This collection of stories presents the implicit background of Hinduism in its most natural form. Beyond this the serious student will also want to read the primary religious literature of Hinduism to provide the foreground. This will include the *Bhagavadgītā*, the *Upanishads* and the *Vedas*. Many suitable and inexpensive editions of the *Bhagavadgītā* and good collections of the *Upanishads* and selections from the *Vedas* are available. All these materials, including the present anthology, are authentic original sources of Indian culture and religious thought. They are delightful and fascinating but unsystematic and often hard to interpret. In order to provide systematic interpretation and some guidance through the labyrinth of Indian literary imagination, this text offers a commentary and outline guide concerning the central issues raised by the stories. This interpretation has little in common with conventional line-by-line commentaries, but is intended to be a selective, rather simple reflection on the implicit assumptions and meanings which the stories themselves take for granted. The marginal notes indicate the essentials of Hinduism discussed in this outline and provide a means for reference back and forth between the issues raised by the stories and the discussion of them later.

These stories come from a wide range of Indian sources and represent rather different types of materials. Their place in Indian literary history is not always clear. Some of them, in one form or another, undoubtedly have a very ancient origin. The primitive character of a few of the stories or of episodes within them will be obvious, but these traditions have probably existed orally through the larger part of their history. Not all of the stories are ancient. Most of these accounts originally had a very specific locale and use. They may have been associated with a particular sacred site or occasion. Sometimes this association is fundamental, but often the same or nearly the same story may be found with very different associations, or the same ceremony may be interpreted by different stories. Each holy place in India has its own cluster of legends which account for significant events which have happened there and thus inspire pilgrims to participate in the major festivals, and simultaneously portray fundamental Hindu values and concepts. Some of the materials in this collection are of this sort, but in some cases the specific original details have been lost or so transformed as to be unrecoverable.

We ask simply that you enjoy the stories. Avoid struggling too hard to understand or believe them—let the story tell itself. You will have to accept certain conventions, perhaps even overcome certain prejudicial interpretations of some symbols or acts, in order to appreciate the work. Let your imagination flow with the story, accepting such conventions as you have to accept to make the story interesting. These are the very implicit assumptions which later we will wish to examine in the commentary. For the moment then, listen to the story of Savitri, a patroness of stability in marriage.

PART I

HERO STORIES

THE SAVITRI CEREMONY

INTRODUCTION

SAVITRI IS NOT A GODDESS. She does not trace her lineage to any deity. She has been deified because of her eminent virtues and is worshipped in the month of May on the fourteenth day after the full moon. She is described in the *Mahābhārata* as a charming young damsel who, though a princess, voluntarily undertook a life of severe austerities in a forest. Afterwards she resumed her place in her palace and, departing from this world when the time was ripe, attained beatitude. Indian women worship her for fourteen years at a stretch, once a year. An earthen jar is placed at the foot of a banyan tree and the spirit of Savitri is supposed to animate it. Only married women perform this ceremony, and, if it is successfully performed, they never lose their husbands, even as Savitri herself did not. The story is used to interpret the ceremony.

Snatched from Death [1]

King Asvapathi of Ujjayinee belonged to the Solar race of monarchs. His vast dominions, which comprised seas and islands, had no joy for him, for though he had been married for

[1] "Snatched from Death," from *Sacred Tales of India*, translated by Dwijendra Nath Neog (London: Macmillan and Co., Ltd., 1916), pp. 14–21, from the Bengali edition of the *Mahābhārata*.

more than twenty years he and his queen had not been blessed with any children. He performed the great *Putreshti* sacrifice to the gods in hope of being blessed with a child and impatiently awaited the result. The gods seemed to listen to his prayers, for the queen conceived and in due time gave birth to a charming daughter. The King named her Savitri. As Savitri grew up, the delight of her parents, she received such education as was appropriate to her sex and rank. Soon the time came when her royal father thought of marriage for her, but he could not find an eligible youth. At last he gave her liberty to choose her own husband, and as a result she visited cities and hermitages, attended only by her maids.

On one of these trips she met a handsome youth, the son, presumably, of a hermit, and was struck with love at first sight. This was Satyaban, who in his turn was also stung by passion. But they both chose to keep their feelings to themselves. A few months later King Asvapathi, under the impression that his daughter had not yet met with anyone whom she could love, called a council of the elders of his court for consultation as to the desirability of holding a regular *svayaṁvara*, or ceremony of self-choice, to which young princes from all the states of Bharatabarsha should be invited. He felt that Savitri could not fail to find a husband worthy of her love among so many guests. These grave councillors had not been long in the council-hall before Savitri, who had guessed their purpose, came like the prudent girl she was to set them right.

"Father," said she, addressing the King, "you need not think of a *svayaṁvara*, for I am already more a married woman than a maid. Please don't be startled, my Lord. You have heard of and seen Satyaban, the son of the hermit. It is he who is the chosen companion of my life here and hereafter. It is he, father, who occupies my heart fully—there is no room for another!"

*Caste,
Wealth
and
Power*
(page 45)
Now the King and his grave councillors were in a quandary. How could a princess be married to the son of a hermit? Bred in the lap of every conceivable luxury, she could not endure the life of an ascetic. Besides, would the hermit allow his son to marry beneath his caste?

But to help them out of this difficulty, who should knock at the door just as that moment but Nārada himself, the celestial hermit, son of Brahmā, the grandsire of all the universe.

After he had been received with the customary *padya* and *arghya* (water to wash the feet and a present of honey, ghee, curd, milk, etc.) and had been conducted to a seat of deerskin with the deepest reverence such as was due to him, the question was referred to him for solution. Nārada, to whom nothing was unknown, said:

"O King, when you have heard my story you will agree that Savitri had better live single than unite herself to Satyaban. For this Satyaban is no son of a hermit: the old, blind man, his father, who wears an ascetic's garb, is none other than King Dyumatsena himself, reduced to this condition by the enemies of his house. He was met in the field, conquered, and driven from his throne and palace. Here you see him now. But what concerns you most," continued the celestial sage, "is that there is a terrible curse upon Satyaban, and he is fated to die within a year of his marriage."

Savitri shuddered involuntarily at this, but quickly regained her self-possession.

"Reverend father," she said, addressing Nārada, "if it is to be as you say, let it be. As for me, I am at this moment a widow if you resolve I am not to marry him. I cannot marry another, for that would be a sin. One can elect a husband only once, not twice. In my heart I have given myself to him. Let me also tell you that I can bear widowhood for eternity after having Satyaban as my husband for a day."

Upon this, and after some further deliberation, it was determined that Savitri should wed the beloved of her heart.

The scene now shifts to the forest—to the hermitage of Dyumatsena, where Savitri and Satyaban, who were now wedded, lived. Savitri made an exemplary wife and an affectionate daughter-in-law, in spite of having discarded every luxury and comfort to which she had been accustomed. She was the stay of her father-in-law and mother-in-law in their old age, and made Satyaban so happy that he did not feel the loss of a prospective throne. He, it may be mentioned, did not know that a heavy curse was hanging over him, and Savitri did not wish to make her husband unhappy with the foretaste of death.

Delivery of Heavenly Knowledge and Omens (page 48)

Month after month passed quickly away; and at last the time came when it lacked only a day to the date on which his doom had been foretold.

Savitri had passed the whole day in worshipping the gods as, indeed, she had done all through the year, praying to them to avert the terrible decree. When she retired to bed at night, she begged Satyaban to take her with him on the following morning on his daily excursion into the woods for fruits, roots, and sacred fuel. He wondered at her unusual request, but consented to comply with her wish.

On the following morning, the loving couple went together into the depths of the forest. Savitri followed her husband like a shadow, and when he climbed up a tree to pluck fruits, she stood beneath with her eyes fixed on him, for there was no way of knowing at what particular moment the curse, like the sword of Damocles, might fall on her dear husband's head.

Satyaban was not many minutes aloft, when he felt a severe headache. Coming hastily down and unable to support himself, he fell prone on the ground at his wife's feet. Although the shock to Savitri was a great one, it was not one for which she was altogether unprepared. "Savitri, my darling," Satyaban gasped, "I am dying. O what a pain there is in my head! Let it rest on your knees—Savitri, my darling!" The next minute all was over.

Savitri wept not. With the remains of her lord in her arms she sat there, a statue of grief, watching what might follow. It was in a happy age when wonderful things were wont to happen. No sooner had Satyaban breathed his last than the messengers of Yama, the King of the dead, came down to take their victim to his place in the other world. But the chastity that hedged in the person of Savitri was like a burning flame, and those grim messengers did not dare approach her for fear of being consumed by it. They returned to their master saying, "Lord, we cannot." Yama was astonished, but he resolved to see for himself what it all meant. So, armed with his club, robed in scarlet, and mounted on his favorite buffalo, the dread deity set off to where Savitri held her dead husband in her embrace. Yama himself felt her influence and he, too, was struck with awe. He did not, however, shrink from his duty, but gently approaching the damsel, "Daughter Savitri," said he in his

Visible Symbols of a God (page 49)

softest voice, "I am here to take your husband away: he is mine now. You, I suppose, know who I am."

"I know you by your words," she replied gently but firmly, "you are Yama. My husband may now be your property, and so will I be too: you can take him, but not without me."

"How can that be?" cried the dread visitor. "Such is not my mission. You must part with your husband, girl. The living cannot accompany the dead."

"You cannot persuade me of that," returned Savitri, holding the corpse tighter in her embrace.

Yama was struck by the devotion of the young wife, and anxious to do what he could for her, said, "Savitri, you may keep your husband's body, and as I am exceedingly pleased with you, I wish to give you anything you may wish for except one thing, that is the life of your husband."

"If you are pleased, great Lord of the Dead, and will grant me a boon, kindly let my father who has no son have one who will live to hand down his name to posterity."

The Boon and the Curse (page 50)

"It shall be so," said the other, "But go home now, for it is not well to stay here alone."

So saying, he turned his back upon her and, taking with him the soul of Satyaban, proceeded on his journey. A few minutes after, he looked back, thinking of the poor faithful wife. Lo! she was at his heels. "Where are you going?" cried he in surprise. "What good is there in following me, child? Go home!"

"Go home?" replied Savitri quietly. "Whither my lord goes I go. I have no home but where he is. O King of the Dead, you know a true wife follows her husband through life and death. A god though you are, you cannot stop me."

And Yama, who was greatly affected, said, "Savitri, ask for still another boon excepting, of course, the life of your husband, and you shall have it."

Savitri replied, "If you are pleased, dread god, let my father-in-law, King Dyumatsena, recover his lost kingdom and his sight."

"He shall," answered Yama, "and now go your way home, and let me go mine."

He held on and lessened not his pace, until out of curiosity, he turned his head once again to see if Savitri was out of sight. Savitri was still close behind him!

"Savitri, why are you following me?" exclaimed Yama, unable to suppress his surprise.

"I cannot choose but do so," was her calm reply, "You have in your possession all that I hold dear in heaven and on earth: and besides, you are so good and kind. Why should I stay behind?"

"My girl," said Yama, his heart melting with pity, "I would give you your husband back, if I could: but ask for a third boon, and if it is not the life of Satyaban, it shall be given to you."

Whereupon said Savitri with folded hands, "Great God, as you have so far granted every request of your poor supplicant, grant that I may have a hundred sons by Satyaban, each born after an interval of a hundred years!"

"It shall be so," said Yama thoughtlessly, bent only upon pleasing his fair petitioner and inducing her to leave him alone.

Then Savitri stood right across Yama's path and smilingly said, "Let me have my husband!"

"How now?" cried Yama. "You are unreasonable, child!"

"Unreasonable? Indeed I am not," answered Savitri gaily. "Consider the boon you have just granted me and say if it can be accomplished without your returning me my Satyaban."

Yama perceived the truth of what she said, and was conquered, as he had never been before; and that too by a girl! But she was strong by virtue of her undying love, her pious and self-sacrificing devotion. Yama yielded his charge not unwillingly, in that it gave the world an example to follow. Savitri returned home with her husband, rejoicing.

Her father-in-law was now no longer a hermit and her husband a hermit's son. The old man regained his sight and with it his kingdom. But the cares of a kingdom are a sore weight to one in the shady vale of life and who has, moreover, tasted the calm of a hermit's life. It was not long before he resigned his crown in favor of his son Satyaban, who mounted the throne of his fathers with Savitri, a queen who was to be forever glorious because of her undying love and chastity.

So, all you that have listened to this sacred *kathā*, cry, "Victory to Savitri," and may you all be even as she was!

THE RISHI WHO ENVIED A FISH[1]

THERE WAS ONCE A KING known as Mandhata who had many The Rishi (page 53) sons and daughters. At the same time there lived in the aquatic regions a *rishi* (*ṛṣi*) sage called Saubhari who was a great ascetic and well versed in the *Vedas*. One day he observed the King of Fish, of enormous size, swimming in the waters and diving into them just as it pleased him. The fish was surrounded by a large shoal of his offspring and descendants sporting all about him, and he appeared to be very happy in the midst of his progeny.

Saubhari saw this and his mind was filled with envy to see the fish so happy. He said to himself, "Why should I not have children and grandchildren myself? How I long for such domestic felicity! Well, I shall marry and beget sons and daughters."

He left his aquatic abode and went to King Mandhata. The king received him with reverence and gave him a seat of honor in his court. Addressing the king, the *rishi* said, "I have been an ascetic, O King, for a long time. Now I wish to marry. Give me one of your daughters to be my wife. Please do not refuse my request. You belong to a line of kings known for their generous gifts. No suitor to your family goes away empty-handed,

---

[1] "The Rishi Who Envied a Fish," from *Stories from Indian Classics*, V. Krishnaswami Aiyar, ed., translated from Sanskrit by P. Sankaranarayanan (Bombay: Bharatiya Vidya Bhavan, 1966), used by permission of the publisher.

and I expect that you will be true to this noble trait of your ancestors."

King Mandhata listened to these words with deep respect mixed with fear. He saw how old and haggard the *rishi* was. He could not consent to marry any of his daughters to him, but was afraid that the *rishi* might curse him if he refused. He was lost in thought and did not speak.

Saubhari noticed the king's hesitation. "What are you thinking about, Mandhata? Have I said anything to make you unhappy? Of course, you don't propose to keep your daughters with you forever, do you? A daughter has to be given away one day or other. Give one of them to me; and you will be doing your duty by her and I too shall gain my desire."

The king could not reconcile himself to his daughter marrying an aged man like that. Yet, he was afraid of the *rishi*'s curse. He thought to find a way out of this predicament. He told the *rishi:* "Holy one! In our family we leave the choice of the husband to our daughters. We agree to whomsoever they choose to wed. If any of my daughters agrees to marry you, I shall have no objection."

Saubhari saw through the king's mind. "By trotting out this family tradition," he thought, "he evidently wishes to evade my request. He believes that none of his daughters in the flush of her youth and beauty would consent to be my wife. Well, we shall see."

Turning to the king, he said, "If it is as you have said, let me be taken to the apartments of your princesses. Let them see me. I suppose that is a fair offer and you can have no objection."

The king agreed and had an attendant take the *rishi* to where the Princesses lived. As he was approaching that part of the palace, in the winking of an eye, Saubhari transformed himself by his yogic powers into a youth of superlative beauty far exceeding that of any mortal or divine being. The attendant went ahead and spoke to the Princesses. "I bring you the King's command. Here is a *rishi*. The king bids me to tell you that he wishes to marry one of you. Which of you will agree to be his wife? Look at him and tell me truly which of you likes him for a husband."

The Princesses heard the king's message and they all looked at the *rishi*. They devoured him with eager eyes, and were enchanted, one and all of them. They all fell in love with him the moment they saw him. They vied with each other to have him.

One of them, more imperious than the rest, exclaimed, "Enough, my sisters, I have chosen to marry him. You had better retire."

Another said, "No, you do not deserve him. See how well my beauty matches with his handsomeness."

A third exclaimed, "Cease your prattle. Don't you see that god has made him for me?"

Thus each Princess said, "He is mine." "He is mine!"

The attendant saw all this clamor for the *rishi*. He went back to the king and reported that every one of the Princesses wished to marry him. Mandhata heard it with amazement. Meanwhile the *rishi* too returned to the royal presence. To the king's eyes he appeared as the old decrepit man that he was. To the Princesses he showed himself in exquisite beauty of form and feature, handsome all over from head to foot.

When every one of his daughters consented to marry the *rishi*, Mandhata agreed to his taking all of them. He celebrated the marriages with due pomp and splendor. After the wedding was over, Saubhari took all of his wives to his hermitage. Arriving there, by his yogic powers, he caused a number of mansions to be constructed in an idyllic setting with gardens and lawns, with rivulets and fountains, orchards and flowerbeds. The interior of every mansion was furnished in the most lavish manner. Nothing was lacking which imagination could conjure or fancy could desire. All the best was provided to feed the body and to delight the mind. Each Princess was accommodated in a separate palace and she had a large retinue of servants to attend on her. Thus they all lived there in the midst of luxury that did not grow stale by enjoyment.

Often the king's thoughts turned to his daughters. He was anxious to know if they fared well in the *rishi*'s rustic home in its rugged surroundings. So he went there to have a look at them and to learn firsthand about the way they lived with their husband.

He went first to his eldest daughter. He was struck with wonder when he beheld her mansion and everything about it. He inquired of her with parental eagerness, "Child, are you happy here? Do you feel unhappy about anything? Does the *rishi* treat you properly? Do you ever think of your home?"

"Father, dear, don't be anxious about me. I cannot tell you how exceedingly happy I am. Yet, who will not think of home, sweet home, forever? Still, father, I am worried over one fact. My husband spends all of his time with me. He does not go to any of my other sisters. I feel guilty that he lavishes his love on me alone, neglecting my sisters. They too have married him, but he does not turn to them at all. When I think of the lot of my sisters I feel unhappy."

Mandhata then went to the palace of his second daughter and made similar inquiries. "Father," said she, "I am delighted with my lord. Oh, how he loves me! He is with me always. I seem to have monopolized him, whole and entire. But should not my sisters too have him to receive his love and affection? But he does not go to them at all. When I think of that, I weep in secret."

Every one of his daughters told the same tale. The king was filled with wonder. He marvelled at the yogic powers of the *rishi*. He spoke to the *rishi* and said, "Holy sir, I misjudged you. I now realize the glory of your austerities."

He stayed with the *rishi* for a few days and then returned to his capital.

As the days passed, Saubhari begot a number of sons by his wives. Looking at them, he said to himself, "Ah! they are my children. How endearing is their sweet babble and their artless laughter. See how they crawl. Very soon they will begin to toddle and learn to walk. When they grow up to be handsome youths, they will be married and they will make me a grand-father."

Thus was he lost in his dreams. He spent a number of days in delightful imagination of the happy time he would spend with his sons, his grandsons and their children. His thoughts turned to the fish king and he felt gratified that he too enjoyed the domestic felicity which he had once envied in the fish.

Suddenly, one day, he woke up to the reality. "Woe is me!" cried he, "What a fool I have been to waste all my austerities.

I have become a victim to my desires and I have fallen from my high estate. First I wished to marry. That was how attachment gained entry into me. One attachment bred another. I then desired to have sons and grandsons. My desire went beyond that too. Desires surge in the heart in unending succession like waves on the bosom of the sea. As one desire is fulfilled, it awakens another. In the grip of my desires, I have lost hold on God. A man who is the slave of his desires does not rest his mind on the Supreme. I was a fool to yearn for a life like the one he lived. I allowed myself to be tempted and have fallen from my spiritual heights.

"Attachment destroys the power of austerities. Even he who has reached the pinnacle of *yoga* falls down when once attachment obtains a lodgment in his breast. What then of those like me who are of inferior mettle?

"Now I have learned the bitter lesson. I shall strive to free my soul from the bonds that bind it to the earth and prevent it from soaring in the regions of the spirit. From this moment onward, I shall spend my days in penance and prayer. I shall meditate without intermission on the Lord of Lords, the God of resplendent Beauty and Supreme Power, He Who is everywhere and in all things, Who abides in the heart of every object small and great. Conquering my passions, killing my desires, freeing myself from every attachment, I shall recover my Soul and attain immortality. I shall surrender myself to Him Who is the Lord of All, Who is without beginning and without end, without Whose consent not a blade of grass can move in this world."

Making this stern resolve, Saubhari gave up his wives, sons and all these earthly possessions and turned into an ascetic once again. Burning out all his desires in the fires of his penance, he reached that bourne from which there is no return.

THE CITY OF GOLD[1]

IN THE CITY of Vardhamana, which is the jewel of the earth, there was once a king named Paropakarin, benefactor of his neighbors, tormentor of his enemies. Even as the thundercloud holds the lightning, so the exalted monarch had a queen, but she was without the lightning's inconstancy. In the course of time this queen, whose name was Kanakaprabha, Golden Lustre, bore her husband a daughter so lovely that it was as though the Creator had fashioned her to humble the pride of the Goddess of Beauty herself. The king called her Kanakarekha, Streak-of-Gold, after her mother, and with the passing of time the princess grew up as a little moon in the eyes of her people.

Arrangement of a Marriage (page 56)   The girl became a woman, and one day her father said to his queen when they were by themselves, "My lady, our daughter, Streak-of-Gold, has grown, and so has my concern to find her a suitable match. My heart is burdened, for a high-born virgin who fails to find her proper place is like a song that is out of tune; the mere sound hurts even a stranger's ears. But a girl who is foolishly given away to an unworthy man is like sacred lore imparted to an unfit pupil; she will bring neither honor nor merit, but infinite regret. So, my dear, my heart grows heavier:

[1] "The City of Gold," from *Tales of Ancient India*, translated by J. A. B. van Buitenen (Chicago: The University of Chicago Press, 1959), from the *Brihatkathasaritsagara* ("The Ocean of the Rivers of the Great Romance," by Somadeva, 12th century), used by permission.

to what king shall I marry my daughter? Who could be equal
to her?"

The queen smiled. "You say this, while the girl herself refuses to marry!" she remarked. "Streak-of-Gold made a doll today, and I said jokingly, 'When is your wedding going to be?'
She reproached me. 'Don't talk like that, mother,' she said. 'I
am not to be married to anyone at all! Fate forbids that I be
separated from you; even as a virgin I shall bring you happiness. If I am forced to marry, I shall surely die. There is a reason.' I was disturbed by her words and came to you, my Lord.
Why should we think about a husband if she refuses to marry?"

When the king heard this story from the queen's own lips,
he was greatly upset and hurried to the princess's chambers.

"Can it be true that you refuse to accept a husband, my
child? Even goddesses and nymphs go to great trouble to find
one!"

Streak-of-Gold lowered her eyes. "Father," she said, "I don't
want to marry, not just now. Why does it concern you so? Why
do you insist?"

Paropakarin, who was a very wise king, replied, "How can a
man ever atone for his sins if he does not marry off his daughter? A girl depends on her family; she cannot afford to be independent. A daughter is in effect born for a husband, and her
parents safeguard her only for a time. Except in her childhood,
how can her father's house ever be a home to a woman without a husband? If a daughter remains a virgin when she is
able to bear children, her kinsmen are ruined. The girl loses
caste, and the man who marries her in the end is the husband
of an outcaste."

When her father had spoken, the princess at last revealed
what she had had in mind all the while. "If it must be so,
father, then I must be married to a brahmin or a nobleman
who has truly visited the City of Gold. This man, and no one
else, shall be my husband. It is useless to force me into marrying another."

The king thought, "At least we are fortunate that she has
agreed to marry at all on those conditions. She must be a goddess who, by some cause, was cast to the earth to be born in
my house. How else could she know so much? She is only a

child." The king agreed to his daughter's condition, and he rose and applied himself to his daily duties.

The following day when the king held court, he asked those present: "Is there anyone among you who knows of a city named the City of Gold? If there is a brahmin or nobleman who has visited that city, I shall give him my daughter and the title to my kingdom!"

They looked at one another in surprise, and all replied, "No, Sire, we have never even heard of such a city, much less seen it."

The king summoned his chamberlain and commanded, "Go and see to it that a proclamation is made throughout the city with the beat of drums and ascertain if any person has seen that city."

The chamberlain departed at once with the king's orders and passed instructions to the king's men. Drummers were sent around to arouse people's curiosity, and all over town the drum was struck and the proclamation made: "If there is a brahmin or a noble youth who has visited the City of Gold, let him speak! The king will bestow his daughter on him and the title of crown prince." When the citizens heard this proclamation, they were astonished. "What is this City of Gold in the proclamation?" they asked one another. "Even the oldest among us have never seen a city of that name, and we have never even heard of it." And no one declared that he knew the city.

Now there lived in Vardhamana a certain Saktideva, a brahmin, the son of Baladeva, and he, too, heard the proclamation. He was still a young man and a slave of his vices; he had gambled away his entire fortune at a game of dice. When Saktideva heard that the king promised to marry off his daughter, he pricked up his ears and thought, "Now that I have lost all my money gambling, I am no longer welcome in my father's house nor in a brothel. I have nowhere to go. The best thing I can do is to pretend to the criers that I know the city. Who is going to find out that I don't? Nobody has ever seen the place. Perhaps I can win the princess this way!"

Having made up his mind, Saktideva went to the king's men and lied. "I know the City of Gold!"

"Bless you," they said. "Come along with us to the chamber-

lain." He went with them straightaway. Before the chamberlain Saktideva repeated his lie, and with great courtesy the
dignitary conducted him to the royal presence. Even when
he faced the king, he did not hesitate to tell the same lie;
what is impossible to a gambler who has been ruined by the
dice?

The king in turn sent the brahmin to his daughter to hear
her decision. Saktideva was announced by the chamberlain.

"Is it true," the princess asked, "that you know the City of
Gold?"

"It is true," he replied. "I visited the city once when I was a
student and traveled about the country in search of knowledge."

"What road did you take to the City," she inquired, "and
what is the City like?"

"I traveled from here to a town called Harapura, from which
I journeyed in stages to Benares. After I had spent a few days
there, I left Benares for the city of Paundravardhana, and from
there I traveled to the town that is called the City of Gold.
Yes, I have seen the City. It is a paradise of pleasure for those
who have earned great merit—and magnificent like Indra's
heaven whose splendor can only be seen by the unblinking eyes
of the gods.

"That was the route by which I traveled, and that is what
the City looks like."

When the crooked Brahmin had told this fictitious story, the
princess laughed in his face.

"Aho!" she cried. "Yes, great brahmin, you certainly know
the City. Please, please, tell me again what road you took!"

Again Saktideva tried to brazen it out, but the princess told
her maids to lead him away. When he had been thrown out,
she went to her father.

"Did that brahmin tell the truth?" the king asked.

"Father," said the princess, "you may be a king, but you do
act thoughtlessly! Don't you know that there are crooks and
that they try to deceive honest people? That brahmin tried to
cheat me; the liar has never seen the City! Don't be too hasty
now in marrying me off. I will remain unmarried; we shall see
what the future has in store."

"My daughter," insisted the king, "it is not right for a woman to remain too long a virgin. Wicked people who are envious of virtue will slander an unmarried woman. And people like best to smear the best. Let me tell you the story of Harasvamin. Listen.

"On the bank of the Ganges lies a town named City of Flowers, and once a certain hermit dwelt there, seeking blessings in the sacred river. The hermit, whose name was Harasvamin, lived on alms in a hut of leaves on the riverbank, and his extraordinary austerities had won him great devotion from the people.

"But one day when the hermit went out to beg his food, a vicious fellow in the crowd that watched the hermit from a distance remarked, 'Do you know what a hypocrite that hermit is? He eats all the little children in town.'

"Another one, equally wicked, added, 'Yes, I have heard people tell the same thing for truth.'

" 'Yes, indeed,' confirmed a third.

"The agreement of the wicked is a chain that ties censure to the righteous. The rumor gradually spread from ear to ear and grew bigger all over town, until all the citizens kept their children inside by force, because, as they said, Harasvamin kidnapped all the children and devoured them.

"At last the brahmins, who were particularly worried lest their lineage be broken, assembled and deliberated and decided to banish the hermit from the town. No one among them dared to go to the hermit for fear that he would devour him in his fury, and they sent messengers. The messengers went and delivered the message from a safe distance: 'The brahmins order you to leave town!'

" 'Why?' asked the hermit in surprise.

" 'You eat our little children,' they said.

"At this the hermit decided to find out for himself, and while the crowd shrank away in terror, he made his way to the brahmins. The brahmins fled and climbed on the roof of their monastery; a man who has been fooled by a rumor is rarely capable of sense. Harasvamin called the brahmins one by one by their names and, standing below, shouted to those who were hiding above.

" 'What foolishness is this now, brahmins! Ask among your-selves which children I have eaten and how many.'

"The Brahmins asked one another, and they found that each of them had all his children alive and well. Thereupon the hermit instructed the other citizens to do the same, and they also found their children accounted for. And all of them, brahmins and merchants alike, exclaimed, 'Aho! In our folly we have made false accusations against a holy man. All our children are alive; who has eaten them then?'

"His innocence proved, Harasvamin proceeded to leave the town. What pleasure can a man find in a bad country of indiscriminate people whose loveless minds turn against him at the slander of unscrupulous crooks? But the brahmins and the merchants all prostrated themselves at the hermit's feet and implored him to stay; and not without difficulty they prevailed on him to consent.

"This shows," concluded the king, "that for vicious people to see a person live righteously is to hate and slander him; and often they will bring false accusations against the just. If they find any opportunity, even the slightest, you will see that they kindle a fire and pour buckets of melted butter upon it. Therefore, if you want to pull this thorn from my flesh, you must try, now that your womanhood has come to flower, not to foster the easy slander of the wicked by remaining at your own choice and for a long time unmarried."

But when her father repeated his admonitions, the princess, who stood firm by her decision, again replied. "Then find me quickly a brahmin or a nobleman who has visited the City of Gold and give me to him; for that is what I have said."

The king thought that his daughter, who was so firm in her resolutions, must have memories from a former life; and seeing no other way to find her the husband she wanted, the king ordered that every day thereafter the same proclamation be heralded with the beating of drums to tell the newcomers in town that "the brahmin or nobleman who has truly visited the City of Gold must speak up, for the king will bestow on him his own daughter and the title to the throne." The proclamation continued to be made, but nobody was found who knew the City of Gold.

The Vow
(page 57) Meanwhile Saktideva, who had been ignominiously thrown out by the princess, thought glumly, "The only thing I have gained by my lies is contempt, and no princess. But now I will conquer her, and I shall travel on the face of the earth until I have found that city or lost my life. What use is my life now, unless I find the city and can return to claim the princess as the stake in this gamble?"

With this solemn vow the brahmin departed from Vardhamana and, turning southward, set out on his journey. After he had traveled for some distance, the wayfarer reached the great jungle ranges of the Vindhya Mountains, abysmal and vast like his own ambitions, and he penetrated into the wastelands. The forest fanned him, when he was hot under the pounding sun, with the tender blossoms of its trees that swayed in the breeze. It was as though the land, which resounded with the tortured cries of deer that were slaughtered by lions and beasts of prey, cried out in grief over the violence of its teeming robbers. Above the vast untamed desert tracts the air quivered so glaringly that the jungle seemed bent on outshining the fierce fires of the sun.

For days he traveled the road through the jungle in a region where no trace of water could be found and danger lurked everywhere; and the country, though endlessly traversed, kept stretching to the horizon. Then he discovered in a secluded spot a large pond with clear, cool water, a king among ponds which bore a regal umbrella of lotus flowers and yak-tail plumes of dancing swans. He bathed in the pond and washed himself. Thereupon he discerned on the northern shore, amidst shady fruit-laden trees, a hermitage. He approached, and he found there a very ancient hermit, Suryatapas by name, who was sitting at the foot of an *asvattha* tree. He was surrounded by a circle of anchorites. A string of beads, which bead by bead seemed to count the centuries of the hermit's life, adorned a beard grizzled and whitened by extreme old age.

Saktideva bowed and drew near and was graciously welcomed by the hermit, who offered him hospitality. The traveler ate some fruits, roots, and other forest fare, and when he had finished eating, the hermit questioned him.

"Whence do you come and whither are you bound, my son?"

"I have come from the city of Vardhamana, Reverend Sir," Saktideva answered with a deep bow," and I am bound by a vow to journey to the City of Gold. But I do not know where that city is. If you know, Sir, tell me!"

"My son, for eight centuries now have I lived in this hermitage, but never have I even heard of a city of that name."

At the hermit's reply Saktideva gave up hope.

"Then nothing remains but to wander over the earth until I die."

Bit by bit the saint found out the whole truth of the matter, and he said, "If you are so determined, then do what I tell you. Three hundred leagues from here is the country of Kampilya. There is a mountain named Mount Uttara, and on this mountain is a hermitage; there lives my eldest brother Dirghatapas. Go to him. He is old and may know about that city."

Saktideva immediately agreed, and having passed the night with the saint, he started out with new hope the next morning and made good speed. After a long journey which took him through rough and perilous jungle ranges, he reached, exhausted, the country of Kampilya and began the ascent of Mount Uttara. He found the hermit Dirghatapas in his hermitage on the mountain and bowed a greeting. The saint offered him hospitality which he gladly accepted.

"Reverend Sir," he said at last, "I am bound for the City of Gold, the name of which was made known to me by the princess of my country. I have sworn an irrevocable vow that I would find the city, and the sage Suryatapas has sent me to you that I may find it."

"In all my long life this is the first time that I have heard of this city," answered the hermit. "None of the wayfarers, from distant countries who have visited me here have acquainted me with its name. This place has never been mentioned within my hearing, much less have I myself ever set eyes on it. But I know that it must be somewhere in a very remote country, perhaps as far as the Archipelago, and I can tell you the way there.

"In the middle of the ocean lies an island named Utsthala.

On this island lives Satyavrata, who is the chieftain of the fisher-tribes and a rich man. He travels back and forth between all the islands of the Archipelago, and he may have seen or at least heard of your city. You must first go to Vitankapura, which is a port on the ocean, and sail with a merchant on his ship to the island of Utsthala where the fisher-tribes live, if you want to reach your goal."

Saktideva at once accepted the saint's advice, took his leave, and departed from the hermitage. He journeyed many leagues through different lands and at last reached the port Vitankapura, which lies as a beauty mark on the brow of the seashore. There he sought out a merchant, by the name of Samudradatta, with whom he made friends. The friendship was sealed with a present of victuals, and the brahmin embarked with the merchant on his ship and set sail on the ocean.

When they were but a short distance from their destination, a thundering black giant of a stormcloud suddenly reared its head, licking its lips with tongues of lightning, and a terrible tempest began to rage which lifted the light and lowered the heavy like fate itself. Huge waves rose from the ocean under the force of the hurricane, like winged mountains of the sea outraged by the violation of their realm. One moment the craft was hurled down, only to rise up again after an instant, as if to illustrate the rise and decline of the wealthy. Then the ship jumped up in the air and the next moment, filled with the agonized cries of the merchants aboard and collapsing under the burden, burst asunder. Samudradatta, the ship's owner, was thrown free when the ship floundered and managed to swim over to a drifting plank from which he was later rescued by another ship.

Saktideva sank into the yawning mouth and throat of a large fish and was swallowed down whole. The fish played around for a while in the ocean and, as fate would have it, drifted toward the island of Utsthala. By a whim of destiny the servants of fisher-king Satyavrata were seining thereabouts for sapharas and caught the fish. They were amazed at the size of their catch and carried the fish to their king. Satyavrata, on seeing the monster, was curious and ordered his servants to slice it open;

and Saktideva stepped out of its belly, alive and well, reborn after a second and remarkable gestation.

When the king saw the young man come out blessing his savior, he asked in astonishment, "Who are you? How did you happen to be in the belly of that monster? Where do you come from, brahmin, and what wonderful adventures did you have?"

"I am a brahmin," he answered. "My name is Saktideva, and I hailed from the city of Vardhamana. I have vowed to visit a city which is called the City of Gold, but not knowing where to seek it I have roamed the farthest corners of the earth. From a hermit whose name is Dirghatapas I learned that the city must be on an island. So I sailed out for the island of Utsthala so that I might learn from Satyavrata the fisher-king where that city is. Our ship was wrecked in a storm. I sank to the deeps of the ocean and was swallowed by this fish, and now I am here."

"I am Satyavrata!" said the king. "This is the island for which you were bound. I have seen many islands but the island you want I have never seen myself, although I have heard about such a place at the fringes of the Archipelago." Then seeing how disappointed Saktideva was, he added, "Don't lose heart, brahmin. Stay here for the night, and tomorrow morning I shall find a way to lead you to your goal."

With these reassuring words the fisher-king sent the brahmin to a brahmin cloister where he found ready hospitality. One of the brahmins who lived there, a certain Vishnudatta, served him his meal and engaged him in conversation. While they were talking, Vishnudatta asked him detailed questions about his country, his family, and all his circumstances, and Saktideva told him everything.

And as soon as Vishnudatta had heard all, he clasped Saktideva in a close embrace and exclaimed in a voice that was muffled with tears of joy: "Oh, blessing, you are my cousin on my mother's side; we are fellow countrymen! I came here from your own country, long ago when I was a child. You must stay here, and before long you will find out what you wish from the reports that are passed on from steersmen and merchants who come here from the Archipelago."

Having established their kinship, Vishnudatta waited on his

cousin with all the proper amenities and Saktideva forgot the trials of the journey and was happy; for finding a kinsman in a foreign land is like nectar in a desert. And he thought that the success of his venture was imminent, for luck on the way spells luck at the end.

When the morning dawned on the island of Utsthala, the fisher-king Satyavrata met Saktideva at the monastery and, true to the promise he had made the day before, said to him: "Brahmin, I have thought of a way that will lead you to your goal. In the middle of the ocean is a beautiful island called Ratna-kuta, Jewel Peak. On that island is a temple of Vishnu which was founded by the Ocean. Every year on the twelfth day of the bright fortnight in the month of Ashadha a festival is cele-brated in the temple, and from all corners of the Archipelago zealous people come on a pilgrimage. Somewhere among them there must be someone who knows the City of Gold. Come with me and let us go there together, for the day of the festival is near." Saktideva agreed and joyfully packed the provisions which his cousin Vishnudatta had prepared for him.

They embarked on a little craft that Satyavrata had pro-cured, and with the king at the helm they set sail immediately on the highway of the ocean. And while they sailed over that treasure house of wonders, infested by whales like floating islands, Saktideva asked Satyavrata at the helm: "What is that *The Use of* beautiful object that is just visible in the sea far away on the *Ancient* horizon? It looks like a lofty winged mountain that can emerge *Symbols* (page 58) from the deeps at will!"

"That is the divine banyan tree," answered Satyavrata. "They say that just below it there is a broad maelstrom which tapers down to the submarine fires. We must steer clear of it, for once a ship is caught in it, there is no escape."

"But even while Satyavrata was speaking, a gust of wind carried the craft in that very direction. When the skipper real-ized it, he cried: "Brahmin, the end has come for us now, no doubt about it. Look, the ship has suddenly started drifting to-ward the maelstrom, and I cannot steer away from it anymore. We shall be hurled into the bottomless whirlpool as into the mouth of Death and swept off by the sea as by the karman that governs our life. I do not care for myself; for whose body is eternal? But it does grieve me that despite all your efforts your goal will be lost forever. So I shall hold the ship for as long as I can, and you must try to get a hold on a branch of the tree, quick now! With your robust build you stand a chance to save your life. Who can fathom the vagaries of fate and the waves of the ocean?"

Even as the magnanimous Satyavrata was speaking, the craft drifted toward the tree, and at the same instant Saktideva jumped up with the strength of terror and grasped one thick branch of the ocean tree. But Satyavrata, sacrificing his body and his ship for the other, was dragged into the submarine fires.

Saktideva, clinging in safety to a branch of the tree which rose out into heaven, thought in despair: "Still I have not seen the City of Gold, and now, after causing the fisher-king's death, I shall perish in desolation. But fate has branded its mark on the forehead of all mortals; who can defy his destiny?" Thinking such thoughts, which indeed suited the occasion, the young man passed the day on the shoulder of the tree. Then, at nightfall, he saw a multitude of giant birds arrive from all directions. Filling the skies with their chatter, they alighted on the tree and were instantly welcomed as old friends by the ocean waves which rose and rolled under the wind of their broad wings. And hidden behind a heavy cover of leaves, Saktideva heard the roosting birds converse with one another in human language. They told one another where they had flown to spend the day—one to an island, the other to a mountain, a third to another region of the sky.

One among them, an ancient bird, said, "I went today to the City of Gold to spend my time leisurely, and tomorrow I shall go there again, for I can no longer bear the fatigue of long flights."

At the bird's words, which were like a sudden shower of nectar, Saktideva's despair was extinguished. "I am saved!" he thought. "The City really exists, and now I have a way to reach it—if I use this monstrous bird as my mount."

He crept slowly nearer and, when the bird had dozed off, installed himself on its back between the wings.

The next morning, after the other birds had flown in different directions, Saktideva's bird rose too like destiny with a wondrous force of wing, carrying Saktideva unseen on his back. After a while the bird reached the City of Gold, and when it alighted in a park to disport itself, Saktideva lowered himself stealthily from its back and made off.

While he sauntered around the park, he encountered two women who were gathering flowers, and cautiously he drew near. The women started in surprise when they saw him.

"What country is this?" he asked. "And who are you, good ladies?"

"This is the City of Gold, realm of the aerial spirits. A fairy queen lives here whose name is Candraprabha, and we, friend, are her gardeners in this park. We are gathering these flowers for her."

"Be kind enough to conduct me to your mistress," he said. Thereupon the women conducted the young man to a regal mansion, which, like a meeting place where all joys held tryst, was splendid with golden walls and gem-studded columns. When the servants saw him approach, they all hastened to tell Queen Candraprabha of the miraculous arrival of a mortal man. At once she ordered her lady chamberlain to conduct the brahmin into the palace without any delay; and he entered and feasted his eyes on her beauty, at which the Creator had toiled to the limits of his divine powers. Long before he was near, she arose courteously from her splendidly jeweled couch and, entranced at the sight of him, gave him a most courteous welcome.

When she was seated, she asked him in great wonder: "Handsome mortal, who may you be? How did you reach this country which is forbidden to human beings?"

Saktideva told her his country, his caste, and his name and narrated how he had staked his life on finding the City of Gold in order to conquer the princess and how he had found it. When he had finished his account, she sat for a moment enwrapped in her thoughts. Then she heaved a deep sigh and addressed him in an intimate tone.

"Listen, I shall tell you a little now, my love. In this country reigns Sasikhanda, Sliver-of-Moon, who rules the aerial spirits. He has four daughters, of whom I, Candraprabha, Radiant Moon, am the oldest. The second is Candrarekha, Streak-of-

Moon; the third Sasirekha, Touch-of-Moon; and the fourth Sasiprabha, Shining Moon. We grew up one after the other, and
one day my three sisters went out together to the Ganges to
bathe while I stayed home to pray for a husband. There was a
hermit in the Ganges, Agryatapas, who did penance in the water; and while my sisters played in the river with the high
spirits of young women, they splashed water over him. They
went too far, and the hermit grew angry and cursed them:
'Wicked girls, all of you shall be reborn in the world of mortal
men!' When my father heard about this, he went to the hermit
and prevailed on his mercy, so that he told under which circumstances the curse of each of them would end. The great
saint granted that even in their mortal state all of them would
have the power to remember their old life and that this power
would be supported by their celestial knowledge. Thereupon
they left their bodies and descended to the mortal realm; and
grieving over his bereavement my father gave me his city and
went to live in the forest.

"Since then I have lived here. One day the great Mother
Goddess appeared to me in a dream and said: 'Daughter, thou
shalt have a mortal husband.' And ever since I have rejected
the many aerial spirits who wooed me, and, to my father's distress, I have remained a virgin until this very day. But now
I am conquered by your miraculous arrival and wonderful
beauty, and I give myself up to you. On the coming fourteenth
day of the moon I shall go to the peak of Mount Rshabha to tell
my father. For on that day every year all the eminent spirits of
the air forgather there from all regions of the sky to worship
God Siva. I shall come back at once, and then you must marry
me. Now rise!" And Radiant Moon thereupon served Saktideva
with the choicest delights that are reserved for the spirits of
the air.

Saktideva agreed to her proposal, and, happy as a man
scorched by a brush fire who plunges into a lake of nectar, he
lived with her. But when the fourteenth day of the moon came,
Radiant Moon said to him: "I shall go to my father today to tell
him about you. All my servants will accompany me, but you
must not be unhappy if you have to remain by yourself here
for a few days. However, while you are staying here alone in

the palace, you must under no circumstances go up and enter the middle storey!"

Radiant Moon departed, leaving her heart in trust with the young man whose thoughts accompanied her on her journey. And alone in the palace Saktideva diverted his mind by wandering from chamber to luxurious chamber. Then he began to wonder why the daughter of the fairy king had forbidden him to ascend to the roof-terrace, and he became curious and went up to the middle storey of the palace: for man's mind will always turn to forbidden sensations. And when he had gone up the stairs, he saw three private pavilions. Two of them were closed, but the door of the third stood ajar, and he entered. And as he entered he saw the shape of a woman wrapped in a sheet of cloth; she was reposing like a beauty mark on a gem-encrusted couch. He lifted a corner of the sheet and stared at the beautiful face of Streak-of-Gold, the Princess Kanakarekha from Vardhamana; and she was dead.

The Snare of Illusion (page 59) "What is this wonderful miracle?" he thought as he looked. "Does she sleep the sleep of no awakening, or am I bedeviled by my imagination? Here she lies dead, the woman for whom I went a-journeying, and at home she was alive! But her beauty has not faded. . . . It must be a snare of illusion in which fate saw fit to enmesh me!"

He left that pavilion and entered the other two on the same storey, and in each pavilion he found a girl lying on a couch, dead. Wonderstruck, he walked out on the terrace. Below he saw an enchanting little lake, and on its bank stood a horse with a jewel-studded saddle. He descended the stairs and walked curiously up to the horse. Seeing that there was nobody to ride it, he wanted to mount it; but the horse kicked at him with its hoof and pushed him into the lake. Saktideva went under; and when he emerged from the water, struggling, he came up in his own city of Vardhamana. And there he suddenly found himself to his consternation in the middle of the garden pond of his home town.

Bereft of his Radiant Moon, his face faded like a night-blooming lotus, and he exclaimed, "Vardhamana! Vardhamana, after the City of the Spirits! Aho, what is the meaning of this bewitching show of jugglery and magic! I must have been

fooled, ill-fated wretch that I am! But is there anybody who
knows the workings of fate?"

Brooding, Saktideva waded out of the pond and went won-
deringly to his father's house. There he pretended that after
he had been ruined by his gambling he had wandered abroad
as a drummer. His father and family rejoiced at his homecom-
ing and welcomed him with a feast.

The next day he left his father's house and went out into the
city. And again he heard the old proclamation that was
heralded about with the beating of drums: "If there is anyone,
brahmin or nobleman, who has truly seen the City of Gold, let
him speak! The king will bestow his daughter upon him and his
throne."

Saktideva went to the drummer—for now he had succeeded
and he said: "I have seen the city!" They conducted him to the
king, but the king recognized him and assumed that he was
lying, as before.

"I now stake my life that I am not lying and that I have
visited the City of Gold! Let the princess question me at once."

The king went and ordered his lackeys to fetch his daughter.
When she recognized the brahmin, she said to the king: "Father, the fellow will lie again."

"I am telling the truth!" Saktideva said, "or, if I lie, then explain to me one curious fact, Your Highness. How is it possible
that I saw you lying dead on a couch in the City of Gold and
now find you here in good health?"

When Saktideva had proved himself with this question,
Princess Kanakarekha immediately turned to her father and
said: "Father, this noble man has really visited the City of
Gold, and soon he shall be my husband when I have returned
there. He will also marry my three sisters and reign in the city
as the sovereign of the aerial spirits. Now I shall have to return
to the City and to my real body, for I was cursed by a hermit
to be reborn in your house. But he set an end to the curse: as
soon as a mortal man looked on my body in the City of Gold
and revealed the truth to me in the realm of mortals, my curse
was to end, and the man would become my husband. I knew
all this, for even in my mortal estate I remembered my former
life.

"I shall return now to the realm of the spirits for the fulfillment of my destiny." Thereupon the princess departed from
her body and disappeared; and there was consternation in the
royal palace and loud lament.

Saktideva now had lost both his women—ultimately defeated
even though his unequaled efforts had been victorious. Yearning for the two women he loved, he blamed himself for his
suffering and the frustration of his desires. But as he wandered
out of the palace, a thought occurred to him.

"Princess Kanakarekha said that my ambitions are destined
to succeed in the end. Then why should I despair? Success depends on character. I shall return again to the City of Gold by
the same route and fate will have to see me through!"

So Saktideva once again set out from Vardhamana; for reso-
lute men who have made great efforts will not desist before
they have achieved their ends. After a long journey he reached
the port of Vitankapura on the dunes of the ocean. And there
he happened to meet the same merchant with whom he had
sailed before and whose ship had foundered.

"That must be Samudradatta!" he thought. "How could he
have been saved after he was thrown into the sea? But small
wonder—I myself am another example!"

When he accosted the merchant, the latter recognized him
and embraced him delightedly. He took Saktideva to his home
and, when the amenities had been complied with, asked him,
"How were you saved from the sea after the shipwreck?"

Saktideva told what had happened to him, how he had been
swallowed by the fish and reached the island of Utsthala. Then
he put the same question to the excellent merchant: "And how
did you cross the ocean in safety? Tell me all!"

"I fell into the sea, and for three days I floated around clinging to a piece of driftwood. Suddenly a ship appeared and
sailed my way. I shouted and the sailors saw me and pulled me
on board. When I climbed aboard, I saw my own father who
had just returned from a long expedition to the Archipelago.
He recognized and embraced me and crying for joy asked what
had befallen me. I told him: 'Father, when you did not return
for a long time after you had sailed away, I thought it my duty
to carry on the business. On a voyage to the Archipelago my

ship was wrecked, and I myself was thrown into the sea, to be found and rescued by yourself!

"My father said reproachfully: 'Why did you venture your life on such perilous enterprises? I am rich, son, and I am getting richer still! Look at the ship I have brought, chockful of gold!' Comforting words indeed! So father took me back on his ship to our home in Vitankapura."

That night Saktideva rested with the merchant. The following morning he said, "Merchant prince, I have to leave again for the island of Utsthala. But tell me how I am to go there."

"Agents of mine are about to sail for Utsthala on business," he said. "You may embark on their ship and travel with them."

So the brahmin took passage with the merchant's agents to the island of Utsthala. On his arrival the sons of the fisher-king Satyavrata saw him in the distance and, as fate would have it, recognized him. And they said to him: "Brahmin, you went with our father to search for the City of Gold. How is it that you now return alone?"

"Your father fell into the sea when heavy waves shattered the ship near the submarine fires."

But the sons of the fisherman were enraged, and they issued orders to their servants: "Fetter this criminal. He has murdered our father! How else is it possible that of two persons on the same ship one falls in the submarine fires and the other escapes? Tomorrow morning we will sacrifice the murderer before the image of the Fierce Goddess."

So the sons of the fisherman had their servants fetter the *Kali* brahmin and lock him in the dreadful sanctuary of the Fierce (page 59) Goddess, in whose swollen belly innumerable lives had been sacrificed—a veritable mouth of death with bones, licked bare of flesh, like protruding tusks. There Saktideva spent the night in chains, despairing of his life; and in his despair he prayed to the Fierce Goddess.

"O Goddess, with your body red like the sun at dawn—as if still bloody with the gore from the throat of Ruru the Demon which you drank when you slew him—you once saved this world. So, O granter of boons, deign to save me, your constant devotee, now that, coming from afar in quest of love, I have fallen in the hands of those who hate me without cause!"

Having prayed to the goddess he at last fell asleep. And in his dream he beheld a divine woman who appeared from the inner sanctum of the temple, and she drew near and spoke with compassion.

"My son, Saktideva, do not fear, for nothing untoward will befall you. The sons of the fisher-king have a sister, Bindumati, and tomorrow she will see you and desire you for her husband. You must agree to marriage, and she shall bring about your release. She is not a fisher-maid but a celestial nymph who has fallen because of a curse."

When he awoke the next morning, the fisher-girl, shower of nectar for his thirsty eyes, came to the temple of the goddess and approached him. She made herself known and said to him lovingly, "I shall have you released from this prison if you do what I wish. I have refused all suitors whom my brothers approved, but the instant I saw you, I fell in love with you. Take me!"

Remembering his dream, Saktideva gladly agreed to Bindumati's proposal. She had him released from his prison, and he married the comely girl with the consent of her brothers who, warned in a dream by the Mother Goddess, had done their sister's bidding. And he lived with the celestial woman who had assumed a mortal form as with the perfect bliss which is the reward solely of virtue.

The Cow (page 61)   One day he stood with her on the roof-terrace of their house and saw below him on the road an outcaste who carried a load of beef. He said to his beloved, "Look, my slender-waisted bride! How is it possible that this evildoer dares eat the flesh of cows, which are honored throughout the three worlds?"

"Indeed, it is an incredible crime," answered Bindumati. "What can one say? Through the power of the cows I myself have been reborn in a fisher-tribe, though my sin was very small. How will he ever atone for it?"

"How curious!" Saktideva said. "Tell me darling, who are you and why have you become a fisher-girl?"

When he insisted, she finally said, "I shall tell you—though the secret must be kept—on condition that you shall do what I am going to ask."

"I promise I shall do it," he said and swore an oath on it.

Thereupon she first told him what she wanted him to do: "You will shortly take another wife on this island, and she will soon become pregnant. In the eighth month you must cut open her belly and tear the fruit from it ruthlessly!"

"What is that?" he asked with surprise and pity.

But his wife continued: "There is a reason why you should do as I tell you. But listen, I shall tell you why I have become a fisher-girl. In a former life I was the daughter of the spirits of the air, while now I am cursed to a sojourn in the realm of mortals. But once when I was still a spirit, I used my teeth to bite off a piece of sinew to make a string on my lute. That caused my birth in a dwelling of fishers! Just because my mouth touched the dry sinew of a cow I have fallen so low now. What fate is there in store for one who eats the flesh of cows?"

Even as she was telling this, one of her brothers came running toward their house in great consternation and cried to Saktideva, "Come out at once! A monstrous boar has suddenly come out and is heading this way. He has killed many people already in his fury!"

Immediately Saktideva came down from the roof, mounted a horse, and with a spear in his hand stormed at the boar. He hit the boar with his spear, and the wounded beast, seeing a hero attack, took to flight and disappeared into a cave. Saktideva followed it into the cave to hunt it down. As he passed through the cavern, he saw a large wooded park with a house; and he entered the park and found there a girl of wondrous beauty who nervously ran toward him like a sylph of the woods sped by love.

"Who are you, beautiful girl?" he asked. "Why are you so excited?"

"I am Bindurekha, daughter of King Candavikrama, protector of the Deccan, my good sir, and I am a virgin. But today suddenly a malignant demon with fiery eyes abducted me treacherously from my father's house and carried me here. Then, yearning for meat, he assumed the shape of a boar and went out; and now, before his hunger was stilled, he was struck by a hero with a spear. I escaped into the open, a virgin still."

"Then why should you be upset?" said Saktideva. "I am the one who hit the boar with my spear, princess."

"Tell me who you are!"

"I am a brahmin, Saktideva."

"Then you must become my husband!" she said.

"So be it," agreed Saktideva and conducted her out of the park through the cave to his house. At home he told his wife Bindumati what had happened and with her consent married the virgin Bindurekha.

While Saktideva was living with his two wives, one of them, Bindurekha, became pregnant. In the eighth month of her pregnancy his first wife, Bindumati, came to him privately and said: "My hero, remember what you have promised to me. This is the eighth month that Bindurekha is with child. Go to her, rip open her belly, and take the child. You cannot belie your own oath!"

Saktideva, overcome with love and compassion but bound by his oath, remained speechless for a while. Then, torn by grief, he went out to where Bindurekha was; and when she saw how dejected he looked, she spoke to him anxiously.

"Why are you so downhearted today, my husband? Tell me, is it because Bindumati has instructed you to tear out my child? But that has to be done, for something is to come of it. And there is no cruelty in it at all; so you must not pity me."

Still Saktideva hesitated, and a Voice was heard from heaven: "My son Saktideva, take the child from the woman's womb and fear not. Hold it by the neck and clench your fist, and it shall become a sword in your hand."

At this divine command the brahmin quickly parted her womb and tore out the child. He grasped it by the neck, and—behold!—when he gripped it like the tress of Luck in a firm grasp, it changed in his hand to a sword. And in the same instant the brahmin was transformed into an aerial spirit, and that very moment Bindurekha vanished.

When he saw that the woman had disappeared, he went in his new form to his first wife, the fisher-king's daughter, and told what had happened.

"My husband," she said, "once we were three sisters, daughters of the king of spirits, and we were cast from the City of

Gold because of a hermit's curse. One of us was born a princess in the city of Vardhamana, under the name of Kanakarekha, and you have seen yourself how her curse ended and she returned to her own city. Just now you have witnessed the wondrous ending of Bindurekha's curse which was ordained by fate. I am the third sister, and now the end of my curse has come too. I must go back to my city, my love. There are the bodies which we have as aerial spirits. Our eldest sister, Radiant Moon, is waiting for us there. Come with me at once, by the power of your magic sword. Our father who now lives in the forest as a hermit will bestow all four of us on you. Even more, he shall enthrone you in his city."

When Bindumati had at last given this true account of herself, she flew with Saktideva along the pathways of the sky to the City of Gold. There he saw again the divine bodies which he had found lying on couches in the pavilions of the middle storey; then they were dead, but now they were brought back to life again by Princess Kanakarekha and her sisters. And he rejoined his three beloved women, who prostrated themselves before him, and also their eldest sister, Radiant Moon, who ceremoniously bade him welcome and feasted her eyes on his presence after the longings of separation. As he entered the inner palace, his coming was hailed by the servants and companions who each of them were engaged at their own tasks.

Radiant Moon said, "Good sir, this is my sister Candrarekha, Streak-of-Moon, whom you knew in Vardhamana as Princess Kanakarekha. This is her younger sister Sasirekha, Touch-of-Moon, whom you have already married in the island of Utsthala as Bindumati, daughter of the fisher-king. This is the youngest of us, Sasiprabha, Shining Moon, who became your wife as Princess Bindurekha after she had been abducted by the demon. Now come with us to meet our father, and when he has given us to you in marriage, do not delay the wedding!"

When Radiant Moon had thus voiced Love's command with urgency and boldness, Saktideva departed in their company to the outskirts of the forest where their father lived. Prostrate at his feet, his daughters told him in unison their desire, and, admonished by a Voice from heaven, the king of spirits joyfully bestowed all the girls at once on Saktideva. And after that he imparted to him the rich domains in the city as well as all the divine sciences which he possessed.

Then he gave Saktideva, who had now achieved his end, a new name to bear among the spirits of the air whom he had now joined. His name was Saktivega, and to Saktivega the king said:

"No one shall ever defeat you. Yet, from the mighty and powerful dynasty of Vatsa an emperor shall arise with the name of Naravahanadatta who shall be your sovereign and to whom you shall bow."

After the old and mighty king Sasikhanda had honored his son-in-law, he gave him leave to depart from the forest where the king performed his austerities and to return with his beloved consorts to their royal residence. And as the sovereign now, Saktivega entered with his wives the City of Gold which is the pennant of the Realm of Spirits. And he lived in his city, which blazed with the golden splendor of its mansions like a magnificent shower of concentrated sunlight from the sky to which it reached, in the constant company of his four loving queens. And dallying with his bright-eyed loves in the gorgeous parks where stairs paved with precious stones led down to charming lakes, he tasted the perfection of happiness.

THE DEFEAT OF DEATH[1]

THERE WAS A GREAT *rishi* whose name was Mirkandu. He had no son to continue his line. He felt very sad. But he knew that there was nothing that sincere prayer to God could not accomplish. So, observing the severest austerities, he prayed to God Shiva. Shiva appeared before Mirkandu and said:

"Mirkandu! I am pleased with your *tapas*. Ask for any boon that you desire."

Mirkandu requested to be favored with a son.

"So be it," said Shiva at once. But He added: "Do you wish to have a son who will live a long time, but will be devoid of every virtue; or do you wish to have a son who will be short-lived? Choose!"

Mirkandu was a *dharmātma* (lover of virtue). So he asked for a good, though short-lived son. But he prayed that he should also be learned and wise.

Shiva granted the prayer. "You shall have a son who will live only for sixteen years. He will be very wise and virtuous." With that Shiva disappeared.

Mirkandu came home extremely happy. He felt a great peace in his mind.

Not long after this, his wife, Marudvati, became pregnant.

[1] "The Defeat of Death," from *Stories from Indian Classics*, V. Krishnaswami Aiyar, ed., translated from Sanskrit by P. Sankaranarayanan (Bombay: Bharatiya Vidya Bhavan, 1966), from the *Skanda Purāṇa*, used by permission.

Ceremonies of a Hindu Home (page 63) On an auspicious day, Mirkandu performed the *puṁsavana* rite for the proper growth of the child which she carried in her womb. In the eighth month of pregnancy, he performed his wife's *sīmanta* with a view to easy delivery.

In the fullness of time, Marudvati gave birth to a charming child who shone dazzling bright like the Sun God himself. Great *rishis* like Veda Vyasa and others came to Mirkandu's hermitage to have a look at the child. Sage Vyasa performed the *jātakarma* (birth-ceremony) and on the eleventh day, *nāmakarana* (naming) was performed with proper ceremony. The boy was named Markandeya. The child received the blessings of the great and good men.

Every one was struck with wonder to see the infant's supremely handsome features and sparkling countenance. "Fortunate is Marudvati," they said, "to bear a child like this."

In the fourth month after birth, the child was taken out of the hermitage, crossing the threshold, and when he was six months old *annaprāshana* was performed (first rice feeding). Tonsure followed in the third year, and in the fifth year Mirkandu performed the boy's *Brahmopadesha* (assignment to a teacher) and *upākarma* (blessings) and initiated him into the sacred lore. Very soon Markandeya acquired a precocious mastery of the *Vedas* and all their branches.

Years passed. One day Mirkandu looked very sad and gave vent to uncontrollable grief. His wife too was in tears. Markandeya approached them and queried, "What ails you that you both weep so bitterly?"

"It is for you that we grieve, my son," said the father. "We got you as a gift from Shiva. But he told me that you would live only for sixteen years. The sixteen years end shortly. What shall we do if you die?"

Markandeya heard this. With great confidence and good cheer, he replied: "Father, do not weep; do not grieve over the prospect of my death. No, I shall not die. I shall strive for immortality. Is not our God, the great Shiva, who is *Mrityunjaya*, the conqueror of death? Is He not *kālakāla*, more powerful than Time? Will Time terminate the life of one who is a devotee of the timeless God?"

Heartened by these words of their son, the parents felt greatly relieved and happy. They said:

"Dear child! Truly you have discovered a way to save us from a great calamity. Yes, Shiva is our sure refuge; seek Him at this moment when death threatens you and live. Long ago, He saved Svetaketu from the jaws of death. He rescued Silada's son who was eight years of age and taking him to Kailās, stationed him as His Nandi. When the whole world was in dread of imminent destruction by the *kālakūta* poison which came to the surface when the celestials churned the Ocean of Milk, Shiva took it in the palm of His hand and swallowed it to save the universe. And so, He will surely save you too in this predicament that threatens you."

Receiving his father's words as his *upādesha* in the worship of Shiva, Markandeya hastened to the shores of the southern ocean and installed a *Linga* of Siva there with due ceremony. Bathing thrice—morning, moon and night—he worshipped Shiva. At the end of each worship, he sang prayers to his God and danced in an ecstasy of devotion. Shiva was mightily pleased with the fervor with which Markandeya worshipped Him.

That night, finishing his worship, Markandeya was about to sing his prayers. Just then, relentless Time, personified as Yama, came there, attended by his instrument, Death. Of terrible aspect and forbidding mien, he was dreadful to see.

Approaching Markandeya, he cast his noose over the boy's person. Turning to him, Markandeya said:

"Stay, stay for a while. Bear with me while I recite this prayer to Shiva. I will not move from here before I finish it. Nothing is dearer to me than these prayers; no, not even my life."

Yama looked at the boy, smiled and said: "Foolish boy! Have you not heard the counsel of your venerable ancestors? If one does not acquire merit in his youth, he will be helpless when he grows old, like a destitute traveller on a lonely way. If you wish to be happy all the year long, you should have striven for it in the early months. To be happy after death, you must have earned merit while alive. Work in the forenoon for what you wish to have in the afternoon. Time marches on and none can stay it. It does not wait while you are acquiring merit; but it drags you to your doom when the fatal hour has struck. None can die before his time even if a hundred darts are aimed at him. But when the moment has come, the point of a gentle blade of grass is enough to finish a man's life. None can escape me. Thousands of kings and hundreds of Indras have succumbed to me and have been led to my abode. Therefore, sinless though you are, your days on earth are over. You must meet your doom. Do not get angry with me. This instant you must die."

Markandeya heard what Yama said. Still engaged in his worship he remonstrated Yama and said: "Remember, those who come in the way of *Shivabhaktas* (devotees of Shiva) during their prayers will surely perish. I warn you: even as a king guards his servants, Shiva keeps his devotees from harm. You are powerless before *Shivabhakta,* you and your emissaries."

Yama's eyes turned red with rage. Thundering a roar that made the worlds tremble, he said: "Fool! Do you hope to escape my clutches? Know that countless Brahmās, as numerous as the sands on the Ganga bed have met with their death at my hands. But why indulge in idle talk? Now look at my power. Let me see!"

With that Yama flung the noose round Markandeya's neck and tried to draw him forcibly to himself. At that moment, the *Linga* burst open and Shiva took shape and emerged from it. Raising His foot, He kicked Yama on his chest with such force that he reeled helplessly and was hurled back from where he stood.

Markandeya saw that Yama was vanquished. He bowed his head before his God and praised Him with heart and voice in a fervent hymn of prayer.

Pleased with his devotee, Shiva assured him that his years on earth would be endless. He made Markandeya one of the immortals and then vanished back into the *Linga.*

Markandeya came home and his parents were intensely happy to see him come back alive. He told them of the boon that Shiva had bestowed on him and they too blessed their son. With their consent, Markandeya left on a pilgrimage to visit the *puṇyakshetras.*

Yama too prayed to Shiva in meek submission and went back to his abode.

COMMENTARY

ASSUMPTIONS AND ATTITUDES

No THOUGHTFUL READER is likely to have mistaken these stories for profound religious documents. They have a certain charm and an obvious but sometimes slightly incidental relation to the religious ceremonies and concepts which they illustrate and presuppose. Literal interpretation is quite impossible. We certainly do not wish to argue whether King Aṣvapáthi "really" belonged to the solar race, or to have to decide whether the Putreshti Sacrifice would make it possible for a middle-aged woman to conceive. Such questions are beside the point and even misleading as regards the real significance of the stories. The stories could have meaning both for those who believe such things literally and for those who do not. Neither is this fundamentally an allegorical literature. There are allegorical values here and there, especially in the names. In the story of Savitri the names reflect the worship of Shiva, and in the story of Sāubhari that of Vishnu, but this is not fundamental to the meanings of the stories. To understand and appreciate such stories it is necessary to set aside the critical function for the moment, to try to enter into the life world of the story itself, to take for granted whatever the story takes for granted, and to believe whatever it asks us to believe. There will be time enough for criticism when the work of understanding is well along. This is not a particularly difficult or unusual demand.

We do it with all imaginative literature, and the fascination of the story which makes this easy for us is a partial measure of its quality. When our familiar life world and that of the story have few elements in common, interpretation is much more difficult.

For many modern Western readers Indian literature is not easily appreciated. It is not simple to step inside the story and to move and feel with the characters and events. The scenes are too unfamiliar. Things which the characters take for granted are often altogether different from the things which we are accustomed to take for granted. The stories themselves are usually complicated, and sometimes move from one dimension to another in strange ways. If we have grown up with Aesop's Fables, the Fairy Tales of Grimm and of Hans Christian Andersen, or the Arabian Nights, we already have become familiar with some of the stories of India in transmuted versions. The Mother-God may have become a "fairy godmother" and the movements from one life-time to another or from one world to another, so conventional in Indian literature, have taken the form of magic spells or transformations in the Western versions. Still the fact that these stories have to be so modified in the West illustrates the different conventions essential to understanding and appreciation of these stories. It is true that these are not primary or profound religious documents, but it is also true that they are grounded in assumptions and attitudes of the most profound religious depth, and perhaps they illustrate some of these religious attitudes more clearly and engagingly than more esoteric philosophical literature does.

A few of the minor conventions are easily noticed and accounted for. Indian literature is inherently gracious and flattering to its characters. In India, praise is a fine art. A beautiful woman must be so lovely that she makes even gods desirous and the goddesses envious. A truly great king controls lands in two or three worlds. Everything worthy of any praise may be praised in superlatives. Indian literature resonates with the eulogies of persons, places, gods and goddesses, each praised as though no other existed. So let it be. We must accept the praise of each as it is and not try to form a ranking of superlatives. This attitude is the surface expression of a much deeper notion widely held in India. Each thing is an example of its own type of thing, and there are many types. Therefore there are many first or best things. Because one thing is good or even best does not mean that another is not good or even best as well. This is a deeply rooted Indian attitude and often differs from our own.

A second rather casual assumption fundamental to many of these stories is the attitude that the present world we live in can best be understood perhaps as a kind of "sample" world. It is by no means the only example of a world, and is not necessarily the most important. There are better worlds and worse. Sometimes these stories relate these worlds to each other. (For example, a person flees into the forest but has in fact entered another world-system.) They may be treated as multiple dimensions of the same essential reality. Sometimes the transit from one world to another is explained in the story by the presence of a god or goddess, by flying, trance, dream, mysterious visitor, etc., and sometimes it is not. The geography and physics of a story do not need to resemble closely the geography or physical laws of this world. It may be only somewhat like this one. This point too is grounded in a profound Indian attitude. Jewish and Christian writers sometimes emphasize the fact that they take history very seriously, that they have and are devoted to a sense of historical progress. Many Hindus believe that this attitude gives altogether disproportionate attention to this particular planet, and to only one of its life-forms, man. They point out that, even by Western scientific procedures, we are convinced that there are billions of planets in the known universe, that the total span of human existence is only a tiny proportion of known natural history, and that our lives are necessarily connected with all other species. They note that the relatively recent Western discovery of the immense dimensions of the universe (which they have always taken for granted) was at first interpreted as a threat to belief in God rather than as testimony to His infinitude, because it appeared to diminish the relevance of human history as the most important testimony for the divine nature and purpose. Hindus point out that we are at least vaguely aware of the great probability of other forms of life and other dimensions of reality, and they point out that it is sometimes very difficult to tell which changes bring authentic progress. Most of our improved material facilities deface, destroy or pollute the environment in which we use them. They insist that one must sometimes take the larger, rather than merely the historical view. In any case, these stories embody a widely populated universe which contains many kinds of beings besides the human and animal. Yet the Hindu attitude holds that in this immense and fertile plurality of systems, not only each world but each individual deserves respect as a potentially perfect example of its own type. There is an integrity of which each individual being is capable, though it may seldom be fully realized. The necessity for the fulfillment of the inner law of each individual being is a recurring theme in Hindu thinking. In this process are integrated some of the most basic concepts of Hinduism, the *dharma,* which is the inner necessity of the individual, the *karma,* which is the connection of all acts with their consequences in the character and fortunes of the actor, and *saṁsāra,* which is the flowing stream of interconnection in the continual "passing through" which constitutes existence as we know it. In Hindu thought are brought together an appreciation for the individual in an incredibly prolific universal process and a sensitivity to the interconnections by which all individual beings, and things too, finally, are related to one another. Some of the beings which populate the universe, such as gods, goddesses, devas, apsaras, nymphs, aerial spirits, etc., are generally both better and more powerful than men. Others, such as rakshas, demons, etc., are generally worse but more powerful than men. Often the character of these beings (like human character) is somewhat mixed and uncertain.

Perhaps with these stories as background we can begin to reflect on the underlying attitudes, values and traditions being exemplified. Some of this reflection will be an effort to clarify unfamiliar details—specific customs, names, literatures, ceremonies, etc., which the stories take for granted. We shall also want to reflect about the atmosphere or climate of the stories and the more general attitudes and values they suggest. On some basic matters the story itself will provide the context and interpretation.[1]

CASTE, WEALTH AND POWER (PAGE 4)

The problem of caste is one of the most difficult in Indian religious and social history. The origins of caste are manifold and obscure; its meanings are confused, and the subject is a matter of sometimes bitter controversy. The *theory* of caste (*varṇa*) offered in the classical religious texts covers only a small part of the actual practice of caste distinctions in India. According to this theory, there are essentially four main types of persons: (1) an intellectual/spiritual type; (2) an active/ executive type; (3) a sensual/indulgent type; (4) a dependent/submissive type. In practical experience all types are more or less mixed. There are both good and bad examples of every type. According to the classical theory, caste represents a recognition of these innate differences in human personality types, and forms the basis for a social structure appropriate to the actual differences among men. When the social system is fully harmonized with the actual variations in human personality types, it should provide varied and fulfilling social opportunities for all the individuals involved—demanding of each what he does best, providing for each what he needs most, establishing conditions essential for compatible marriages and a stable social order. Corresponding to each predominant personality type there is a social role. Each of these general roles demands a certain temperament, provides specific vocations and appropriate types of satisfactions for each. For the intellectual/spiritual type there are the roles of priests, teachers, advisors of rulers and preservers of the traditions. These are the *Brahmins*.[2] For the active/executive type there

[1] Note: References to the appropriate materials in the stories can be facilitated by the use of the heading notations and page numbers on which they appear.

[2] As a device to promote clarity, this text will use the term "brahmin" in reference to the priestly caste. The term for the ultimate principle of reality, the impersonal absolute, will be Brahman. The priestly scriptures written as commentaries on the *Vedas* will be called *Brāhmaṇas,* and the four-faced god, creator of the world order (in most accounts) is Brahmā.

are the princely, war-making and administrative roles. They are warriors, decision makers, managers. They handle both wealth and power. These are the *Kshatriya,* often called the "princely" or noble class. For the sensual/indulgent type there are numerous roles as the fundamental producers of basic goods. They are the traders, manufacturers and some farmers. These are the³*Vāishya,* most commonly called "merchants" in the stories. Finally, the dependent/submissive type also has a role. Under the leadership of the other castes, they will be assigned tasks consonant with their powers and limitations as laborers, assistants and servants. Free from the necessity of decision-making, they find satisfaction in their important role in the total economy. These are the *Shūdra.* The objectives and values of each caste differ along with the roles. Spiritual fulfillment and knowledge of the truth are primary *Brahmin* virtues, though as several of the stories will suggest, this is sometimes inconsistent with "common sense." Reputation, the exercise of power and restraint, status and generosity (and the wealth necessary to sustain them) are *Kshatriya* values. Courage and decisive action are their critical virtues. The great heroes of the *Rāmāyana* and the *Mahābhārata* are *Kshatriyas.* Satisfaction, a pleasant and secure life in terms of home, food, family and friends, the gratification of the desires for comfort, ease and pleasure are primary values of *Vāishyas.* This may lead to overindulgence, but that is not characteristic of the type. A prosperous and hard-working merchant or a farmer, satisfied with his plain but nourishing meals, the pleasures of a rustic home, gentle wife, obedient children, numerous grandchildren, good friends, and ability to work with persistent skill and to sleep with clear conscience is more nearly the "ideal" of the type. The *Shūdra* too works for satisfaction, but needs the protection of wiser minds to direct his actions and appropriate tasks to exercise his specific skills. He is a man who has been born once, that is into human existence but not yet into the privilege of Vedic study or the services of a high-born priest.

Although this device is not perfectly justified on linguistic grounds, it is rather common. I have taken the liberty of making the various texts quoted here also conform to this spelling in order to avoid confusion.

This ideological structure of caste is only one of its elements, and the functional differentiations which it provides have been supplemented in numerous ways. In general in Indian life the members of a particular caste are bound together by a common traditional occupation and by the belief in a common ancestry. The functional caste distinctions which are based on occupation are enormously diverse and are not uniform all over India either in caste rules and customs or in their names. Along with occupational and ancestral distinctions, the rules of caste generally control customs connected with marriage, birth and death ceremonies, and particularly food and drink and those with whom it may be shared, as well as social relations with members of other castes. Though the origins of caste are sometimes connected with race, with vocation, with the incorporation of whole independent tribes into the larger culture, with certain kinds of occupational and/or geographical mobility, with crossing of established castes, and with conversion to or from other social groups, the traditional foundations as illustrated in the *Institutes of Manu* press all of these distinctions together into the general outline of the four castes and their many precise variations. In village life, where occupations have been relatively fixed and entirely traditional, and where marriage arrangements are more or less rigidly controlled, a specific caste leadership (pañchāyat) controls the meaning and imposes the powerful sanctions for caste. Where urbanization and industrialization are more fully developed, these controls are much weaker.

Fundamentally, the Indian view of caste as it developed following the Aryan immigrations and early settlement is an organic interpretation of society. A person's identity is found in the group of which he is a member, which inducts him into its expectations and controls many of the intimate details of his life, but which gives him security, satisfaction and self-confidence. It is this fundamental notion and its values to which Dr. S. Radhakrishnan refers when he describes caste as a system for harmonizing the races and occupational groups who have lived together in India.[3]

[3] S. Radhakrishnan, *The Hindu View of Life* (New York: The Macmillan Co., 1968), Chapter 4.

These stories reveal interesting characteristics of caste. For example, in the story of Savitri the wealthy royal family is concerned that their beautiful daughter might be rejected by her beloved, impoverished hermit, whom they believe to be a *Brahmin,* because she is below him in rank. Wealth and power are not the primary measures of status. The highest kingdom is not of this earth, and those who aspire to live in it are dependent in this world upon the generosity and respect of those whose ambitions and responsibilities are merely mundane. Many *Brahmins* covet and sometimes achieve power and wealth, but usually it demonstrates that they are "foolish" *Brahmins.* Many of these stories reflect a rather flexible attitude toward caste. There is a certain openness between *Brahmins* and the higher *Kshatriyas* on marriage rules. Some of the stories have merchant heroes who rival *Kshatriyas* in cleverness, wealth and power. It would seem that these stories document the notion that caste has been sometimes more and sometimes less rigid. Always there is the distinction between the three upper castes (the twice-born) and the *Shūdra* and out-of-caste people. Caste will sometimes be more important, sometimes less, in these accounts, but it is a part of the assumptions of Indian society that men are fundamentally of different sorts and need to find out just who they are, and to function in organic relation with all the other sorts of men which society requires.

DELIVERY OF HEAVENLY KNOWLEDGE AND OMENS (PAGE 5)

Hindu stories abound in auspicious moments, omens and divine messages, promises and threats. Some of this is merely literary. It adds poignancy and significance to the story. But the idea reflected by the delivery of such supernatural knowledge is fundamental. There are episodes and movements in Hindu thought which would seem to be entirely fatalistic, to insist that the whole course of life for every individual is predetermined and unchangeable. But such extreme fatalism is not predominant. It seems safe to say that all Indian religion teaches that a great many of the fundamental circumstances of life are already fixed and constitute the conditions to be respected in all decisions. Assertions of radical indeterminism are not common in India, but the situation is complex. Almost always there is a recognition of some margin of choice within the context of conditions. The future will be determined by the choice made, but the choice itself involves some room for genuine initiative. All sorts of omens, warnings and suggestions may be provided. For the pious it is most commonly the visit of a god or goddess. For others any of the supernatural sorts of beings may deliver the message, openly or cryptically. Astralism, virtually universal in India, may be consulted for omens, and palmistry (or occasionally dream analysis) may be used in the same way. These clues will enter into the decision-making process, if the individual will attend to them. These suggestions will have to be related to the discussion of *karma* to be taken up later, but for the moment it should be seen that there is a popular tradition which insists that men should be alert for the omens and signs coming to them from the superior ones of the higher worlds, to warn them of dangers, assure them of triumph, or condition their existence. Just as praise is sometimes exaggerated, so these omens are sometimes given an absolute form which later seems to be modified. One can understand much apparent inconsistency as natural in the type of literature we have here. Notice, for example, in "The Defeat of Death" that Shiva promises early death and then prevents and punishes Yama, his agent, for attempting to fulfill his decree. Man must have a chance if an omen or warning is to have real meaning.

VISIBLE SYMBOLS OF A GOD (PAGE 6)

In the story of Savitri, for the first time, there is a brief description of *Yama*, the God of Death. He is obviously anthropomorphized, armed with a club, robed in scarlet, and mounted on a water buffalo. Each of the principal gods of the Hindu pantheon also has his or her equivalent description. A full description would include a direction (Yama is south, for example), weapons or other characteristic objects held in the hands, costume, mount, and consorts. In some situations there may be special ornaments or headdress and characteristic postures as well. These traditional characterizations are modes of recognition, generally artistic traditions emerging from religious dance, sculpture and painting as well as expressions of the character, experience and concept of deity. The whole question of images and worship and polytheism will be taken up much later, but for now it may be noticed that the deities are not altogether vague abstractions; each of them has a character and can be recognized in a variety of ways. One may wish to begin to establish the major themes expressed by the principal deities as they appear in the stories.

THE BOON AND THE CURSE (PAGE 7)

Two recurrent themes in this literature are the boon and the curse. These may sometimes appear merely as literary devices serving obvious functions in the stories, but they are expressions of fundamental attitudes. There are various ways in which the boon and the curse appear. The boon usually represents the attitude that the gods will respond to human demands if they are properly presented. One of the forms of this underlying attitude is the "Act of Truth" (*satyakriyā* or *satyavrata*) as discussed by E. W. Burlingame and particularly by W. Norman Brown.[4] He points out that beginning as early as the *Rig Veda* and continuing through the Brāhmaṇas to the Epic and Purāṇic literature are accounts of incidents in which individuals demonstrate magical power to accomplish their will based upon the singleness of their integrity and truth. Formally the act requires a declaration of fact concerning the integrity and singleness of purpose of the individual, a command or resolution that some particular event shall occur, and a prayer that in the light of the integrity of the person his purpose shall be accomplished. In the accounts we have before us here these formal conditions of the "act of truth" may not be present, nor is it necessarily a demon-

---

[4] Cf. W. Norman Brown, "The Basis for the Hindu Act of Truth," *Review of Religion*, Vol. 5 (Nov. 1940), pp. 36–45 and E. W. Burlingame, "The Hindu Acts of Truth," *Journal of the Royal Asiatic Society* (1917), pp. 429–467.

stration of the power of one's integrity, but in the boon and curse, as in the act of truth, it is the singleness, the persistence, the absolute and unswerving determination of the individual which is the basis of the power. In the earliest of the Vedic literature (*Rig Veda*) there appears the concept of an inexorable and impersonal cosmic order, called *ṛta*. This is the ultimate pattern which all things, including the gods, observe. Anything in harmony with this order must be fulfilled. Anything out of harmony with the ultimate order must finally fail. Sacrifice is the means of coming into harmony with the cosmic order. Any who will perform the proper act in the proper way will achieve the power of the sacrifice. In ordinary terms, this is not a moral question. As Professor Brown put it: "Whether priest, king, thief or prostitute, a person should be scientific and efficient. In this way the individual achieves personal integrity and fits the cosmic purpose. Life then becomes a sacrificial act, a rite (*kriyā*) and as such, when perfectly executed, it can accomplish any wish, compelling even the gods, as we are taught in the Vedas and the Brāhmaṇas is possible through sacrifice." [5])

The "boon" represents the attitude that the gods will respond to human demands if they are properly presented. Absolute sincerity must have its benevolent result. The proper presentation of the demands may involve very different sorts of things. In the story of Savitri it was her dogged persistence, love and courage which earned the boon. The "Rishi Who Envied the Fish" had generated power by his enormous austerities to accomplish his purpose. This is a common feature. Saktideva achieved his objectives and was assured of ultimate success by persistently maintaining the vow to clear himself. Total devotion to Shiva won the necessary protection for Markandeya. In all of this we see that moral character in the usual sense may or may not be required in order to receive certain divine rewards. Austerity, persistence and self-disciplined preparation seem to be the most common basis for the granting of a boon.

When the recipient's initial response to the offer of such a gift is to wish for a good thing for someone else, to use up

[5] Brown, *op. cit.*, p. 39.

the reserve of merit which one has built up in an unselfish and intercessory act for another, it is common that the boon will be granted again. Ultimately, however, the hero or heroine must be clever enough to distract attention or to exhibit such overwhelming sincerity and unselfish devotion as to secure the promise of the one forbidden wish. Boons may be granted by anyone with the power to fulfill the request or promise—gods, devas, rishis, kings. They are absolutely binding without any regard whatsoever to convenience or appropriateness of the request. It is this feature which gives the dramatic conflict of the *Rāmāyana* (see Part III of this text) its particular intensity. The deeper attitude reflected here has two parts: (1) wishes, hopes, fears, the inner attitudes with which one responds to fortune or misfortune are enormously important in the conduct of life; and (2) in the cosmic order of the universe the various powers which may lead to success are essentially amoral in themselves; they may belong to anyone who will pay the price to acquire them. In a culture which gives so much attention to the fixed conditions of life (caste, karma, saṁsāra), wishes, hopes, aspirations and integrity play an enormously important role. In a culture which is especially sensitive to the variations in the moral rules which govern different classes of men there is an equally clear recognition that the conditions which give a person a particular kind of competence can be met by individuals of very different moral character or intent. These powers can be attained either for evil or for good ends, depending only upon whether one meets the required conditions for their attainment.

The *curse* is another common element in many Indian stories. Perhaps it should be understood as a kind of commentary on human nature. A curse once pronounced by a figure of proper authority (most often *rishis*) must be fulfilled. Nothing can interfere or prevent its accomplishment. Even if the one who made the curse instantly repents and regrets his hasty words, he cannot take them back or avoid their consequences. One slight out is provided. He may continue to state the limiting conditions of the curse, but it will remain in effect until all these condtions are fulfilled. The insight draws attention to the fact that inexorably one must live with the consequences of his words and acts no matter how impulsive and thoughtless they may have been. A second dimension of the insight corresponds to the proverb, "Pride goes before a fall." A curse often is the explosive release of the pent-up energy created by years (or in the Hindu view perhaps even lifetimes) of austerity and devotion. As one's reserves of spiritual power build up by means of such intense and austere discipline, one's situation becomes increasingly precarious. One may use this power and achievement to reach the ultimate fulfillment of existence in liberation (*moksha*) or one may dissipate the power through some impulsive outburst. Such a lapse is, of course, an indication of an actual failure on the part of the *rishi* to be as totally dedicated and sincere as he had seemed. One of his goals must be to pass beyond all irritability, where annoyances, no matter how provocative, are ignored and transcended. Pronouncing a curse both reveals one's inner weakness and dissipates some portion of his spiritual merit. Time and again the stories suggest that the problems of life are the result of a curse which one may have carried for years as a result of some stupid childish prank, and that the flash of anger which the curse expresses is an occupational hazard of holy men.

THE RISHI (PAGE 9)

In Hinduism there are a number of religious roles which have no exact counterparts in Western religions. The Brahmin is a caste position of considerable complexity. Some Brahmins (but not all) function in the temple and community as priests, performing the important ceremonies of worship (*pūjā*) before the temple images, or conducting the major ceremonies in the home. These people are religious professionals, technicians and specialists. It is a vocation for which they are trained through exacting apprenticeship. They are expected to receive a major portion of the offerings brought before the gods and to be given appropriate gifts by the families for whom they perform various services. This is their means of livelihood. Brahmins are religious professionals, but they are not necessarily deeply religious persons.

Cutting across the whole structure of caste is another kind of religious elite, which depends not on name or descent but on personal religious power. Some of the members of this group are members of the *saṁnyāsa* order as men who have put aside or abandoned worldly concerns. The term applies as well to those who have reached the fourth and final stage of life in the orthodox Brahmin tradition. Sometimes called *sādhu* (straight, holy, pure) hermits, ascetics, forest dwellers or wanderers, they invariably practice rigid austerities (*tápas*) as part of their way of life. These men have voluntarily chosen some means of religious self-discovery as the sole concern of their lives and devote themselves to it entirely. Although as indicated before and throughout the stories, the Hindus enjoy all the pleasures of life, they understand that in the final analysis the truly religious person will outgrow and go beyond all such pleasures for the still greater good of ultimate fulfillment. No such deeply religious person either possesses or has any concern about any form of wealth or personal status. He is a free man, with only the most slender and inconsequential strings to hold him to this earth. He has his spiritual eye on goods that man can't give and cares little for anything that man can take away. Therefore he is beyond the possibility of either seduction or threat. The term *rishi*, meaning singer of sacred songs, has come to mean one of the patriarchal saints or sages of ancient times, but is also used more popularly to mean a person renowned for piety and wisdom. The poet-singers of the basic Hindu scriptures (*Vedas, Āraṇyakas, Upanishads, Mahābhārata, Rāmāyana, Purāṇas*, etc.) all were *rishis*. In these stories we find the term used more loosely and meet rishis of a different character. For the most part serious religious thinking in India has been done in poetry or song. The rishis are the authors of this religious poetry, these holy accounts of which they were given direct vision for the benefit of mankind, and these songs of personal devotion in which their faith is expressed. Because the rishi is the saint and sage of the Hindu heritage it is all the more tragic when he misuses his enormous spiritual and psychic powers. Although these stories may at times represent the rishi as silly, irritable, vicious and hypocritical, he is in his authentic version the very highest form of the religious' life for men, a kind of divine being in his own right, through whom the eternal message of the Vedas continues to be the living truth for man.

PLEASURE AND AUSTERITY (PAGE 11)

One of the common misconceptions concerning Hinduism is that it is essentially other-worldly. Some Hindu literature, especially philosophical literature and that in which the life of the ascetic is eulogized, gives basis to this conception, but the stories here will show clearly that it is only a half-truth. The desires of the rishi who envied a fish are for the best that earth has to offer—pleasant surroundings, comfort, family, numerous children and grandchildren. More erotic values are suggested in the delights of the "City of Gold," while the process of development and maturity in one's ability to work for longer-range satisfactions is indicated in the conversation between Yama and Markandeya. The net result must be the recognition that Hindus appreciate all sorts of values; comfort and delight; wealth, sex, family joy, adventure, ease, reputation, and anything else which people may regard as valuable. Over and above all these good things, which may be called simply "pleasures" there is, however, another kind of good. This kind of good is spiritual, absolute and ultimate. It takes a special kind of spiritual vision to see this ultimate release, this freedom, as good, especially since it involves the rejection of so much that others call good. It is to be approached through austerity and self-discipline, which then have their value as the means of ultimate liberation. Many of these stories assume that such a perspective is indeed the supreme point of view. They recognize, in fact often accentuate, the idea that the standards of a holy man will appear absurd when measured by ordinary human standards of pleasure, cleverness and success. Pleasure is to be enjoyed in its way, perhaps for many lifetimes, but beyond all pleasures are the authentic goods of life for which the spirit of man ultimately will yearn.

ARRANGEMENT OF A MARRIAGE (PAGE 14)

It is neither possible nor essential to understand all the historical and legal circumstances concerning marriage arrangements in India. One theme, however, does recur in several forms and should be mentioned. The general pattern throughout Indian history has been that marriage must be arranged by the heads of families for their children. This is a most important responsibility—especially for the father of a daughter. These arrangements must take into account many factors which the young persons themselves might not at first be able to appreciate properly. The marriage is a permanent social relationship which will have profound effect on the social status of the families involved (not merely the individuals to be married) so that matters of caste must be respected even though they may be quite restrictive. There should be auspicious signs in the comparison of astrologies. There must be appropriate financial arrangements designed to reflect both the relative status of the families involved and to protect or enlarge the families' interests and give stability to the marriage. The young people themselves should approve of the choice, though it would be taken for granted that no objection would arise from this quarter. Many different forms of marriage were legally recognized—love marriages (*Shakuntalā*), marriage with captured women (*Rāmāyana*), polygynous and polyandrous marriages (*Mahābhārata*), in-caste and out-of-caste marriages, but these are all exceptions to the rule that marriage ought to be fully and properly arranged. Hindu stories frequently suggest that a happy and fulfilling marriage is often the result of a uniting and reuniting of the same couple through many different lifetimes and in many different forms.

In these stories polygamy and bride's choice (*svayaṁvara*) are rather frequently mentioned. These patterns may have been authentic, but probably only occasionally and usually in the higher castes. From the literary standpoint, however, such marriages are especially interesting, since the relationships among the various wives (or husbands) or the competition among the young princes for an especially desirable princess

provide ready-made bases for conflict and intrigue. Even today in much of India the early years of the marriage of Rāma
and Sita are regarded as the ideal of married bliss, while the
licentious and adulterous designs of the mistress, Prabhavati,
who was prevented from meeting numerous lovers only by
the enchanting tales of the parrot left behind by her husband,
are regarded as much more common and probable attitudes
on the part of women.

THE VOW (PAGE 20)

Throughout these stories fundamental psychological principles and insights are clothed in the flesh of concrete characters and their motivations. A person's actions and attitudes
seem bewildering until they are seen in relation to the vow
which motivates his life. Not everyone is under a vow, of
course. It is a mark of a certain kind of maturity. It means that
a person has voluntarily taken upon himself the achievement
of some value. This achievement may be inferior to other values, but for the moment at least the individual will have
clarity of purpose and a measure of his success or failure. The
most serious and profound vows as illustrated in Indian literature usually take several generations for their realization. The
fact that one lifetime may have closed without the vow having
been realized does not at all mean that the vow will forever
remain unrealized. The conditions for its fulfillment must all
be met, and it is not always possible to see what conditions
one will have to meet in order to fulfill his deepest purposes.
The elements of continuity in existence, according to the
Hindu testimony, are most likely to be purposes, expressed in
the form of the vow and continuing as a latent motive which
will spring into action the moment the conditions are right.
A person's life should cross several thresholds. Each of these
will be marked by progressively more serious and enduring
vows, until at last one vows to be free from rebirth and separation. This is the vow which leads to liberation. From the moment that one makes this vow in the depths of his being, he
begins to live in a new dimension in which all that happens
is somehow an expression of the intent which motivates his

life. The "Acts of Truth" which were discussed earlier may be
seen as one of the expressions of the relation between the integrity of the person and his capacity to accomplish what he
intends—no matter what that may be.

THE USE OF ANCIENT SYMBOLS (PAGE 24)

There are many human projects which seem virtually impossible because everything has to be done first. This is true
of the incidents, symbols and allusions of these stories. The
stories emerge in a stream of literary tradition each element
of which takes most of the other elements for granted. If we
had grown up in Indian culture, many of these allusions
would have been familiar proverbs or sayings which would
have aroused old memories of other stories heard. There is
an incredible interconnectedness which pervades most Hindu
literature. This is true both of the serious and profound religious writings such as the *Vedas, Brāhmaṇas,* and *Upanishads,* but also of the more popular religious literature such
as the Epics (*Mahābhārata* and *Rāmāyana*), the *Purāṇas,* and
the later folk literature from which many of these stories are
taken. The familiar episodes, poems, hymns, or characters of
the ancient books are often used as illustrations or metaphors
in the later writings. Such interconnections are common.
Many of these stories assume that the reader is already familiar with many such traditions. In other cases the characters
in a story begin to tell other stories to illustrate some point
which they have brought up. This process of digression can
go on so far that the original issue becomes entirely lost, but
usually the main line of the argument is clear enough even
when the illustrations are not. Later there will be a more systematic discussion of Hindu literature. In the particular case
mentioned here there is a reference to the ancient story of the
mountains flying about and upsetting the earth's balance until
Indra cut off their wings. The next sentence uses the ancient
symbol of the banyan tree as an indicator of the divine presence, here connected with the bottom of the ocean, submarine fires, and a broad whirlpool. All of these are allusions to
ancient myths. Generally we will not attempt to develop these

allusions unless they are essential to understanding the story at hand. The principal point is that even in a popular literature such as this, there is constant reference to the mainstream of Hindu tradition such as one would find embodied in the *Upanishads* and in the earlier *Vedas*.

THE SNARE OF ILLUSION (PAGE 28)

In the Western tradition it has been common to take seriously only the wakened and sober state of consciousness. Those things which "appear" to us in dreams, or in flights of fancy, may be strangely perplexing but are not to be given credence as sources of knowledge. The Hindu tradition on the whole finds the wakened, sensory state of consciousness equally perplexing as dreams and fancies, and sees no reason to deny the possibility of truth to any state of consciousness. They recognize that we are often fooled by our imagination, by our senses, by our desires and interests. This foolishness, however, may often be a clue to the deeper dimensions of our experience, to the real meaning behind the bewilderment. In the Hindu philosophical tradition this notion assumes enormous importance. It becomes the basis for an analysis of knowing which puts ordinary sensory experience into a secondary role and allows the testimony of the more subtle dream and "beyond dream" worlds to count for more. This notion also becomes the expression of the doctrine of *māyā*, a mode for interpreting our experience in the present world. These more specialized uses will await later development, but one may already see how this popular literature expresses the Indian appreciation of the many worlds which we may inhabit and of the "snare of illusion" in which we may be trapped if we do not regard the world from the proper perspective.

KALI (PAGE 31)

It has always been difficult for most Westerners (and for some Hindus, for that matter), to understand the worship of Kali. She is "The Mother," but unlike our images of motherhood she is the "Fierce Goddess." The necklace she wears is made of children's skulls; her body is fiery red and she is worshipped by blood sacrifice. It is obvious that this conception represents something very primitive in human experience. Archaeological discoveries in ancient North Indian sites and recent research on the reading of the seals found there have given some support to the hypothesis that she was known by name in the Indus Valley civilization about 4,500 years ago.[6] In fact Kali is known by many names (Durgā, Devi, Uma, Pārvatī, Kapalini, among the more important) and is rather obviously composed of traditions from many groups and times. Mentioned in *Rig Veda* as one of the tongues of Agni (fire) she became popular in the following periods. She is associated particularly with fire, mountains, childbirth, terror, fever. The most famous stories about her deal with her fight with a great demon in the form of a buffalo, and a second fight in which each drop of spilled blood of the demon Raktabiya formed a new *asura* just as powerful. She drank up all the blood before it struck the ground and thus saved the *devas* (and became known as bloodthirsty also). She also has been associated particularly with the later forms of Hindu tantrism in which worship in forms of drunkenness and blood sacrifice have been developed.

In Kali we find a recognition of the mutuality of destruction and creation, of the mutuality of the flow of blood and milk, the death and destruction of the many that some may survive. She embodies the writhing of labor, the trauma of birth, the authentic act of creation, not shorn of its bloody afterbirth or the sense of the precariousness of survival. She represents the primitive recognition of the fierce power of creation in volcanic fires and smoking hills. She is the *shakti* or creative energy of the great god Shiva, one of his manifestations. She is by no means pure destructivity, and is the great support of her devotees, but this is no "mother" to be wrapped around one's little finger, to be subject to the wheedling and soft appeals of those whom she has spewed into the world. She is not to be approached easily, but it is well to be her

[6] Cf. Asko Parpola, "The Indus Script Decipherment," *Journal of Tamil Studies*, Vol. II, No. 1 (May, 1970), p. 94.

devotee just the same. In Kali is the ancient recognition of the mingled fury and compassion which encloses all creative action, the recognition of the stillborn and soon dead who are represented by every surviving individual.

THE COW (PAGE 32)

The Hindu attitudes toward the cow are sometimes perplexing to Westerners. The visitor to India lands at a modern jet airport, passes through the usual labyrinth of customs and emerges into India itself, where his bus or taxi into town is required to dodge slow-moving cows in the streets (among many other kinds of obstacles). The airport scene is familiar. The idea that cows have priority over traffic is not. The contrast makes one wonder. The cow is in fact a very complex symbol in Hindu history. Her sanctity was recognized in prehistoric times and is related to the "Guardian of Living Things" in Iranian mythology. In *Rig Veda* a mystical relation between the cow and the universe is established, which continues to be developed through the later literature. She is seen as a kind of generating principle of the universe. She is intimately related to *Earth* and also to heaven, rays of light, of the sun, rain, clouds, speech, and holy song. A particular image of importance emerges as early as the *Atharva Veda*. *Virāj*, as universal cow, comes to divine beings and to men who milk her of all the things they need, including cultivation and grain. It is this myth which is fully developed in the story of Vena and Prithu which appears in Part II.

The origins of the taboos against cow slaughter and eating beef are difficult to discern. Though early Aryans were apparently herdsmen and beef eaters, even in the *Vedas* we find the beginnings of the attitude of reluctance to use beef. It is specifically forbidden in the *Shātapatha Brāhmaṇa*, but a curious exception (for tender meat) was mentioned. One of the major ceremonies which occurs on the occasion of receiving a distinguished guest, especially perhaps a Brahmin, say for an important wedding, is the slaughter and eating of a cow as part of the required hospitality. Later it became customary for the guest to decline the formal offer, while appreciating the thoughtful and generous gesture of his host. In later times the prohibition was much stronger. In the *Mahābhārata* the veneration of the cow is explained by the necessity of her products (milk, curds, ghee, dung, urine) for religious sacrifice. These are also seen as purifying agents for men, with urine and dung thought to have special therapeutic and purifying powers. A curious legend also accounts for the name "the fragrant one" for Surabhi, mother of cows, as she was born from the satisfied belch of the creator having drunk his fill of nectar. Much later we see Krishna related to the cowherds and milkmaids, again suggesting their high status. The cow as the patient mother, source of nourishment, symbol of fertility (rain) and prosperity, came ultimately to share in the inviolability of the holy caste for whom she was a gift, and of the gods to whom their sacrifices were offered. In South Indian legend there is another story of a reckless young prince whose careening chariot killed a calf. The bereaved cow rang the temple bell and demanded justice from the King. So the cow was to be associated with justice as well as prosperity and with the favor of all benevolent divine beings. The association of Vishnu (via Krishna and Surabhi) with the cow and of Shiva with the bull (Nandi) strengthen these attitudes of veneration and respect. The late texts also describe *Goloka,* the cowheaven, in glowing terms.

The passage in our story obviously is designed to support the rejection of beef for food. Vegetarianism has never been anywhere nearly universal in Indian religion, but the rejection of the use of beef by Hindus has become very widespread. Cows are protected by the attitudes of the people. On the other hand, it ought also to be recognized that in India cows are herded, milked, beaten, shooed away, fed, and ultimately usually slaughtered and the hides tanned. Some cows serve as scavengers in the cities and their wandering has much to do with the absence of fenced pastures and the needs of the poor for dung for fuel. It may be that in the light of modern conditions of life, the increasing burden of traffic in the cities, the demand for purification of milk, and the emergence of new awareness of the population/food problem, Hindu attitudes toward the cow will undergo significant change, but the symbol of the cow lies deep in Indian consciousness. The reasons are very different, but the emotional impact of the use of cows for food for many Indian persons would perhaps be very similar to the reaction of Western readers that we use pet dogs and cats for food.

CEREMONIES OF A HINDU HOUSE (PAGE 38)

Every Hindu sect provides a full round of ceremonies which identify and intensify the crucial events of family life, mark with appropriate rites the stages of development, and secure the blessings of the gods upon the home. Many of these ceremonies are simple family affairs to which a few friends and relatives may be invited. Some of them are spectacular public occasions which virtually turn into festivals. In many rites (especially daily ones) the father and mother officiate, but for others it is desirable or mandatory to invite a Brahmin priest to perform at least some part of the ceremony. Since this function cannot involve inappropriate crossing of caste lines there are different priests to serve each different kind of caste. Though all are known by the name of Brahmin and license to perform such services is rigidly controlled, it is obvious that they do not all come from the same ancestry.

Taken as a whole this topic would become enormously complex. This is due to various factors. There are numerous events which may be marked by ceremony—when pregnancy has been established, the first perceptible movement in the womb, birth, naming, the taking of the first solid food, crossing the threshold to the "outer world," the first recital of a religious text, mastery of each of the stages of learning, puberty, marriage arrangements, the marriage itself, religious initiations of various sorts, certifications of one's experience or skill, completion of religious studies, death of relatives, inheritance, employment, retirement, illness, and death. Secondly, there is a daily rhythm of life—awakening, rising, first sight of the day, physical and spiritual preparation for the day ahead, first greetings, daily tasks, meals, meditation, worship, work, study, reflection, last sight in the evening, sleep, etc., which may to greater or lesser extent be sanctified or marked by religious features. Thirdly, each sect will have its own sequence of notable events and its own particular ways to mark those it regards as important, such as events in the life of founders or great leaders, historical events, annual or monthly cycles of events. Fourthly, there is an additional monthly and yearly cycle of public holidays which families are likely to celebrate at home as well as in the community or temple. There will be special rites for such holidays,[7] often involving processions, music, fireworks, special costumes or activities and gifts to all servants and also perhaps to Brahmins and to the poor. There are a great many of these in the course of the year.

In an orthodox Hindu home there would ordinarily be a *pūja* (worship) room in which are kept the treasured religious symbols of the family—god images housed in a special cabinet, implements and utensils of worship, etc. Before this shrine the mother and father conduct the daily and seasonal worship of the home—the blessing of the food to be eaten there, the protection of the gods and goddesses for each family member through the day. In such a home, religion is very much a part of everyday life.

In India as elsewhere the conditions of modern life in the cities have tended to weaken the hold of many of these traditions over large numbers of the people. Great public holidays are still very widely celebrated, but there is increasing neglect of some of the ceremonial forms. Whether Hinduism can successfully resist this secularization, or what modifications it may be required to make in the light of it, is for the future to determine. It seems probable that changes will be substantial.

[7] A fascinating series of films has been produced by Professor H. Daniel Smith, of Syracuse University, which illustrate and show some of these ceremonies. For information and/or rental please write: Marketing Division of Film Rental Library, 1455 E. Colvin St., Syracuse, New York 13210.

PART II

RELIGIOUS MEDITATIONS AND TEACHINGS

HOW SHRI BHĀGAVATA
CAME TO BE WRITTEN[1]

BĀDARĀYANA, KNOWN ALSO as Vyāsa, was one day seated on the bank of the Sarasvatī with his mind ill at ease. He thought within himself as follows: "I have written the *Mahābhārata*, explaining the meaning of the *Veda* and making it available even to women and *shūdras*. Yet my mind is not at ease. Perhaps I have not emphasized *Bhāgavata dharmas* (accounts of Bhagavan) in the manner which will be appreciated by the great yogis who are dear to Bhagavan."

Just then the divine sage Nārada appeared before him and stated that his suspicion was well-founded; and that though he had described all the *dharmas* in the *Mahābhārata*, he did not give prominence to the *Bhāgavata dharmas*.

He said: "A work may be well-written, but if it does not relate the pure deeds of Bhagavan, it will be like a pool which is resorted to by crows but in which the swans will find no pleasure. A work may show defects of grammar and of prosody in every verse; but if it contains Bhagavan's Names, descriptive of his noble deeds, it will wash out the sins of the world, and great men (*sādhus*) will hear it read; they will sing it to others or relate it to themselves.

"People are by nature drawn to *dharma*, wealth and enjoy-

[1] "How Shri Bhagavata Came to Be Written," from *Sribhāgavatam: Being an Analysis in English,* translated and published by Diwan Bahadur V. K. Ramanujachari (Kumbakonam, Madras, 1933), pp. 1–5 (as translated and adapted from the *Bhāgavata Purāṇa*).

Values:
Proximate
and
Ultimate
(page 134)
ment. By pointing out the means of attaining them you intended to do them good, but the result will be the reverse; for they will regard those ends alone as worthy of being sought and they will not pay any attention to their defects and turn away from them towards Bhagavan.

"There may be here and there a clever person that will do action only as the worship of Bhagavan and may be able to perceive with ease his noble deeds. But most people do not know what their own nature is and are made to do worldly actions by their *guṇas;* for their sake it is necessary for you to write a separate work dealing only with *Bhāgavata dharmas.* For this purpose do *yoga* and find out what those deeds are."

Nārada then praised *bhakti* (love for Bhagavan) as the means of obtaining the only good that is worthy of being sought, and in order to show the importance of *Bhāgavata dharmas* in creating a love for Bhagavan he related the story of his own life.

Nārada

In the previous *kalpa* (world age) I was a Gandharva (musician) named Upabarhana; I had a fine person and was full of conceit on that account. Certain great sages assembled at a sacrifice asked me to sing songs about Bhagavan. I, however, sang worldly songs, and the sages being enraged at this cursed me, saying, "Do you become the son of a *shūdra* woman."

Accordingly I became the son of a sweeper woman. Fortunately for me, my mother was engaged to do service to certain sages, who were assembled at a place during the rainy season, and who were spending their time in relating stories of Bhagavan.

Though I was a boy only five years old, I was made to attend upon them, and I listened to the stories with great attention, giving up my toys, and ate 'the remains of the food partaken by them. By listening to their stories of Bhagavan, by taking the remains of the food partaken by them, and by the service which I rendered to them, my mind became pure and a love for Bhagavan sprang up in me.

Prasāda—
Sharing of
Holy Food
(page 137)

When the sages departed, they imparted to me *jñāna*

(knowledge), which was given by Bhagavan Himself, and which is carefully preserved and taught only to proper students. I pondered over this instruction every day, and Bhagavān was pleased to give me fuller knowledge.

Soon after my mother died of a snake bite, and pleased with being rid of this encumbrance, I went to a jungle in order to do *tapas*. I sat at the foot of a peepul tree, and as taught by the sages, I meditated upon Bhagavan who is within myself. I was so wrapped in the meditation that I even forgot my body.

For one moment, Bhagavan was pleased to show His form to me in my mind, and then He disappeared. Then I became unhappy and made efforts to see Him again. Then I heard a voice in the air saying, "You are not fit to see Me in this birth of yours; for your mind has not become pure. My appearing before you for a moment was to stimulate your desire. Continue in this practice and you will in due course become so truly pure that you will give up every object of desire and you will become My *bhakta*. Your knowledge of Me which you have now acquired will never leave you and you will remember Me even if you go through a period of dissolution and be born in another *kalpa*."

When the proper time came, my *shūdra* body fell down and I entered the bosom of Brahmā, when He lay on the ocean during the ensuing *pralaya*. At the beginning of this *kalpa*, I came out from Brahmā and was then born as Nārada along with nine *Prajāpatis*.

Nārada then advised Badarayana to write a book on *Bhāgavata dharmas* in particular, so that men who now suffer from the three kinds of sufferings might know whatever they have to know to end them. He then repeated to him the instruction which Brahmā received from Bhagavan and which he received from Brahmā. Brahmā directed Nārada to amplify this teaching so that a love might be created in men for Bhagavān. This direction was communicated by him to Badarayana. *Shri Bhāgavata* was the book written by him in accordance with this direction from Bhagavān through Brahmā and Nārada.

A PURĀṆIC ACCOUNT
OF CREATION[1]

THE FOLLOWING ACCOUNT has been paraphrased from the *Bhāgavata Purāṇa*. It begins with a description of the topics treated by the *Purāṇa* as a whole and then provides an account of creation as described by Brahmā to Nārada, the celestial sage.

A *Purāṇa* should deal with ten matters: (1) *sarga*—that is, the creation of the universal process, the five great elements and the instruments of the Self; (2) *visarga*—the creation of the several orders of living beings by Brahmā; (3) *sthana*—the greatness of Bhagavān shown by the destruction of his enemies; (4) *poshana*—the protection of the created world; (5) *ûti*—the tendency created in men by the actions which they do to procure fruits of different kinds; (6) *manvatārakathā*—stories of the several *Manus* who held sway; (7) *ishankathā*—stories of the *avatāras* of Bhagavān and of those who love Him only; (8) *nirodhā*—the dissolution of the world; (9) *mukti*—the relief of *ātmas* from the bondage of *karma* and the attainment of their true nature; and (10) *āshraya-Bhagavan*—praise of the divine power who supports the world.

[1] "A Purāṇic Account of Creation," adapted from *Sribhāgavatam: Being an Analysis in English*, translated and published by Diwan Bahadur V. K. Ramanujachari (Kumbakonam, Madras, 1933), pp. 8–22 (from the *Bhāgavata Purāṇa*).

SARGA CREATION

This world, full of beings and objects appearing in various forms and bearing various names, was at one time without names and forms. The matter of which they were the forms was dissolved in subtle matter known as *prakriti*. The *ātmas* (Souls, Selfs) being deprived of their bodies, were all exactly alike, and the world then consisted of three essences—matter (*prakriti*), Selfs (*ātmas*) and God (*Bhagavan*) who controls both. They were so intimately blended that it was not possible to separate them even in thought. The *Veda* therefore states that before creation being (*sat*) alone existed, one only.

When the proper time came, Bhagavan decided to become many, that is, to become the present world with its numerous forms and names. He gave a shake to matter, which ever forms his body (i.e., a thing supported and controlled by an intelligent being for his own purposes). In the condition of rest (*pralaya*) the three *guṇas* of matter—*sattva* (being, existence, goodness), *rajas* (activity, passion) and *tamas* (darkness, idleness, inertia, degeneration) were in equipoise. Creations (page 137)

By this shaking, the equipoise was disturbed and one or another of the *guṇas* predominated in each of the stages or products which emerge (as the curd, the buttermilk and the butter emerge from the process of churning). The result of this shaking was that the portion of matter which was marked out for the future world became gross and visible and some became elements. From the most gross elements came the five great *bhūtas*—ether, air, fire, water, and earth successively, each grade of matter being grosser than the one from which it was formed. From the least gross elements came forth minds, the five classes of senses of perception and of senses of action which serve the *ātmas* as their instruments in their embodied condition. These interacting processes form the creation of the univeral system.

VISARGA CREATION

The fundamental substances and forms of being were unable to do anything by themselves. The *devatas* (divine aspects) in charge of them praised Bhagavan, who then entered into the twenty-three substances and mixed and compounded them in various ways. The substances thus mixed and compounded appeared in the form of a lotus bud in the navel of Bhagavan, who floated in the water envelope. In this Bhagavan entered also as Brahmā, who was to be the ruler of the universe to come. It took a thousand years for the lotus bud to grow in size and to develop fully. During all this time Brahmā and the *ātmas* that were to take birth in the universe dwelt in the lotus bud.

Great Gods and Others (page 138) Brahmā then came forth and looking all around saw no one other than himself. He thought that the lotus flower should have come forth from some cause; and in search of it, he went down through the stalk of the lotus flower into the water envelope and looked for a long time. Failing in this attempt, he came up and sat on his seat. He considered how he should create the world but did not then perceive it.

He then heard the word *"tapa, tapa"* in the air, which means to do *tapas* (meditation, austerities). He looked all around to see from whom the word came, but found no one. He made *tapas* for one thousand divine years (an unimaginably vast time). Bhagavan then showed him His own world, known as *Vaikuṇṭha*. Brahmā was greatly pleased, and being directed to create the world, he requested Bhagavan to impart to him such knowledge as would help him in that work; that he might do the work with due diligence; that he might not be touched with the charge of partiality when he should create differences in the world according to the *karmas* of the various individuals, and that he might not be intoxicated with the thought that he was the creator of the world.

The creation of the various orders of living beings takes place on the same general plan in every *kalpa* (age). It will therefore be sufficient to state how this creation was made in the present *kalpa*. At the beginning Brahmā found that the worlds *bhu* (earth), *bhuvas* (higher worlds) and *svarga* (highest worlds) were submerged in water. The first step was to drink the water. He then considered how he might create the three worlds and meditated on Bhagavan. Bhagavan said, "Do not yield to depression; make efforts to create. What you desire

has already been arranged by Me. Do *tapas* again and meditate on Me. With these you will clearly see in your heart the
three worlds as they were before. You will see Me pervading
yourself and the three worlds, and the three worlds in Me.
When one thus sees Me dwelling in all beings, as fire is in a
piece of wood, he abandons his depression. In addition he
should see himself, i.e., the *ātman*, divested of the material body
with its instruments, as resting on Me. He will then be released from bondage.

"You have now to create numerous beings in accordance
with their past *karma;* but this will not affect your mind;
for you will have My blessing with you, and though you will
be engaged in this work, the quality *rajas* will not bind you.
You have already had several proofs of My blessing. You know
Me who cannot be known by embodied beings; you perceive
that I am connected as their controller with the elments, the
senses, their three qualities (*guṇas*) and the *ātma*. Also you
saw Me outside of yourself, when you wished to know Me,
and searched going down through the stalk of the lotus
flower into the water below; and you have praised Me, dwelling on the stories of My deeds, and have done *tapas*. I am
pleased with this praise of yours. I impart to you the knowledge of the *Veda*, with which create as in the previous *kalpa*
all the beings that have rested upon Me." With these words
Bhagavan disappeared. Brahmā carried out Bhagavan's directions.

The first order of living beings created by Brahmā under
the command of Bhagavan was the vegetable kingdom, consisting of trees forming the lords of the forest, trees bearing
flowers and fruits, shrubs, herbs and creepers. Among these
should be included also as the sixth variety those that are required only for the skin, like the plantain and the bamboo.
Next came the creation of beasts consisting of the beasts that
roam on land, the birds that fly in the air, and the fish that
swim in the sea. . . . This order of beings is full of the quality
of *tamas*, and cannot distinguish between the past, the present
and the future; they perceive with their senses of smell and
feel pleasure and pain that are present, but cannot look beyond
them. Then came the creation of human beings, who are full
of the quality of *rajas* and do *karma;* they regard what is really

pain as pleasure. Lastly came the creation of the *devas* (supernatural beings) which consist of eight classes.

The *devas* themselves were created by Brahmā when he shone brightly; and they came forth from his face turned to the east. The *devas* are therefore bright beings and powerful in the day. The *spirits of the forefathers* were created when Brahmā felt himself strong. They are worshipped by men with offerings, when they desire strength. The *asuras* were created from the back of Brahmā, and they are powerful during the time between the departing day and the coming night. They are addicted to the pleasure of sex union. The demonic *yakshas* and *rakshas* were created when Brahmā was overpowered by the quality of *tamas*. These classes therefore show this quality prominently, and are powerful during nights. When Brahmā laughed, enjoying the beauty of his own person, the musicians and dancers came forth from him (that is, from his mood or state of mind). The ghosts and magicians were made when Brahmā thought of the power of making oneself imperceptible. These classes have therefore the power of disappearing at their will. The evil and lustful spirits came from Brahmā's shadows; they sing every morning and praise Brahmā, each together with his wife. When he was indolent, the demons came forth from him, and when he lay down and was angry the great snakes like Takshaka were born.

Kurmāra Shristi Brahmā meditated upon Bhagavan, and when his mind became pure thereby, four sons came out of him, Sanāka (Eternal One), Sanānda (Eternal Bliss), Sanātana (Eternity), and Sanātkumāra (Eternal Youth). The father directed them to propagate the human race, but as they liked Bhagavan alone, they declined. The father (Brahmā) became angry, and could not control his anger, even though he tried to do so. In this state Rudra (Shiva) came out of him from between the eyebrows. Brahmā directed Rudra to multiply the human race. He complied with this command; but those whom he created were full of the quality *tamas* and began to devour things around them. Brahmā then said, "Enough! Go and do *tapas* on Bhagavan." Then came out of Brahmā, Nārada, the Celestial Sage, and nine *Prajāpatis* (creative agents) from whom the world evolved and was filled.

MEDITATION ON THE WORLDS[1]

THE UNIVERSE, formed from the body of Bhagavān, consists of fourteen worlds (*lokas*). *Bhuloka* (earth-world) is in the center and it is the world in which we live. Above this but below the sun is the *Bhuvarloka*. Immediately below the sun is the world of the eclipse-planet; below this is the world of strange magical ones; and below this is the world of various demons. Below this but above the earth is the world in which the wind moves. The higher limit of the *Bhuloka* is the place where the swan and other superior birds fly about. Between the sun and *Dhruva* is the *svarga* world. It is the abode of the *devas* (gods and goddesses) under the command of Indra. In this region are the following in order of their distances from the moon: Sukra (Venus), Buddha (Mercury), Bhauma (Mars), Brihaspati (Jupiter), Manda (Saturn) and the Seven Rishis, and above them all is the star known as Dhruva. Around him the whole of the starry sphere moves round like bulls tethered to a central post. Above the *Svargaloka* are the worlds *Worlds* (page 140) Mahar, Janas, Tapas, and Satya. In the Mahar reside seers like Sanāka and the other three sons of Brahmā. In the *Tapasloka* (meditation world) reside the *devas* known as Vairājas. The *Satyaloka* (World of Being) is the abode of Brahmā. The three worlds, Bhu, Bhuvar and Svarga, are known as *krītaka*

[1] "Meditation on the Worlds," from *Sribhāgavatam: Being an Analysis in English,* translated and published by Diwan Bahadur V. K. Ramanu-jachari (Kumbakonam, Madras, 1933), pp. 23–28.

from the fact that they are destroyed at the end of each *kalpa,* and are reformed at the beginning of the next *kalpa.* The three worlds, Janas, Tepas and Satya, are known as *akrītaka* from the fact that they suffer no change at the end of a *kalpa.* The *mahar* world which is between these two groups is known as *krītaka-akrītaka* from the fact that it is abandoned at the end of a *kalpa,* but not destroyed. Above the *Satyaloka* is the region known as *Vishnu-pada,* in which the sacred river Ganges (that is, the heavenly river) took its rise. Beyond this are the seven *avarnas* (envelopes).

There are seven *lokas* below the earth— *atala, vitala, sutāla, talātala, mahātala, rasātala* and *pātāla.* These afford greater sense enjoyment than the *svar* world of the *devas.* In the first, Bala, the son of the *asura,* Māyā, holds sway. He has created ninety-six *māyās* of which some are even now practiced in the place. In it are found three classes of beautiful women, who give sense enjoyment to any one that enters that world. This is done to such an extent that the person is so intoxicated that he regards himself as the controller of everyone and as one that has attained whatever has to be attained. In the second, Rudra [2] is surrounded by his attendants (the *bhūta gaṇas*) and is engaged in sexual intercourse with his wife, Bhāvanī. The semen that comes out of their union flows in a stream, which is drunk by fire and wind, and which is then thrown out by them. This becomes gold which is utilized by the residents for making ornaments. In the third lower world resides Bali, the grandson of Prahlāda, he from whom Bhagavan in his *avatāra* as Vāmana took away the three worlds and restored them to Indra. Here Bhagavan is present with his *gadā* (club) in his hand and is protecting Bali. Rāvaṇa (the demon of the *Rāmāyana*) came to this place in the course of a conquering expedition. Bhagavan told him that he was the servant of Bali, and that he should overcome him first before going on to his master. With these words he picked Rāvaṇa up by one of his toes and he was thrown off to a great distance. In the fourth

---

[2] Since this text comes from a Vaisnava source, Rudra, who is normally identified with Shiva, has been demoted from Kailasa to a lower world and lower task. Notice, however, in a later passage, that it is still acknowledged that he will protect his devotees securely.

lower world, Māyā the *Asura* resides. He formerly made three cities for the *asuras* and when they were destroyed by Rudra, he fell at his feet, and by his grace he lives in the place from the fear of Bhagavan's *chakra* (discus). In the fifth the great serpents, the sons of Kadru, reside. In the sixth, Rasātala, reside the enemies of the *devas* which are very strong. In the seventh, Pātāla, the lowest world, reside Vāsuke and other lords of the Nāga (serpent) underworld. Only the luster from the gems in their hoods dispels the darkness of that world. Below them is Bhagavān in the form of a thousand-hooded serpent, known as Sankarshaṇa. He supports the nether worlds and the earth.

The world system consists of seven islands. In the center is Jambūdvīpa, surrounded by the ocean of salt water. Around it are six other *dvīpas* [galaxies?] each surrounded by an ocean. Beyond the ocean of pure water are the *lokaloka* (world's end) mountains. Beyond them are no living beings, the sun, the moon, and the stars do not shine there. Jambūdvīpa (Center Island—Earth) consists of nine portions. In each Bhagavān is worshipped in a particular form and by particular personages. These forms are the *avatāras* of Vishnu. Of the nine earthly continents only Bharata (India) is the place where good and bad deeds yielding fruits can properly be done. The others are places where men of meritorious deeds reap the fruits of their good deeds which may remain after their enjoyment in the *svarga* world.

MEDITATION ON TIME[1]

TAKING AS THE UNIT the *Muhūrta* ("hour"—equivalent to 48 minutes of English time), 30 *muhūrtas* make one day. Three hundred and sixty days make one year for men. This is one day for the *devas*. Three hundred and sixty-six such days make a divine year. Twelve thousand divine years make a *catur yuga*, a period of time consisting of *Krita, Treta, Dvapara* and *Kali yugas*. The duration of the four *yugas* is: *Krita* 4,800 divine years; *Treta* 3,600 divine years; *Dvapara* 2,400 divine years; *Kali* 1,200 divine years.

Of these a portion at the beginning and a portion at the end of each *yuga* are known as *samdhyā*, i.e., the time during which two *yugas* met. Taking the two *samdhyās* together, the period is 800 divine years for *Krita*, 600 for *Treta*, 400 for *Dvapara*, and 200 for *Kali*.[2]

One thousand *chatur yugas* form a day of Brahmā, which is known as a *kalpa*. His night is of the same duration. Brahmā's life consists of 100 years each of 360 days and 360 nights. His life is known as *para*, being longer in duration than

---

[1] "Meditation on Time," adapted from *Sribhāgavatam: Being an Analysis in English*, translated and published by Diwan Bahadur V. K. Ramanujachari (Kumbakonam, Madras, 1933), pp. 29–32 (from the *Bhāgavata Purāṇa*).

[2] This works out to 4,392,000 human years to form one *chatur yuga* and about eight and three quarter billion years for one day and night in the life of Brahmā.

that of any other being. Brahmā is now in the first day of the second half of his lifetime. The present *kalpa* is known as *svetararāha kalpa* from the fact that Bhagavan appeared at the very beginning of the *kalpa* in the form of a white boar and brought up the earth from the lower world into which it had been carried by an *asura.* The previous *kalpa* was known as *padmakalpa.*

In each *kalpa* fourteen *Manus* (Patriarchal earth-rulers) hold sway, so that the duration of the rule of each Manu is seventy-one *chatur yugas* roughly. Six Manus have held sway and we are now in the rule of the seventh Manu. In each *Manu-antāra* there is a separate Manu, a separate Indra and the seven *rishis,* and Bhagavan comes down in *avatāra* (incarnation). The next Manu will be Savarani and the next Indra will be Bali.

In each *Manu-antāra* Indra holds sway over the three worlds. The *Veda* being forgotten and spoiled in each *Kali yuga* of a *chatur yuga,* the *rishis* reproduce it by doing *tapas* in the *treta yuga.* In the first *yuga* (*Krita*) men are naturally pure-minded, and they do *tapas* on Bhagavan, and they require no guidance. In the second *yuga* (*Treta*) men worship Bhagavan by *yajñas* (sacrifices) and therefore *Veda* in its threefold form should appear. This is reproduced by the seven *rishis.* Manu rules over the earth and propagates the human race. He also compiles the rules scattered in the various parts of the *Veda* and reproduces them in a convenient form for the guidance of men (that is, *The Laws of Manu*).

Towards the end of the third *yuga* of each *chatur yuga,* owing to the growing disability of men to learn the whole of the *Veda,* it is divided into four parts, and each is subdivided into many branches and each branch of the *Veda* is entrusted to the care of a particular group of men. The officer employed on this work is known as Vyāsa. This work of division has been done twenty-eight times, so that we are in the twenty-eighth *chatur yuga.*

Decline
(page 141)

MEDITATION ON DISSOLUTION[1]

THERE ARE TWO KINDS of dissolution. When the purpose of the evolution has been completed, the material products in the universe are dissolved into the elements. This takes place in the following manner. For a hundred years there is no rain, and every drop of water is evaporated. Then the universe is burnt up by a huge fire from below, and the whole is reduced to the form of ashes. Then for a hundred years there is torrential rain and all the compounds are dissolved into the elements. Then earth is reabsorbed in water, similarly water in fire, fire in air, air in ether, ether in the inert variety of self-awareness; mind, the senses of perception and action are all absorbed in the *sātvika* variety of consciousness, and all the varieties of consciousness are reabsorbed in *mahat* and *mahat* in *prakriti* without name and form. This is *prakrita pralaya* (the sleep of all nature). In the other dissolution only the three *lokas,* Bhu, Bhuvar and Svarga, are destroyed and this takes place as each *kalpa* ends, and the night of Brahmā begins.

The same process—absence of rain, evaporation, burning up and torrential rain—is repeated here also, but only the three worlds are affected. The Seers in the *mahar* world, unable to bear the heat, leave for the Janaloka.

Thus the creation, sustenance and the dissolution of the

[1] "Meditation on Dissolution," adapted from *Sribhāgavatam: Being an Analysis in English,* translated and published by Diwan Bahadur V. K. Ramanujachari (Kumbakonam, Madras, 1933), pp. 33–35.

universe have been described. Of these the fundamental substances, mind, and instruments of the soul are the work of
Bhagavan Himself. Creation of differences is done by Him
through Brahmā. In the classes thus created there are differences in the quality of the matter—*satva, rajas,* and *tamas,* that
predominate in the individual making up the class. The universe is sustained by Bhagavan Himself appearing in the form
of *dharma* (embodied righteousness) and coming down in
avatāra as animals, men and *devas.* The dissolution is done
by him in the form of time, fire and Rudra, when the time for
it comes, as clouds are scattered and made to disappear by
the wind.

The description of the creation, sustenance and dissolution
of the universe reflects the greatness of Bhagavan—His infinite capacity to know and His ability to do what is impossible for others. All this He does by mere willing, and it
never becomes futile. His infinite mercy is also exhibited. He
has nothing to gain for Himself by this work; for He can command whatever He may desire. His only wish is to help the
ātma that are in the universe resting on Him. They do not
truly know their own nature, and regard their bodies as themselves, and those that are connected with those bodies as
belonging to them. This ignorance makes them seek the gratification of their senses. They do *karma* of various kinds, and
are connected with one body after another. This is *samsāra.*
Bhagavan wishes to lift them from this. He gives them bodies
and instruments (souls). He informs them through the *Veda*
as to what they should do, and what they should not do. He
expects that the *ātma* with these helps will realize their own
nature, kill their hankering after sense-enjoyment, develop a
love for Him and identify themselves with Him in the end,
having the same thoughts and feelings, and serving Him for
Himself only. This is their true goal.

The Career of a Soul (page 142)

THE STORY OF VENA
AND PRITHU[1]

MAITREYA: "BEST OF MUNIS (sages), tell me why was the right hand of Vena rubbed by the holy sages, in consequence of which the heroic Prithu was produced."

Parashara: "Sunitha was originally the daughter of Mṛtyu, by whom she was given to Anga to wife. She bore him Vena, who inherited the evil propensities of his maternal grandfather. When he was inaugurated by the Rishis "Monarch of the Earth," he caused it to be everywhere proclaimed, that no worship should be performed, no oblations offered, no gifts bestowed upon the Brahmins.

"I, the king," said he, "am the Lord of Sacrifice; I alone am entitled to the oblations."

The Rishis, respectfully approaching the sovereign, addressed him in melodious accents, and said: "Gracious prince, we salute you; hear what we have to represent. For the preservation of your kingdom and your life, and for the benefit of all your subjects, permit us to worship Hari (Vishnu), the lord of all sacrifice, the god of gods, with solemn and protracted rites; a portion of the fruit of which will revert to you. (That is, the land will be fertile in proportion as the gods are propitiated, and the king will benefit accordingly, as

Sacrifice Supports the World (page 143)

[1] "The Story of Vena and Prithu," adapted from *The Vishnu Purāṇa: A System of Hindu Mythology and Tradition*, translated by H. H. Wilson (First Edition, London: 1840; Third Edition, Calcutta: Punthi Pustak, 1961), pp. 82–88.

a sixth part of the merit and of the produce will be his.)
"Vishnu, the god of oblations, being propitiated with sacrifice by us, will grant you, O king, all your desires. Those princes have all their wishes gratified in whose realms Hari, the lord of sacrifice, is adored with sacrificial rites."

"Who," exclaimed Vena, "is superior to me? Who besides me is entitled to worship? Who is this Hari, whom you style the lord of sacrifice? Brahmā, Janārdhana, Śambhu, Indra, Vāyu, Yama, Ravi (the sun), Hutabhak (fire), Varuṇa, Dhātā, Pusha (sun), Bhūmi (earth), the Lord of Night (moon); all these, and whatever other gods there be who listen to our vows; all these are present in the person of a king: the essence of a sovereign is all that is divine. Conscious of this, I have issued my commands and look that you obey them. You are not to sacrifice, not to offer oblations, not to give alms! As the first duty of women is obedience to their lords, so observance of my orders is incumbent, holy men, on you!"

"Give command, great king," replied the Rishis, "that piety may suffer no decrease. All this world is but a transmutation of the oblations, and if devotion be suppressed, the world is at an end."

But Vena was entreated in vain; and although this request was repeated by the sages, he refused to give the order they suggested.

Then those pious Munis were filled with wrath, and cried out to each other, "Let this wicked wretch be slain. The impious man who has reviled the god of sacrifice, who is without beginning or end, is not fit to reign over the earth."

And they fell upon the king and beat him with blades of holy grass, consecrated by prayer, and slew him, who had first been destroyed by his impiety towards god.

Afterwards the Munis beheld a great dust arise, and they said to the people who were near, "What is this?" and the people answered and said, "Now that the kingdom is without a king, the dishonest men have begun to seize the property of their neighbors. The great dust that you behold, excellent Munis, is raised by troops of clustering robbers, hastening to fall upon their prey."

The sages, hearing this, consulted, and together rubbed the

thigh of the slain king, who had left no offspring, to produce a son. From the thigh, thus rubbed, came forth a being of the complexion of a charred stake, with flattened features, and of dwarfish stature.

"What am I to do?" cried he eagerly to the Munis. "Sit down (nishida)," said they, and thence his name was Nishada. His descendents, the inhabitants of the Vindhya mountains, great Muni, are still called Nishadas, and are characterized by the exterior tokens of depravity (outcasts, barbarous mountaineers or forest people). By this means the wickedness of Vena was expelled; those Nishadas being born of his sins, and carrying them away.

The Brahmins then proceeded to rub the right arm of the dead king, from which friction was engendered the illustrious son of Vena, named Prithu, resplendent in person, as if the blazing deity of Fire had been manifested.

There then fell from the sky the primitive bow (of Mahādeva) named Ajagava, and celestial arrows, and panoply from heaven.

At the birth of Prithu all living creatures rejoiced; and Vena, delivered by his being born from the hell named Put, ascended to the realms above. The seas and rivers, bringing jewels from their depths, and water to perform the ablutions of his installation, appeared.

The great parent of all, Brahmā, with the gods and the descendents of the Angiras (the fires), with all things animate or inanimate assembled and performed the ceremony of consecrating the son of Vena. Beholding in his right hand the mark of the discus of Vishnu, Brahma recognized a portion of that divinity in Prithu, and was much pleased; for the mark of the discus of Vishnu, Brahmā recognized a portion born to be a universal emperor, one whose power is invincible even by the gods.

The mighty Prithu, the son of Vena, being thus invested with universal dominion by those who were skilled in the rite, soon removed the grievances of the people whom his father had oppressed, and from winning their affections he derived the title of *Rāja* or king. (This reading assumes the term from "rāga" meaning "passion" or "affection.")

The waters became solid when he traversed the ocean; the

mountains opened him a path: his banner passed unbroken through the forests: the earth needed no cultivation; but at a thought food was prepared: all kine were like the cow of plenty: honey was stored in every flower.

At the sacrifice of the birth of Prithu, which was performed by Brahmā, the intelligent *Sūta* (herald or bard) was produced, in the juice of the moonplant, on the very birth-day; at that great sacrifice also was produced the accomplished Magadha: and the holy sages said to these two persons, "Praise ye the king, Prithu, the illustrious son of Vena; for this is your especial function, and here is a fit subject for your praise."

But they respectfully replied to the Brahmins, "We know not the acts of the new-born king of the earth; his merits are not understood by us; his fame is not spread abroad: inform us upon what subject we may dilate in his praise."

"Praise the king," said the rishis, "for the acts this heroic monarch will perform; praise him for the virtues he will display."

The king, hearing these words, was much pleased, and reflected that persons acquire commendation by virtuous actions, and that consequently his virtuous conduct would be the theme of the eulogium which the bards were about to pronounce; whatever merits, then, they should panegyrize in their encomium, he determined that he would endeavor to acquire; and if they should point out what faults ought to be avoided, he would try to shun them. He therefore listened attentively, as the sweet-voiced encomiasts celebrated the future virtues of Prithu, the enlightened son of Vena.

"The king is a speaker of truth, bounteous, an observer of his promises; he is wise, benevolent, patient, valiant, and a terror to the wicked; he knows his duties; he acknowledges services; he is compassionate and kind-spoken; he respects the venerable; he performs sacrifices; he reverences the Brahmins; he cherishes the good; and in administering justice is indifferent to friend or foe."

The virtues thus celebrated by Sūta and Magadha were cherished in the remembrance of the Rāja and practiced by him when occasion arose. Protecting this earth, the monarch performed many great sacrificial ceremonies, accompanied by liberal donations.

His subjects soon approached him, suffering from the famine by which they were afflicted, as all the edible plants had perished during the season of anarchy. In reply to his question of the cause of their coming, they told him that in the interval in which the earth was without a king, all vegetable products had been withheld, and that consequently the people had perished. "Thou," said they, "art the bestower of subsistence to us; thou art appointed by the creator for the protection of the people; grant us vegetables, the support of the lives of thy subjects, who are perishing with hunger."

On hearing this, Prithu took up his divine bow, Ajagava, and his celestial arrows, and in great wrath marched forth to assail the Earth. Earth, assuming the form of a cow, fled hastily from him, and traversed, through fear of the king, the regions of Brahmā and the heavenly spheres; but wherever went the supporter of living things, there she beheld Vainya with uplifted weapons: at last, trembling with terror, and anxious to escape his arrows, the Earth addressed Prithu, the hero of resistless prowess.

"Know you not, king of men," said the Earth, "the sin of killing a female, that you thus perseveringly seek to slay me?"

The prince replied, "When the happiness of many is secured by the destruction of one malignant being, the death of that being is an act of virtue."

"But," said the Earth, "if in order to promote the welfare of your subjects you put an end to me, whence, best of monarchs, will thy people derive their support?"

"Disobedient to my rule," rejoined Prithu, "if I destroy thee, I will support my people by the efficacy of my own devotions."

Then the Earth, overcome with apprehension and trembling in every limb, respectfully saluted the king, and thus spake: "All undertakings are successful, if suitable means of effecting them are employed. I will impart to you the means of success, which you can make use of if you please.

"All vegetable products are old, and destroyed by me; but at your command I will restore them, as developed from milk. Do you therefore, for the benefit of mankind, most virtuous of princes, give me that calf, by which I may be able to secrete milk. Make also all places level, so that I may cause my milk, the seed of all vegetation, to flow everywhere around."

Prithu, accordingly, uprooted the mountains, by hundreds and thousands, for myriads of leagues, and they were thenceforth piled upon one another. Before his time there were no defined boundaries of villages or towns, upon the irregular surface of the earth; there was no cultivation, no pasture, no agriculture, no highway for merchants: all these things (or all civilization) was originated in the reign of Prithu.

Where the ground was made level, the king induced his subjects to take up their abode. Before his time also the fruits and roots which constituted the food of the people were procured with great difficulty, all vegetables having been destroyed; and he therefore, having made Svayambhūva Manu, the calf, milked the Earth, and received the milk into his own hand for the benefit of mankind.

Thence proceeded all kinds of corn and vegetables upon which the people subsist now and perpetually. By granting life to the Earth, Prithu was as her father, and she then derived the patronymic appellation Prithivī (the daughter of Prithu).

Then the gods, the sages, the demons, the rakshas, the gandharvhas, yakshas, pitris, serpents, mountains, and trees, each took a milking vessel suited to their kind, and milked the earth of appropriate milk, and the milker and the calf were both peculiar to their own species.

This Earth, the Mother, the Nurse, the Receptacle, the Nourisher of all existent things, was produced from the sole of the foot of Vishnu.

And thus was born the mighty Prithu, the heroic son of Vena who was lord of the earth, and who from conciliating the affections of the people, was first ruler to whom the title of *Rāja* was ascribed.

Whoever shall recite this story of the birth of Prithu, son of Vena, shall never suffer any retribution for the evil he may have committed; and such is the virtue of the tale of Prithu's birth, that those who hear it repeated shall be relieved from affliction.

THE LEGEND OF THE MOTHER OF KARAIKAL[1]

INTRODUCTION

SOME OF THE LEGENDS in the Tamil Periya Puranam relate to the period between the first and second great revivals of Shaivism (sectarian worship of Shiva), and a few are anterior to both. It seems pretty certain that, while the Jains and Buddhists were active and apparently triumphant everywhere, there, were a great multitude of the faithful Shaivites who, like the Covenanters in Scotland, were rendered more zealous by the persecutions to which they were exposed. Among these was the "Mother" of Karaikal, who was a poetess, many of whose verses are still preserved. The legend gives a most interesting picture of some phases of South Indian life a thousand years ago.

THE LEGEND

The "Mother" was the wife of a rich merchant of Karaikal, whose name was Paramadattan ("Endowed with heavenly gifts"). Her own name was Punithavathiyar ("The pure"). She was very devout, and especially careful to entertain all Shiva devotees that came to her door. One day her husband

[1] "The Legend of the Mother of Karaikal," from The *Tiruvaçagam: or Sacred Utterances of the Tamil Poet, Saint and Sage, Manikkavacagar*, translated by G. U. Pope (Oxford: at the Clarendon Press, 1900), pp. 111–113.

received from some persons who had come to him on business a present of two mangoes, of a very superior kind, which he sent home to his wife. Soon afterwards, a holy devotee arrived at the house as a mendicant guest; but she had nothing ready to offer him except some boiled rice. This she set before him, and having no other condiment to present, gave him one of the aforesaid mangoes. At noon her husband returned, and after his meal ate the remaining mango, which pleased him so much that he said to his wife, "There were two; bring me the other." She went away in dismay; but remembering that the god to whose servant—because he was His servant—she had given the fruit, never deserts those who serve Him, she offered a mental prayer, and straightway found a mango in her hand, which she carried to her husband. Being a divine gift, it was of incomparable sweetness, and he said to her, "Where did you obtain this?" She hesitated at first to reveal the wonder that had been wrought on her behalf, but reflected that she ought to have no concealments from her husband, and so told him everything. He gave no credence to her words, but roughly replied, "If that is so, get me another like it."

She went away, and said in her heart to the god, "If thou givest me not one more fruit, my word will be disbelieved!" Forthwith she found another fruit still more lovely in her hand. When she carried this to her husband he took it in astonishment; but behold! It forthwith vanished. Utterly confounded by these wonderful things, he came to the conclusion that his wife was a supernatural being, and resolved to separate at once from her. He revealed the matter, however, to no one, but quietly equipped a ship in which he invested a great part of his wealth, and then on a lucky day, worshipping the god of the sea, with sailors and a skillful captain, he set sail for another country where he made merchandise, accumulated a fortune, and after some time, re-embarking, he came back to India to another city in the Pandiyan land, where he married a merchant's daughter and lived in great luxury. A daughter was born to him, to whom he gave the name of the wife with whom he feared to remain, but for whom he retained exceeding reverence.

After a while his return and prosperity became known to

his friends in Karaikal, who resolved to compel him to receive again his first wife, their kinswoman, whom he had deserted. They accordingly proceeded to his new residence, carrying with them in a litter his saintly spouse, the "Mother" of Karaikal. When he heard that they had arrived and were halting in a grove outside the town, he was seized with a great dread, and proceeded with his second wife and daughter to where the "Mother" was encamped surrounded by her kindred. He at once prostrated himself with profoundest reverence before her, saying, "Your slave is happy here and prosperous through your benediction. To my daughter I have given your sacred name, and I constantly adore you as my tutelary goddess!!"

Poor Punithavathiyar, utterly confounded by this salutation and worship, took refuge among her kinsfolk, who all cried out, "Why is this madman worshipping his own wife?"

To this Paramadattan replied, "I myself beheld her work a miracle, and I know that she is no daughter of the human race, but a supernatural being, and so I have separated myself from her, and I worship her as my tutelary divinity, and have dedicated my daughter to her, and therefore have I worshipped her and call upon you to do the same."

But Punithavathiyar pondered the matter and prayed within herself to Shiva, the Supreme, saying: "Lord, this is my husband's persuasion! Take from me the beauty that I have hitherto cherished for his sake alone. Remove from me the burden of the flesh, and give to me the form and features of one of the demon hosts who evermore attend on Thee and praise Thee." That very instant, by the grace of the god, her flesh dried up, and she became a demoness, one of Shiva's hosts, whom the earthly world and the heavenly world hold in reverence. Then the gods poured down a rain of flowers, heavenly minstrels resounded, and her relatives, fearing, paid her adoration and departed. So she had now become a demoness, and her abode was the wild jungle of Alankadu; but through the inspiration of the god she sang several sacred poems, which are preserved. Afterwards there came upon her an irresistible desire to behold the sacred hill of Kailasa, and with inconceivable speed she fled northwards till she arrived at the foot of the mountain, and reflecting that it was not right with her feet to tread the heavenly ascent, she threw herself down and measured the distance with her head. The goddess Uma, Shiva's bride, beheld her thus ascending and said to her spouse, "Who is this that in this strange fashion draws near, a gaunt, fleshless skeleton, sustained only by the energy of love?"

To which Shiva replied, "She that cometh is the 'Mother,' devoted to my praises, and this mighty demon-form she has obtained by her prayers."

Caste and Spiritual Status (page 145)

When she drew near he addressed her with words of love, calling her by the name of "Mother," which she forever bears. As soon as she heard the word she fell at his feet worshipping Him and crying, "Father!"

Shiva then said to her, "What boon dost thou ask of me?" She worshipped and replied, "Lord, to me your slave, give love which is undying and infinite blessedness. I would fain be born on earth no more; but if I must be born, grant me at least that I may never in any form, at any time, forget Thee my God, and when thou dost perform thy sacred mystic dance, beneath thy feet in rapture may I stand and sing thy praise."

To which the God replied, "In Alankadu, thou shalt see my dance, and with rapture thou shalt sing."

Then the sacred "Mother" of Karaikal returned, measuring the distance still on her head to holy Alankadu, where she beheld the God's sacred dance, and sang her renowned lyrics in his praise.

THE FOUR BRAHMINS[1]

IN A CERTAIN TOWN there were four Brahmins who lived in friendship. Three of them had reached the far shore of all scholarship, but lacked common sense. The other found scholarship distasteful; he had nothing but practical, good sense.

One day they met for consultation. "What is the use of attainments," said they, "if one does not travel, win the favor of kings, and acquire money? Whatever we do, let us all travel."

But when they had gone a little way, the eldest of them said: "One of us is a dullard, having nothing but ordinary sense. Now nobody gains the favorable attention of kings by simple sense without scholarship. Therefore we will not share our earnings with him. Let him turn back and go home."

Then the second said: "My friend, you lack scholarship. Please go home."

But the third said, "No, no. This is no way to behave. For we have played together since we were little boys. Come along, friend. You shall have a share of the money we earn."

With this agreement they continued their journey, and in a forest they found the bones of a dead lion. Thereupon one of them said, "A good opportunity to test the ripeness of our scholarship. Here lies some kind of creature, dead. Let us

[1] "The Four Brahmins," as translated by Arthur W. Ryder, *The Panchatañtra* (Chicago: University of Chicago Press, 1925), pp. 442–444.

bring it to life by means of the scholarship we have honestly won."

Then the first said, "I know how to assemble the skeleton." The second said, "I can supply skin, flesh, and blood." The third said, "I can give it life."

So the first assembled the skeleton, the second provided skin, flesh, and blood. But while the third was intent on giving the breath of life, the man of sense advised against it, remarking, "This is a lion. If you bring it to life, he will kill every one of us."

"You simpleton!" said the other, "It is not I who will reduce scholarship to a nullity."

"In that case," came the reply, "wait a moment, while I climb this convenient tree."

When this had been done, the lion was brought to life, rose up, and killed all three. But the man of sense, after the lion had gone elsewhere, climbed down and went home.

And that is why I say:

> Scholarship is less than sense;
> Therefore seek intelligence:
> Senseless scholars in their pride
> Made a lion, then they died.

THE FISHERMAN TAKES A BRIDE[1]

PĀRVATĪ WAS ONE DAY inattentive while Shiva was expounding to her the Vedic mysteries, for which she was condemned by her angry husband and preceptor to be born on earth as the wife of a fisherman. Accordingly, one day she was discovered lying as a tender infant under a *Pinnai* tree, by the headman of the Paravar, a great clan of fishermen found everywhere along the coasts of the Tamil lands. By him she was adopted and grew up a maiden of surpassing beauty. At this time *Nandi,* the chamberlain of Shiva, in order to bring about the accomplishment of the god's purposes with regard to the banished Pārvatī, assumed the form of a monstrous shark, and in various ways annoyed the poor fishermen, breaking their nets and wrecking their boats. On this the headman of the Paravars issued a proclamation that whoever should catch the seamonster should be rewarded with the hand of this beautiful adopted daughter. Shiva forthwith made his appearance as a youth of noble aspect who had come from Madura, and at the first throw of his net caught the shark and brought it to land. He accordingly, having himself become a fisherman, received the fisherman's daughter in marriage. The god now assumed his ancient form, and restored Pārvatī to hers, and with many gracious words took the foster-father with him to Kailāsa, the paradise of the Silver Hill.

[1] "The Fisherman Takes a Bride," translated by G. U. Pope, *The Tiruvaçagam* (Oxford: at the Clarendon Press, 1900), p. 118.

THE LEGEND OF THE
LOWLY DEVOTEE[1]

IN THE TOWN of Tiru-cenkattan-kudi, in the Chora land (the
Tamil country round about Tanjore), there lived a man called
Paranjotiyar, who was skilled as a physician, and adept in the
management of horses and elephants, and also a mighty warrior. But he was a saint also. Day and night this noble and
highly gifted man meditated on the perfections of Shiva the
Supreme, and so humbly devoted himself and his wealth to
the service of the poor mendicant devotees of Shiva that he
always bore the name of the "Lowly Devotee."

On a certain occasion he had gained a great victory for his
Rāja, and as he returned laden with rich spoil the courtiers
sneeringly told the king that it was the singular devotion of
the brave hero to his God that had gained for him the victory,
which was therefore due solely to the favor of Shiva.

"What," cried the Rāja, who before this knew nothing of
the saintliness of his Commander-in-Chief, "have I exposed so
great a saint to peril of death in battle for my petty affairs?
He shall fight no more!"

The "lowly devotee" replied: "Nay, I have merely performed the ancestral duties of my caste. No evil there, though
I slew your foes!"

But the king, giving up to him the spoils of the campaign,

---

[1] "The Legend of the Lowly Devotee," from *The Tiruvaçagam*, translated by G. U. Pope (Oxford: at the Clarendon Press, 1900), Appendix 1,
pp. xxxviii–xxxix.

released him at once from all further service, and bade him occupy himself henceforth wholly in the service of God, and of his devotees. So the *Nayanar* (devotee) went home, and thenceforth devoted himself exclusively to the worship and service of Shiva in the temple of his native town. And, as domestic virtue is the highest of all virtue (a Tamil proverb) . . . he married a lady called Nangaiyar of Tiru-venkadu, by whom he had one son, Cirala-devar. At five years of age the boy was sent to school to learn Shiva's sacred books.

Now Shiva the Supreme was graciously pleased to make proof of the love of his devotee, and to test especially his obedience: and, therefore from among the various forms the God assumes, and under which he is worshipped by the six Shaiva sects, he chose that of Bhairava—"the terrible, the destroyer" and descended from Kailasa, his own peculiar heaven, in that dread shape, loaded with matted hair, his body smeared with ashes—weird and terrible. Yet he seemed a holy man, though of the most repellent type of fanatical mendicants. The "lowly devotee" found him thus seated under a banyan tree, and immediately discerning the sign of the sacred ashes, went to offer him hospitality.

The Uses of Opposition (page 146)

The disguised one inquires: "Art thou the renowned 'lowly devotee'?"

The Nayanar meekly replies: "The servants of my God deign in love to style me so. I have sought in vain today for guests among the pilgrim-servants of our God. I have now found thee. Graciously take thy holy meal in my house."

"Thou cannot find me the food I need."

"If Shiva's servants need anything, the difficult becomes easy, because of Him whom they serve: I can and will provide whatever thou can require."

"Once in six months I eat the flesh of a slain victim: this is the day."

"I have flocks and herds; I can supply and offer the victim, and my wife shall prepare the food."

(To an orthodox Shaivite the slaying of any living thing is a great crime; yet this devotee is represented as overcoming his natural repugnance to it and to the use of animal food, because he believed that what the servant of Shiva wished must somehow or other, there and then, be right. The whole story—one of the very oldest of the religious legends of South India—takes us back to the time of Abraham, and it seems to illustrate a faith resembling his. [Note by G. U. Pope])

The Bhairava replies: "What I eat must be a HUMAN victim. It must be five years of age, its limbs without a blemish; the only child in the household; a sacrifice willingly offered. Such a little one the mother must herself hold with joyous mind while the father slays. Such food alone I eat this day."

"Such food, if THOU require, is not difficult to supply," replies the "lowly devotee," and hastens homeward with cheerful countenance. His wife meets him with wifely obeisance at the door, and asks: "What does the holy one command?"

He repeats to her the awful words.

She asks: "Where shall such an offering be obtained?"

"My life, my wife," says he, "for much wealth might even such a one be bought, but where are the mother and father able with glad and pious mind so to sacrifice? It must be our own little son and it is we who must so offer him to the servant of God."

She, with a like unflinching devotion, consents and adds: "Go, bring from the school our little one, born to be the guardian of our lives."

The devotee, with pious mind, eagerly hastens to the school. . . . Soon the food is ready, the fearful guest is brought in, and the father with courteous deference begs him to eat of the sacrifice.

"I cannot eat alone. None so worthy to share with me as thyself."

Another plate is set in all lowly loving obedience. But the Bhairava interposes yet another objection.

"Thou has a son, let him eat too."

"My son cannot help us in this!"

"Till he come I eat not; go, seek, call, and bring him here."

The father rises, calls the mother and they, simply obedient, but bewildered, stand without the door and cry, "Come, O son."

Then lo, even as he was wont, his bright eyes beaming with joy, his long black silken curls glistening in the sunlight, his silver anklets tinkling as he runs, their son is seen hastening on, and rushes into his mother's arms. . . . When they would bring him into the presence of the disguised God, the dread guest had vanished, and the dish was empty, bright and clean. It had all been delusion, the sport of the Deity!

No death, no offering—but in pious will.

Then, because what the God caused them to seem to do in a loving ecstasy was right in its motive, though forbidden in itself, all the gods appeared to them in the sky and applauded them; and while they worshipped in speechless rapture, the father, mother, son, and nurse were carried away to Kailāsa, there to adore the God and Pārvatī, his wife, and Subramanya, his son, in bliss unending.

THE LEGEND OF KANNAPPA NAYANAR (EYE-DEVOTEE)[1]

THE IMAGE OF THIS renowned South Indian devotee stands in the temple at Kalahasti near the Pulicat hills. He was a Rāja of Uduppur, of the Shepherd caste, a *Vedan* or hillman. The story represents the ancient clan as possessing great wealth and authority in a wild, hilly district, where their whole occupation was hunting. The old chieftain, whose name was Nāgan (the dragon-man), is represented to us as moving about attended by fierce hunting dogs, armed with every kind of rustic weapon; a skillful archer, around whose mountain dwelling innumerable forest animals of every kind had their home, and where the cries of "shoot," "hurl," "strike!" were mingled from morning to night with the howlings of wild beasts, the barking of dogs, and the sound of the horns and drums of the hunters. He had no son, and therefore he and his wife went to the temple of Subramanya (a son of Shiva)—the favorite of mountaineers, and offered him cocks and peafowl, and a great feast with copious libations of strong drink and wild orgiastic dances. The result was that by the favor of their deity a son was born to them, who from his early childhood shared in his father's pursuits, being brought up, it is expressly said, "like a tiger's cub." The proud, happy father used to carry him about on his shoulder, but finding him one day too heavy to be thus

[1] "The Legend of Kannappa Nayanar," from *The Tiruvaçagam*, translated by G. U. Pope (Oxford: at the Clarendon Press, 1900), pp. 141–145.

borne, gave him the name of Tinnan (the sturdy one), which remained his pet household name. He was eventually to bear a more honorable and enduring title. Soon after this the old chief, finding himself unable any longer to conduct the hunting expeditions of the tribe, made over his authority to his son, with whom this story is concerned.

Henceforth the young hero was ever in the dense jungles with his veteran huntsmen. One day a gigantic wild boar that had been caught in their nets escaped, and ran off with prodigious speed up the mountainside. Tinnan pursued it with two faithful attendants, but it led them a weary chase and did not stop until, exhausted with fatigue, it fell down in the shade of a tree on the slope of a distant hill. There Tinnan with his sword cut it in two. His attendants came up, and were astonished and delighted at his success, and said, "We will roast the boar here and refresh ourselves." But there was no water at hand, so they took up the carcass of the boar and carried it some distance onward, till they came in sight of the sacred hill of "Kalahatti." At the sight of the mountain one of the attendants remembered that on that mountain summit there was an image of the "God with Flowing Hair" (Shiva). "If we go there, we may worship him," he added.

Lingam and Salāgāma (page 147)

Hearing this, the young giant Tinnan again shouldered the boar and strode on, exclaiming, "With every step that I move ahead towards that mountain, the burden of the boar diminishes. There is some miraculous power here; I must find out what it is!" So saying he rushed on with great eagerness until he came to the bank of a river, where he deposited his burden, told his companions to make a fire and prepare the feast, while he himself hurried onward until he beheld on the slope of the hill, on the further bank of the stream, a stone *lingam,* the upper part of which was fashioned into a rude image of the head of the god. The moment he beheld it, as the magnet draws the iron, it drew his soul which had been somehow prepared by the merit of good deeds and austerities performed in some former birth,[2] and his whole nature was changed,

[2] This sudden illumination and influx of devout feeling towards Shiva, the Supreme, is in strict accordance with the fundamental dogma of *Karma,* "old deeds" which suddenly, after many transmigrations, at the

every feeling being swallowed up in intense love for the god,
whom for the first time he now beheld.

As a mother seeing her long lost son return, tarries not, but
rushes to embrace him, so he threw himself upon the image,
tenderly embraced it, and fervently kissed it. With tears of
rapture his soul dissolving like wax in the sunshine, he cried
out, "Ah, wondrous blessedness! to me, a slave, this divinity
has been given! But how is it that the god remains here alone
in the wilderness where lions, elephants, tigers, bears, and
other wild beasts dwell, as though he were some rude mountaineer like me?"

Then examining the image more closely, he saw that water
had recently been poured upon it and green leaves strewn
over it. "Who can have done this?" he asked.

His attendant, who had in the meantime come up, replied,
"In the olden times, when I came here on a hunting expedition with your father, a Brahmin, I remember, came here,
poured water and placed leaves upon this image, repeating
some mysterious words; perhaps he is here still."

So it dawned upon the mind of Tinnan that these and other
services, which he himself could render, might be acceptable
to the god. "But," said he, "there is no one here to supply him
with food. He is alone, and I cannot leave him for an instant;
yet, I must perforce go and bring for him some of the boar's
flesh cooked for our feast." So after much hesitation and un-
willingness to lose sight for a moment of his new-found
treasure, he went back, crossed the stream, where he found
the food already prepared and his servants wondering at the
delay in his return. Tinnan, paying no attention to them, took
some of the boar's flesh, and cutting off the tenderest portions,
roasted them on the point of an arrow, tasted them, to ascertain that they were savory, carefully selected the best, put
them into a cup of teak leaves which he had sewn together,
and prepared to return to the woodland deity with his offering. The servants seeing all this, very reasonably concluded
that their master had suddenly gone mad, and hurried home

appointed time yield their assured, though long-delayed fruit. This subject demands the careful study of all who would gain an insight into any
Hindu system. (Note by G. U. Pope)

to ask the priestess of their tribe to return with them and
exorcise the evil spirit that they supposed had taken possession of their lord. Tinnan, unaware of their departure, hurried
back with the food in one hand, and his bow and arrows in
the other. As he crossed the river, he filled his mouth with
water, with which, coming before the image, he besprinkled it.
He then took the wild jungle flowers from his own hair, and
put them over it, and presented the coarse boar's flesh he had
brought, saying: "My Lord, I have chosen for thee the dain-
tiest portions, have carefully prepared them with fire, have
tasted them, and softened them with my own teeth. I have
sprinkled thee with water from the stream, and have put on
thee flowers thou mayest love. Accept my gifts!"

Meanwhile the sun went down, and during the whole night
Tinnan with his arrow on the strung bow kept watch around
the god, and at dawn went forth to the mountain to hunt, that
he might provide for the daily wants of his new master. While
he was gone on this errand, the Brahmin in charge of the
lingam, who was a learned ascetic of renowned virtue and holiness, came at daybreak, and having performed his own ablutions in the river, provided himself with a vessel of pure water
for the purification of the divine image, and a basket of sacred
flowers and fresh leaves for its adornment, and uttering the
mystic Five Syllables, devoutly drew near. A scene of unutterable pollution met his horrified gaze. Flesh and bones
were strewed around, and the image itself had been defiled
with filthy water and common wild flowers! With trembling
horror he sprang aside, exclaiming, "O God of Gods! What
unhallowed, impious hands of mountaineers have brought
these pollutions here? How didst thou permit them to profane
thy presence?" So saying, he wept, he fell down, and rolled in
anguish before the god. But reflecting that at any rate it was
wrong to delay any longer the sacred service, he carefully
removed the unhallowed things from the precincts, and proceeded to perform his daily worship according to the *Vedic*
rites; and having sung the appointed hymn, and many times
gone round the right of the image, and prostrated himself in
adoration, departed to his hermitage.

Meanwhile, the servants, having taken the news of Tinnan's

madness to old Nagan, his father, returned with him and the priestess of their demon temple. They both attempted to reason with the young enthusiast, and to recall him to the worship to which he had been accustomed; but its wild orgies delighted him no more. His whole affection was centered on the new-found Shiva; so they, regarding him as hopelessly mad, returned sorrowing to their village.[3]

Meanwhile the mountaineer guarded the god by night, returned each eventide to offer his gifts and perform his rude service, and spent the day in providing the flesh of beasts for the god's enjoyment. At dawn, when the young woodman had departed, duly came the pure and exclusive Brahmin, having scrupulously made his own ablutions, cleansed the precincts, and performed the ceremonious worship. These men, so different, serve by turns before the same *lingam,* which they both regard with equal reverence.

But this could not long continue so. The Brahmin made a passionate appeal to Shiva to guard himself from these pollutions. He then returned to his hermitage, sad and deeply perplexed. But in the night the god appeared to him, and spoke: "That which you complain of is to me most dear and acceptable! Your rival ministrant is a chieftain of the rude foresters. He is absolutely ignorant of the *Vedas* and the Shaiva texts. He does not know the ordinances of worship. But don't judge him, judge the spirit and motive of his acts. His rough and

[3] One object of this legend seems to be in the reconciliation of the orthodox Shiva worship with the ruder forms of demon worship then in use. The contrast is exceedingly striking when the refined and thoroughly instructed Brahmin, with his scrupulous attention to all the minutiae of Vedic worship who regarded the slaying of animals as a crime, and the eating of their flesh as an unspeakable abomination, and considered that whatever had touched a man's mouth was polluted, and that the wild human inhabitants of the jungle were a lower order of creation, is brought face to face with the youthful chieftain of an almost savage tribe, whose chief delight is to hunt down, slay and devour the birds and beasts of the forest; who brings boar's flesh for the unpolluted Shiva to eat, and carries water in his mouth wherewith to besprinkle the image; who actually uses his leather slippers to brush away the refuse leaves from the head of the god; who knows no sacred texts; and who worships the same god, indeed, but has nothing to commend him save a rude and uninstructed though zealous devotion. (Note by G. U. Pope)

gigantic frame is instinct with love to me, his whole knowledge—in your eyes crass ignorance—is summed up in the
knowledge of Me! The touch of his leather slipper is as pleasant to me as that of the tender hand of my son Skanda. The
water with which he sprinkles me from his mouth is holy to
me as the water of the Ganges. The food he offers to me—to
you so abominable—is pure love. I regard not the externals of
the worship. He utterly loves me, even as you do: but come
tomorrow when you will see his worship, and I will give you
proof of his devotion to me."

The Brahmin slept no more that night, but at daybreak was
put in hiding behind the *lingam* by the god himself. And now
Shiva, who knows the hearts of his worshippers, in order that
Tinnan's truth might be manifest, caused blood to trickle down
from the right eye of the image. The young worshipper draw-
ing near saw this, and exclaimed, "O my Master, who has
wounded you? What sacrilegious hand, evading my watchful-
ness, has done this evil?"

Then seizing his weapons he proceeded to search the neigh-
borhood to see if any mountaineer or wild animal could be
detected as the source of the mischief. Finding none, he threw
himself upon the ground in despair; but at length reflected
that he had heard of remedies which would staunch the flow of
blood. So he went and sought out in the jungle some good
herbs and applied them, but the wound bled all the more
copiously. Then a happy idea struck him: "For a wounded eye
the remedy is another eye applied," said he, and, pausing not
an instant, with his arrow he scooped out his own right eye,
and applied it to the bleeding eye of the image, from which
at once the blood ceased to flow! At this his rapture knew no
bounds. He sang and danced, and poured forth uncouth expressions of ardent thanksgiving; but on looking at the image
once more, alas! blood was seen issuing from the other eye.
After a moment or two of bewildered sorrow, his countenance
was lit up with a radiant light of gladness; for he had still one
eye left, and the efficacy of the remedy had been tried already.
So he raised himself up, put his foot up close to the image's
suffering eye, that he would be able to feel, when he could no
longer see, where to apply the remedy and proceeded to scoop

out the other eye. But this last sacrifice was too much for Shiva to permit to be consummated. Out of the *lingam* he put forth a sacred hand, and grasped that of the youthful enthusiast, who still held the arrow ready to accomplish its pious intention, and said: "Stay, Tinnan, stay your hand, my loving son! Henceforth your place for ever shall be at my right hand, on my holy mountain." The Brahmin had learned the lesson, that love and self-devotion are more than ceremonial purity, and fell prostrate, while the choirs of heaven chanted the beatification of the Saint, who is from age to age adored under his title of *Kann-appan*—the devotee who gave his eye for the service of God.

TEACHINGS OF THE
SAGE UMAPATHI[1]

IN HINDUISM THERE ARE numerous mystic syllables which are believed to possess special powers. The pronunciation of these magic words under the proper circumstances will release supernormal power by putting the individual into mystic harmony with the fundamental sound, rhythm, texture and meaning of the universe, that is, of the god of whose power the visible/audible universe is a manifestation. In Sanskrit and *Vedic* tradition the term "OM" (composed of the three sound components, "A," "U," and "M") and the *Gāyatrī mantra* are the most familiar. In the Tamil traditions of South India the *names* of Shiva and of Vishnu are used in a similar way by their respective votaries. In the Krishna bhakti movement the names "Hari," "Krishna," "Rāma" have a similar function. On the surface such words or phrases are very simple. The one used here is simply *"Shivayanama"* which is the name of Shiva in honorific form and could be translated "adoration to Shiva" or "praise Shiva." Such passages are never taken at the obvious level, however. They are subject to expansive development and elaboration. The following selection is a good example of one of these interpretations.

Each section consists of a question by the disciple, a poetic answer by the *Guru* (master teacher), and the commentator's

[1] "Teachings of the Sage Umapathi," from *The Tiruvaçagam*, translated by G. U. Pope (Oxford: at the Clarendon Press, 1900), Appendix 1, pp. xxxix–xlvi.

summary of the meaning which had been expounded, but often somewhat esoterically, by the *Guru*.

The Mystic Formula of the Five Letters (Syllables)

A SHAIVA ROSARY

SHI–VA–YA–NA–MA

Adoration to Shiva. . . . A help to those votaries who cannot otherwise attain to the bliss of mystic quietude (*samādhi*).

The disciple asks: If the unutterable rapture has not been gained by means already explained, is there any other method?

The Guru answers:

> The systems of grace,
>> the Vedas,
>>> and other sacred scriptures,
> Have as their object
>> the mystic meaning
>>> of the "Five Syllables."

Commentary: The substance of the teaching of the sacred "Five Letters" is the LORD, the FLOCK, and the BOND. Such is the conclusion of those mighty in the *Ágamas* (twenty-eight books of Shaiva teachings), the *Vedas* and other sacred books.

Summary: The substance of all truth is contained in the "Five Letters."

Disciple: What does this pentad of letters declare?

Guru:

> The King, the Energy,
>> The Bond, fair Maya,
>>> Soul—
> All these are contained
>> in the *Om-garam.*

Commentary: These contain (1) the Grace of Shiva, and (2) of Shakti, his Divine Energy, with (3) the knowledge of the bonds of finite ignorance, darkness and delusion, (4) the knowledge of fair *Māya* (world), and (5) of the Soul (*Ātman*). These are symbolized by the "Five Syllables" and in *OM* the whole are concentrated.

Summary: Here is expounded the doctrine of the mystic *OM*, which is the subtle form of the "Five Letters."

Disciple: What is the order in which the "Five Letters" stand?

Guru:

On the one side—
   mystic dance of "Weakness"
On the other
   dance of mystic "Wisdom"
Soul between the two.

Commentary: The syllables MA and NA represent the energetic whirl of Impurity itself, and as operating in the Soul; the syllables SHI and VA represent the mystic action of Shiva and of Grace. Between these stands YA, which represents the Soul.

Summary: Thus are explained the five letters by the mystic dance and sport of Shiva in the world and in the soul.

Disciple: Will impurity depart from those who repeat the "Five Letters?"

Guru:

Ah, worship;
   but if the foundation be not known,
   since SHI precedes not,
Impurity will still assert itself.

Commentary: When men repeat the sacred formula unmindful of the foundation, which is Shiva, desire will reassert itself, still clinging to the NA and MA.

Summary: Here he commiserates those who thus recite them, and still suffer, having no Divine assistance.

Disciple: Why is this pentad of letters recited thus?

Guru:

If Shiva come first,
   and thou so recite it,
Embodiment will cease.
   This is your method.

Commentary: If the devotee recites the pentad so that SHI and VA precede, by this position the embodiment will be removed. Thou, O Disciple, who desirest release, recite it thus!

Summary: This teaches that the released say, "Shi-va-ya-na-ma," and never Na-ma-shi-va-ya.

Disciple: What benefit accrues from this order of recitation?
Guru:
> VA will in grace give SHI
> and bring prosperity.
> To such souls this is the spotless Form
> which will appear.

Commentary: When thus recited, VA, which is Grace, points out SHI, which is Shiva, and establishes YA, which is the Soul, in the abode of delight. And that is the faultless, sacred form of Shiva.

Summary: Here the significance of the sacred formula of VA (the energy of Grace—Shakti) is taught.

Disciple: How will that soul exist in the heaven of liberation?
Guru:
> No longer placed between the spotless NA and VA,
> The Soul will stand in grace between VA and SHI.

Commentary: The Soul (YA) standing no longer between the spotted NA (Bond) and the spotless VA (Shakti—energy of Grace), now stands between VA (Grace) and SHI (the Power of Shiva).

Summary: This defines the position attained by those who rightly use the formula.

Guru:
> The sacred writings teach
> in every possible way
> To fix the mind on the path
> that leads not away from Him.

The Soul's Emancipation
(Tamil—"mutti"; Sanskrit—"mukti" or "moksha")

Ten faulty (or imperfect) theories of the consummation of liberation so devoutly wished for by all Hindus are enumerated in Umapathi's works or in the commentaries on them:

(1) There is the bliss aspired to by the worldlings. This is simply gross sensual enjoyment in this world. . . . These were atheistic Epicureans, followers of the Charvāka (Materialistic) philosophy.

(2) There is the cessation of the five skandhas (elements of

personality). This is the Buddhist *nirvāna,* and is always considered by Tamil Shaiva authors to be mere annihilation.

(3) The destruction of the three (or eight) qualities is pronounced to be the final emancipation by some Jains, and by the teachers of the atheistic Sāṅkhya system. This would reduce the human Soul to the condition of an unqualified mass, a mere chaos of thought and feeling.

(4) There is the cessation of deeds by mystic wisdom. This is the system of *Prabhākara,* a type of yogic discipline. The deeds mentioned are "all rites and services whatsoever." The devotee becomes in this case, so the Shaivite urges, like a mere image of clay or stone.

(5) *Mutti* is represented by some Shaiva sectaries as consisting in the removal from the soul of all impurity, as a copper vessel is supposed to be cleansed from verdigris by the action of mercury. There is a good deal of abstruse reasoning about the pollution aforesaid. "Copper is not really in this sense purified by the removal of the green stain on its surface; the innate weakness of the metal is in its constant liability to this defilement. Gold is never coated by such impure matter. Copper will always be so. It is, as it were, congenital. Now these sectarians preach that, by the grace of Shiva, the innate corruption of the Soul may be removed, from which will necessarily follow permanent release from all bonds." This seems to resemble very closely the Christian idea of the sanctification of the souls of men by divine grace infused. The Siddhānta, however, insists upon it that for ever, even in the emancipated state, the power of defilement, the potentiality of corruption, remains. The corruption cannot, it is true, operate any longer in the emancipated condition; but it is still there, dead unilluminated, the dark part of the Soul, turned away from the central light, like the unilluminated part of the moon's orb. Personal identity, and the imperfections necessarily clinging to a nature eternally finite, are not destroyed even in *Mutti.*

(6) Another class of Shaiva sectaries taught that in emancipation the body itself is transformed, irradiated with Shiva's light and rendered immortal. This system supposed that intimate union with Shiva transmuted rather than sanctified the Soul.

(7) There is then the system of the Vedāntis, who taught the absolute union of the Soul with the Infinite Wisdom, its commingling with the Divine Spirit, as the air in a jar becomes one with the circumambient air when the jar is broken. But here personality is lost.

(8) The doctrine of the Palkariyam, followers of Bhāṣkara, is that in emancipation there is an absolute destruction of the human Soul, which is entirely absorbed in the supreme essence.

(9) There were some Shaivites who taught that in emancipation the Soul acquires mystic miraculous powers; that, in fact, the emancipated one is so made a partaker of the divine nature and attributes, that he is able to gain possession of and exercise miraculous powers, which are called the eight "Siddhis." Persons professing to wield such magical powers are not unfrequently found in India, and there is in them very often a bewildering mixture of enthusiasm and fraud.

(10) There were also some who taught that in emancipation the Soul becomes like a stone, insensible. This stationary, apathetic existence, if existence it can be called, is the refuge of the Soul from the sufferings and struggles of embodiment.

In opposition to all these faulty theories, the true doctrine of emancipation is thus defined: When the Soul, finally set free from the influence of threefold defilement through the grace of Shiva, obtains divine wisdom, and so rises to live eternally in the conscious, full enjoyment of Shiva's presence, in conclusive bliss, this is *emancipation* according to Siddhānta philosophy.

The Guru—Venerable Teacher

The Guru plays a most important part in all Hindu religion. He is the "venerable preceptor," master, and embodied god. In the Shaiva system his dignity culminates. He is the one who, in successive embodiments, has drawn nearer and nearer to final deliverance (*mutti*), and is now in his last stage of embodiment. Shiva lives in him, looks lovingly on the true disciple through his eyes, blesses with his hands, with his mouth whispers into the disciple's ear the mystic words of initiation, and

crowns with the lotus flowers of his feet the bowed head of the
postulant, who thus is to become as his Master. The exact doctrine is set forth in the following couplets from Umapathi's
authoritative work, "The Fruit of Divine Grace."

GRACE IN THE FORM OF THE GURU

Disciple: Who comes when two-fold deeds are balanced?
Guru:
> Grace that in times of ignorance
>   abode within;
> Now made manifest by visible signs—
> The King
>   who departs not.

Commentary: While man was in this state of ignorant bondage He (Shiva) by latent grace abode within. Now the Divine
Lord, the very center of knowledge, appears in bodily shape
as Guru. Neither from before the eyes, nor from within the
Soul, does this King henceforth depart.

Summary: Divine grace assumes the form of a Guru.

Disciple: Is it essentially necessary that He Himself should
come as a Guru? Would not a learned man suffice?
Guru:
> None can know the disease within
>   but those of the household.
> Can the outer world discern it too?

Commentary: In any house if one be diseased, those in the
house will be aware of it, but the distant world knows it not;
so, if Shiva, who dwells within the Soul, comes as a Guru, our
disease shall be healed.

Summary: This removes the doubt as to the necessity of
Shiva's advent as a Guru.

Disciple: Can all recognize the Guru thus appearing?
Guru:
> Who born on this earth
>   is able to discern
>   such a Divine Dispenser of Grace
>   not ever given before?

Commentary: He (Shiva) performed the works of creation,
preservation, destruction and "veiling" without any manifest

appearance; but now His work of grace is performed in a way not known before, while He wears a human form as a robe, and thus conceals himself. This men know not.

Summary: Men think of the Guru, who is Shiva Himself made manifest, as though He were a mere man like themselves.

Disciple: How is it that inferior souls know not the Guru?

Guru:

> Souls immersed in the false darkness of sense-perception
> cannot see the two:
> Teachings of Grace Divine
> and the Teacher.

Commentary: Those who live in the enjoyment of fleeting, worldly enjoyments, and whose understandings are veiled by the darkness of ignorance (*anavam*) cannot know the two great truths of the blessedness of mystic Wisdom, and of the grace embodied in the Guru, by which it may be reached.

Disciple: Is it necessary that His sacred form should be visible like ours?

Guru:

> The world does not discern the bodily form
> As the cloak assumed
> to take and hold men fast.

Commentary: It is common in the world to ensnare beasts and birds by exhibiting their own shape as a lure. Here men would dread any appearance manifestly Divine, and so Grace clothes itself in a human dress, beneath which men, alas! fail to discern the Divine.

Summary: In this and the two preceeding verses, the ignorance of men in not recognizing the Guru is reproved.

Disciple: May not any teacher be thus cloaked in the image of Shiva?

Guru:

> What would this accrue?
> Who knows anything?
> Seek Him, and be freed.
> The true meaning is known only from Him.

Commentary: Whether you ordinarily rely upon a particular Guru or not signifies nothing; seek Him alone who can interpret the truth. So only can you escape from impurity and emerge into pure light.

Summary: The real meaning of any scientific treatise cannot be understood without the assistance of the true Teacher.

Disciple: Is it not enough that divine Grace is the core of your knowledge? Must He come as a Guru too?

Guru:

> When snake-poison has entered the system,
>> —not the mere presence of the "Mangus" (snake-charmer)—
> A skillful physician is necessary
> to remove the poison.

Commentary: The mystic art beyond that of the snake-charmer is necessary to cure one bitten by a poisonous serpent. Thus a Guru bearing Shiva's very image must look upon us with the eye of mystic Wisdom, and darkness will disappear, not otherwise.

Summary: The Bond (ignorance) is only loosened by the Divine Teacher.

Disciple: Is this His gracious manifestation as a Teacher for all, or for only one class?

Guru:

> To those become *a-kālar* He gives
> precious gifts of grace, and cancels deeds.
> To those still *sha-kālar*, as a Guru,
> He gives his grace.

Commentary: To the *Vinnāna-kālar* and to the *Pralaiya-kālar* (i.e., subject to only one or two of the three Bonds), who are freed from *Kalai* (sense deception). He reveals Himself in their inner consciousness, and removes *anavam* (the Bond of Ignorance). To others in the form of a Guru, He comes and bestows Grace.

Summary: This shows why, and for the sake of whom, He puts on the vestment of humanity.

Disciple: Can salvation be effected without the coming of the Guru?

Guru:

> Who can know unless the gracious Revealer
> Of the wide extended way,

the great Knower,
shall appear?

Commentary: Unless the Lord, possessed of the wisdom surpassing the six *Aṭṭuva* (elements of being), and the Revealer of the way of release, shall come in the form of Guru, who can know these things?

Summary: The knowledge of the really existent can only be given by the manifested Lord, possessed of perfect knowledge.

Disciple: Is it necessary that He should come in the form of another devotee? Is it not enough that He is within my sentient mind?

Guru:

Mystic knowledge may visit us
without His intervention—
When the fair crystal kindles fire
without the sun!

Commentary: The crystal may be faultless, but will not act as a burning glass in the absence of the sun; even so divine and mystic Wisdom enters not the mind, whatever knowledge it may possess, without the Guru, who is Shiva's grace made manifest.

Summary: In this it is taught that religious knowledge has no excellence without the teaching of the Guru.

THE STORY OF PRAHLĀDA

THE EVIL KING Hiranyakasipu, son of Diti, resting his confidence on a boon bestowed upon him by Brahmā, had brought the three worlds under his control. Displacing Indra, Kuvara and many other gods, he himself exercised the functions of sun and air, waters, fire and the moon. He was god of riches, judge of the dead, and appropriated to himself all the sacrifices to the gods. The true deities, therefore, wandered on the earth disguised in mortal forms.

Having conquered the three worlds, Hiranyakasipu was inflated with pride and enjoyed whatever he desired. Eulogized by demons, he was entertained by heretic sages, seductive nymphs and drunken *asuras*.

Hindu Reflection (page 150) His illustrious son, Prahlāda, was still a boy, living with his teacher and reading the lessons young boys study. One day he was brought by his teacher to the court where his father was engaged in drinking with his friends.

[1] "The Story of Prahlāda," from *The Vishnu Purāṇa,* translated by H. H. Wilson (First Edition, London: 1840; Third Edition, Calcutta: Punthi Pustak, 1961), pp. 82–88.
This story has been quoted here at considerable length because the prayers it contains are excellent examples of Hindu liturgical literature, the scenes it depicts are so filled with the assumptions and spirit of Hindu thought, and the lengthy speeches of Prahlāda are convenient summaries of basic Hindu teachings. The story has sufficient clarity in its own right that no additional commentary will be provided.

"Here now! Get up and recite what you have learned," said the King.

"Hear, sire," replied Prahlāda, "what in obedience to your command I will recite, the substance of all I have learned. I have learned to adore him who is without beginning, middle or end, increase or diminution, the imperishable lord of the world, the universal cause."

On hearing this King Hiranyakasipu, his eyes red with wrath and his lips swollen with indignation, turned to the teacher and said, "Vile Brahmin, what is this preposterous praise of my foe that, with disrespect to me, you have taught this boy to utter?"

"King of the Dāityas," replied the Guru, "it is not worthy of you to give way to such passion. That which your son has uttered has not been taught by me."

"By whom then?" said Hiranyakasipu to the lad, "By whom has this lesson been taught you? Your teacher denies that it proceeds from him."

"Vishnu, father," answered Prahlāda, "is the instructor of the whole world: what else should anyone teach or learn save him, the supreme spirit?"

"Blockhead!" exclaimed the king. "Who is this Vishnu, whose name you reiterate so impertinently before me, the sovereign of the three worlds?"

GLORY BEYOND DESCRIPTION

"The glory of Vishnu is to be meditated upon by the devout; it cannot be described. He is the supreme lord who is all things and from whom all things proceed."

"Are you so desirous of death, fool," responded the king, "that you would give the title of the supreme lord to anyone else, while I survive?"

"Vishnu, who is Brahmā," said Prahlāda, "is the creator and and protector not of me alone, but of all human beings and even, father, of you. He *is* the supreme lord of all. Why should you be offended, sire?"

Hiranyakasipu then exclaimed, "What evil spirit has entered

into the breast of this silly boy, that like one possessed, he utters such profanity?"

"Not into my heart alone has Vishnu entered, but he pervades all the regions of the universe, and by his omnipresence influences the conduct of all beings, mine, father, and thine."

"Away with the wretch," cried the king. "Take him to his teacher and teach him not to repeat the lying praises of my foe."

Prahlāda was conducted back to the house of his guru, where he continued to grow in wisdom. After a considerable time his father sent for him again, and on his arrival requested him to recite a poetical composition. Prahlāda immediately began:

> "May he from whom matter and soul originate,
> From whom all that moves or is unconscious proceeds,
> He who is the cause of all this creation, Vishnu,
> Be favorable unto us."

On hearing this Hiranyakasipu exploded, "Kill the wretch: he is not fit to live, who is a traitor to his friends, a burning brand to his own race."

The attendants, obedient to the king's order, snatched up their weapons and rushed in crowds upon Prahlāda to destroy him. The prince looked calmly upon them and said, "O Dāityas, as truly as Vishnu is present in your weapons and in my body, so truly shall these weapons fail to harm me."

Although struck heavily and repeatedly by hundreds of the demons the prince felt not the least pain and his strength was ever renewed.

His father then attempted to persuade him to refrain from the praise of Vishnu and promised him immunity. But Prahlāda replied that he felt no fear as long as his immortal guardian was in his mind, the recollection of whom was alone sufficient to dissipate all perils consequent upon birth or human infirmities.

Hiranyakasipu, completely exasperated, commanded the poisonous serpents to bite him to death, and they attacked with their fatal poison and bit him in every part of his body.

But he, with thoughts immovably fixed on Krishna, felt no pain from their wounds, being immersed in rapturous recollections of the divinity. Then the snakes cried to the king, "Our fangs are broken, our jewelled crests are burst, there is fever in our hoods, and fear in our hearts, but the skin of the youth is still unscathed. Have recourse, we beg, to some other way."

"Ho! Elephants of the skies!" exclaimed the demon-king, "Unite your tusks and destroy this disloyal son and traitor. How often our progeny are our destruction, as fire consumes the wood from which it springs."

The young prince was then assailed by the elephants of the skies, as vast as mountain peaks cast down upon the earth, trampled on and gored by their tusks. But he continued to call to mind Govinda, and the tusks of the elephants were blunted against his breast. "Behold, father," he said, "the blunting of these tusks is not through any strength of mine. Calling upon Janardana is my defense against such fearful affliction."

Then said the king to his attendants, "Dismiss the elephants, and let fire consume him; and you, deity of the winds, blow up the fire, that this wicked wretch may be consumed." The Dānavas piled a mighty heap of wood around the prince, and kindled a fire, to burn him as their master had commanded.

But Prahlāda cried, "Father, this fire, though blown up by the winds, burns me not; and all around I behold the face of the skies, cool and fragrant, with beds of lotus flowers."

Then the Brahmins who were the sons of Bhargava, illustrious priests and reciters of the Sama-veda, said to the king of the Dāityas, "Sire, restrain your wrath against your son. How should anger succeed in finding a place in heavenly mansions? As for this lad, we will be his instructors, and teach him obediently to labor for the destruction of your foes. Youth is the season of many errors; and you should not therefore be relentlessly offended with a child. If he will not listen to us, and abandon the cause of Hari, we will adopt infallible measures to work his death." The king of the Dāityas, thus solicited by the priests, commanded the prince to be liberated from the midst of the flames.

THE LESSONS OF SORROW

Established again in the home of his teacher, Prahlāda himself began to give lessons to the sons of the demons during his free time. "Sons of the offspring of Diti," he used to say to them, "hear from me the supreme truth; nothing else is fit to be regarded; nothing else here is an object to be coveted. Birth, infancy, and youth are the portion of all creatures; and then succeeds gradual and inevitable decay, terminating with death for all beings. This is manifestly visible to all; to you as it is to me. That the dead are born again, and that it cannot be otherwise, the sacred texts are warrant. Production cannot be without a material cause, and as long as conception and parturition are the material causes of repeated birth, so long, be sure, is pain inseparable from every period of existence. The simpleton, in his inexperience, fancies that the alleviation of hunger, thirst, cold, and the like is pleasure; but of a truth it is pain: for suffering gives delight to those whose vision is darkened by delusion, as fatigue would be enjoyment to limbs that are incapable of movement. This vile body is a compound of phlegm and other humors. Where are its beauty, grace, fragrance, or other estimable qualities? The fool that is fond of a body composed of flesh, blood, matter, ordure, urine, membrane, marrow, and bones will be enamored of hell. The agreeableness of fire is caused by cold, of water by thirst, of food by hunger; by other circumstances their contraries are equally agreeable. The child of the Dāitya who takes to himself a wife introduces only so much misery into his bosom; for as many as are the cherished affections of a living creature, so many are the throes of anxiety implanted in his heart; and he who has large possessions in his house is haunted, wherever he goes, with the apprehension that they may be lost or burnt or stolen. Thus there is great pain in being born: for the dying man there are the tortures of the judge of the deceased, and of passing again into the womb. If you conclude that there is little enjoyment in the embryo state, you must then admit that the world is made up of pain. Yes, I tell you, in this ocean of the world, this sea of many sorrows, Vishnu is your only hope.

"If you cannot understand this, saying, 'We are spiritual children; embodied spirit is eternal. Birth, youth, decay are the properties of the body, not of the soul.' In this way we deceive ourselves: 'I am yet a child; but it is my purpose to exert myself when I am a youth. I am yet a youth; but when I become old I will do what is needful for the good of my soul. I am now old, and all my duties are still to be fulfilled. How shall I, now that my faculties fail me, do what was left undone when my strength was unimpaired?' In this manner do men, while their minds are distracted by sensual pleasure, ever propose and never attain final beatitude: They die thirsting. Devoted in childhood to play, and in youth to pleasure: ignorant and impotent they find that old age is come upon them. Therefore even in childhood let the embodied soul acquire discriminative wisdom, and, independent of the conditions of infancy, youth or age, strive incessantly to be free. This is what I declare to you; and since you know that it is not untrue, do you out of regard to me, call to your minds Vishnu, the Liberator From All Bondage. What difficulty is there in thinking upon him, who, when remembered, bestows prosperity, and by recalling whom to memory, day and night, all sin is cleansed away? Let all your thoughts and affections be fixed on him who is present in all beings, and you shall laugh at every care. The whole world is suffering under a triple affliction. What wise man would feel hatred towards beings who are objects of compassion? If fortune be propitious to them, and I am unable to partake of similar enjoyments, yet why should I cherish malignity towards those who are more prosperous than myself? I should rather sympathize with their happiness; for the suppression of malignant feelings is of itself a reward. If beings are hostile and indulge in hatred, they are objects of pity to the wise, as encompassed by profound delusion. These are the reasons for repressing hate, which are adapted to the capacities of those who see the deity as distinct from his creatures.

"Hear, briefly, what influences those who have approached the truth. This whole world is but a manifestation of Vishnu, who is identical with all things; and it is therefore to be regarded by the wise as not differing from, but as the same with themselves. Let us therefore lay aside the angry passions of our race, and so strive that we obtain that perfect, pure and eternal happiness, which shall be beyond the power of the elements or of their deities, of fire, of the sun, of the moon, of wind, of Indra, of the regent of the sea; which shall be unmolested by the spirits of air or earth, by Yakshas, Dāityas, or their chiefs; by the serpent-gods or monstrous demigods of Svarga; which shall be uninterrupted by men or beasts, or by the infirmities of human nature, by bodily sickness and disease, or hatred, envy, malice, passion, or desire; which nothing shall molest, and which every one who fixes his whole heart on Kesava shall enjoy. I tell you that you shall have no satisfaction in various revolutions through this treacherous world, but that you will obtain placidity forever by propitiating Vishnu, whose adoration is perfect calm. What here is difficult of attainment, when he is pleased? Wealth, pleasure, virtue, are things of little moment. Precious is the fruit that you shall gather, be assured, from the exhaustless store of the tree of true wisdom."

The Dānavas, observing the conduct of Prahlāda, reported it to the king, lest they should incur his displeasure. He sent for his cooks, and said to them, "My vile and unprincipled son is now teaching others his impious doctrines: be quick, and put an end to him. Let deadly poison be mixed up with all his food without his knowledge. Hesitate not, but destroy the wretch without delay."

Accordingly they did so, and administered poison to the virtuous Prahlāda, as his father had commanded them. Prahlāda, repeating the name of the imperishable, ate and digested the food in which the deadly poison had been infused, and suffered no harm from it, either in body or mind, for it had been rendered innocuous by the name of the eternal. Beholding the strong poison digested, those who had prepared the food were filled with dismay, and hastened to the king, and fell down before him, and said, "King of the Dāityas, the fearful poison given by us to your son has been digested by him along with his food, as if it were innocent."

Hiranyakasipu, on hearing this, exclaimed, "Hurry, hurry,

ministrant priests of the Dāitya race! Instantly perform the
rites that will effect his destruction!"

Then the priests went to Prahlāda, and having repeated the
hymns of the *Sama-veda,* said to him, as he respectfully listened, "Thou hast been born prince, in the family of Brahmā,
celebrated in the three worlds, the son of Hiranyakasipu, the
king of the Dāityas; why shouldest thou acknowledge dependence upon the gods? Why upon the eternal? Thy father is
the stay of all worlds, as thou thyself in turn shalt be. Desist,
then, from celebrating the praises of an enemy; and remember
that of all venerable preceptors, a father is most venerable."

THE NEED FOR THE ETERNAL

Prahlāda replied to them, "Illustrious Brahmins, it is true
that the family of Marichi is renowned in the three worlds;
this cannot be denied: and I also admit, what is equally in-
disputable, that my father is mighty over the universe. There
is no error, not the least, in what you have said, 'That a father
is the most venerable of all holy teachers.' He is a venerable
instructor no doubt and is ever to be devoutly reverenced. To
all these things I have nothing to object: they find a ready
assent in my mind. But when you say, 'Why should I depend
upon the eternal?' Who can give assent to this as right? The
words are void of meaning."

Having said this much, he was silent awhile, being re-
strained by respect to their sacred functions; but he was unable to repress his smile, and again said, "What need is there
of the eternal? Admirable! Most worthy of you who are my
venerable preceptors! Hear what need there is of the eternal,
if to listen will not give you pain. The fourfold objects of men
are said to be virtue, desire, wealth, final emancipation. Is he
who is the source of all these of no avail? Virtue (*dharma*)
was derived from the eternal by Daksha, Marichi, and other
patriarchs; wealth (*artha*) has been obtained from Him by
others; and by others the enjoyment of their desires (*kama*):
while those who, through true wisdom and holy contemplation, have come to know his essence, have been released from

their bondage, and have attained freedom from existence for ever. The glorification of Hari, attainable by unity, is the root of all riches, dignity, renown, wisdom, progeny, righteousness and liberation. Virtue, wealth, desire, and even final freedom, Brahmins, are fruits bestowed by Him. How then can it be said, 'What need is there of the eternal?' But enough of this: what occasion is there to say more? You are my venerable teachers, and whether you speak good or evil is not for my weak judgment to decide."

The priests said to him, "We preserved you, boy, when you were about to be consumed by fire, confiding that you would no longer eulogize your father's foes: we knew not how un-wise you were: but if you will not desist from this infatuation at our advice, we shall even proceed to perform the rites that will inevitably destroy you."

KARMA AND CHARACTER

To this menace, Prahlāda answered, "What living creature slays, or is slain? What living creature preserves or is preserved? Each is his own destroyer or preserver, as he follows good or evil. Death or immunity, prosperity or adversity, in this life are the inevitable consequences of conduct in prior existence. No man can suffer a penalty which his vices in a previous state of being have not incurred, nor can he avoid it if they have."

Thus spoken to by the youth, the priests of the Dāitya sovereign were incensed, and instantly had recourse to magic incantations, by which a female form, enwreathed with fierce flame, was engendered. She was of fearful aspect, and the earth was parched beneath her tread, as she approached Prahlāda, and smote him with a fiery trident on the breast. In vain! For the weapon fell, broken into a hundred pieces upon the ground. Against the breast in which the imperishable Hari resides the thunderbolt would be shivered, or even split in pieces. The magic being first directed against the virtuous prince by the wicked priests, then turned upon them instead, and having quickly destroyed them, disappeared.

PRAYER FOR ONE'S ENEMIES

Prahlāda, beholding the Brahmins perish, hastily appealed to Krishna, the eternal, for succor and said, "Oh Janārdana! who art everywhere, the creator and substance of the world, preserve these Brahmins from this magical and insupportable fire. As thou art Vishnu, present in all creatures, and the protector of the world, so let these priests be restored to life. If, while devoted to the omnipresent Vishnu, I think no sinful resentment against my foes, let those priests be restored to life. If those who have come to slay me, those by whom poison was given me, the fire that would have burned, the elephants that would have crushed, the snakes that would have stung me, have been regarded by me as friends, if I have been unshaken in soul, and am without fault in thy sight; then, I implore thee, let these priests of the Asuras be now restored to life."

Having prayed in this way, the Brahmins immediately rose up uninjured and rejoicing; and bowing respectfully to Prahlāda, they blessed him, and said, "Excellent prince, may thy days be many; irresistible be thy prowess, and power and wealth and posterity be thine." Having thus spoken they withdrew and went and told the king of the Dāityas all that had passed.

When Hiranyakasipu heard that the powerful incantations of his priests had been defeated, he sent for his son, and demanded of him the secret of his extraordinary might. "Prahlāda," he said, "you are possessed by marvelous powers; where are they from? Are they the result of magic rites? Or have they accompanied you from birth?"

LOVE FOR ALL CREATURES

Prahlāda, thus interrogated, bowed down to his father's feet and replied, "Whatever power I possess, father, is neither the result of magic rites, nor is it inseparable from my nature. It is no more than that which is possessed by all in whose hearts Achyuta abides. He who meditates not of wrong to others, but considers them as himself, is free from the effects of sin, inasmuch as the cause does not exist; but he who inflicts pain upon others, in act, thought, or speech, sows the seed of future birth, and the fruit that awaits him after birth is pain. I wish no evil to any, and do and speak no offence; for I behold Kesava in all beings, as in my own soul. When should corporeal or mental suffering or pain, inflicted by elements or the gods, affect me whose heart is thoroughly purified by Him? Love then for all creatures will be assiduously cherished by all those who are wise in the knowledge that Hari is all things."

When he had thus spoken, the Dāitya monarch, his face darkened with fury, commanded his attendants to cast his son from the summit of the palace where he was sitting, and which was many yojanas in height, down upon the tops of the mountains, where his body should be dashed to pieces against the rocks. Accordingly the Dāityas hurled the boy down, and he fell, cherishing Hari in his heart, and Earth, the nurse of all creatures, received him gently on her lap, thus entirely devoted to Kesava, the protector of the world.

Beholding him uninjured by the fall, and sound in every bone, Hiranyakasipu addressed himself to Samvara, the mightiest of enchanters, and said to him, "This perverse boy is not to be destroyed by us. You, who are potent in the arts of delusion, contrive some device for his destruction."

Samvara replied, "I will destroy him. You shall behold, king of the Dāityas, the power of delusion, the thousand and the myriad artifices that it can employ."

Then the ignorant Asura Samvara practiced subtle wiles for the extermination of the firm-minded Prahlāda. But he, with a tranquil heart, and void of malice towards Samvara, directed his thoughts uninterruptedly to the destroyer of Madhu; by whom the excellent discus, Sudardana, was dispatched to defend the youth. The flaming devices and the thousand tricks of the evil-destined Samvara were every one foiled by this defender of the prince. The king of the Dāityas then commanded the withering wind to breathe its blighting blast upon his son, and thus commanded, the wind immediately penetrated into his frame, cold, cutting, drying, and insufferable. Knowing that the wind had entered into his body, the Dāitya boy applied his whole heart to the mighty upholder of the earth; and Janardana, seated in his heart, waxed wroth and drank up the fearful wind, which had thus hastened to its own annihilation.

THE SCIENCE OF GOVERNMENT

When the devices of Samvara were all frustrated, and the blighting wind had perished, the prudent prince repaired to the residence of his preceptor. His teacher instructed him daily in the science of polity, as essential to the administration of government, and invented by Usanas for the benefit of kings; and when he thought that the modest prince was well grounded in the principles of the science, he told the king that Prahlāda was thoroughly conversant with the rules of government as laid down by the descendant of Bhṛigu. Hiranyakasipu therefore summoned the prince to his presence, and desired him to repeat what he had learned: how a king should conduct himself towards friends or foes; what measures he should adopt at the three periods (of advance, retrogression or stagnation); how he should treat his councillors, his ministers, the officers of his government and of his household, his emissaries, his subjects, those of doubtful allegiance, and his foes: with whom he should contract alliance; with whom engage in war: what sort of fortress he should construct; how forest and mountain tribes should be reduced; how internal grievances should be rooted out; all this, and what else he had studied, the youth was commanded by his father to explain. To this, Prahlāda, having bowed affectionately and reverentially to the feet of the king, touched his forehead to the ground and replied:

"It is true that I have been instructed in all these matters by my venerable preceptor, and I have learnt them, but I cannot in all approve them. It is said that conciliation, gifts, punishment, and sowing dissension are the means of securing friends or overcoming foes, but I, father—don't be angry— know neither friends nor foes; and where no object is to be accomplished, the means of effecting it are superfluous. It would be idle to talk of friend or foe in Govinda, who is the supreme soul, lord of the world, consisting of the world, and who is identical with all beings. The divine Vishnu is in thee, father, in me, and in all, everywhere else. Hence how can I speak of friend or foe as distinct from myself? It is therefore a waste of time to cultivate such tedious and unprofitable sciences, which are but false knowledge, and all our energies should be dedicated to the acquirement of true wisdom. The notion that ignorance is knowledge arises, father, from ignorance. Does not a child imagine the firefly to be a spark of fire? That is active duty, which is not for our bondage; that is knowledge which is for our liberation. All other duty is good only for weariness. All other knowledge is only the cleverness of an artist. Knowing this, I look upon all such acquirement as profitless. That which is really profitable, hear me, oh mighty monarch, thus prostrate before thee, proclaim. He who cares not for dominion, he who cares not for wealth, shall assuredly obtain both in a life to come. All men, illustrious prince, are toiling to be great; but the destinies of men, and not their own exertions, are the cause of greatness. Kingdoms are the gifts of fate, and are bestowed upon the stupid, the ignorant, the cowardly, and those to whom the science of government is unknown. Let him, therefore, who covets the goods of fortune be assiduous in the practice of virtue. Let him who hopes for final liberation learn to look upon all things as equal and the same. Gods, men, animals, birds, reptiles, all are but forms of the one eternal Vishnu, existing, as it were, detached from himself. By him who knows this all the existing world, fixed or movable, is to be regarded as identical with himself, as proceeding alike from Vishnu, assuming a universal form. When this is known the glorious god of all, who is without beginning or end, is pleased; and when he is pleased, there is an end of affliction."

On hearing this, Hiranyakasipu started up from his throne in a fury, and spurned his son on the breast with his foot. Burning with rage, he wrung his hands and exclaimed, "Ho Viprachitti! Ho Hahu! Ho Bali! (celebrated Dāitya leaders) Bind him with strong bands and cast him into the ocean, or everyone may become converts to the doctrines of this silly wretch. Repeatedly prohibited by us, he still persists in the praise of our enemies. Death is the just retribution for the disobedient."

The Dāityas accordingly bound the prince with strong bands as their lord had commanded, and threw him into the sea. As he floated on the waters, the ocean was convulsed throughout its whole extent, and rose in mighty undulations, threatening to submerge the earth. When Hiranyakasipu observed this, he commanded the Dāityas to hurl rocks into the sea and pile them closely on one another, burying beneath their incumbent mass him whom fire would not burn, nor weapons pierce, nor serpents bite; whom the pestilential gale could not blast, nor poison, nor magic spirits, nor incantations destroy; who fell from the loftiest heights unhurt; who foiled the elephants of the spheres: a son of depraved heart, whose life was a perpetual curse.

"Here," he cried, "since he cannot die, here let him live for thousands of years at the bottom of the ocean overwhelmed by mountains." Accordingly the Dāityas and Dānavas hurled upon Prahlāda, while in the great ocean, ponderous rocks, and piled them over him for many thousands of miles: but he, still with mind undisturbed, thus offered daily praise to Vishnu, lying at the bottom of the sea, under the mountain heap.

A HYMN OF PRAISE

"Glory to thee, God of the lotus eye: glory to thee, most excellent of spiritual things: glory to thee, soul of all worlds: glory to thee, wielder of the sharp discus: glory to the best of Brahmins, to the friend of Brahmins and of cattle, to Krishna, the preserver of the world: to Govinda be glory! To him who, as Brahmā, creates the universe, who in its existence is its preserver; be praise. To thee, who at the end of the kalpa takes the form of Rudra; to thee, who art triform; be adoration! Thou, Achyuta, art the gods, Yakshas, demons, saints, serpents, choristers and dancers of heaven, goblins, evil spirits, men, animals, birds, insects, reptiles, plants, and stones, earth, water, fire, sky, wind, sound, touch, taste, color, flavor, mind, intellect, soul, time and the qualities of nature. Thou art all these, and the chief object of them all. Thou art knowledge

and ignorance, truth and falsehood, poison and ambrosia.
Thou art the performance and the discontinuance of the acts
of devotional sacrifice. Thou art the acts which the *Vedas*
enjoin: thou art the enjoyer of the fruit of all acts, and the
means by which they are accomplished. Thou, Vishnu, who
art the soul of all, art the fruit of all acts of piety. Thy universal diffusion, indicating might and goodness, is in me, in
others, in all creatures, in all worlds. Holy ascetics meditate
on thee: pious priests sacrifice to thee. Thou alone, identical
with the gods and fathers of mankind, receive burnt-offerings
and oblations. The universe is thy intellectual form; whence
proceeded thy subtle form to this world. Thence art thou all
subtle elements and elementary beings, and the subtle principle that is called soul within them. Hence the supreme soul
of all objects distinguished as subtle or gross, which is imperceptible and which cannot be conceived, is even a form of
thee. Glory be to thee, Purushottama; and glory to that imperishable form which, soul of all, is another manifestation of
thy might, the asylum of all qualities, existing in all creatures.
I salute her, the supreme goddess, who is beyond the senses;
whom the mind, the tongue, cannot define; who is to be distinguished alone by the wisdom of the truly wise. *OM!* Salutation to Vasudeva: to him who is the eternal lord; he from
whom nothing is distinct; he who is distinct from all. Glory
be to the great spirit again and again: to him who is without
name or shape; who is only to be known by adoration; whom,
in the forms manifested in his descents upon the earth, the
dwellers in heaven adore; for they behold not his inscrutable
nature. I glorify the supreme deity, Vishnu, the universal witness, who seated internally, beholds the good and ill of all.
Glory to that Vishnu from whom this world is not distinct.
May he, ever to be meditated upon as the beginning of the
universe, have compassion upon me; may he, the supporter of
all, in whom everything is warped and woven, undecaying,
imperishable, have compassion upon me. Glory, again and
again, to that being to whom all returns, from whom all proceeds; who is all, and in whom all things are; to him whom I
also am. For he is everywhere; and through whom all things
are from me. I am all things; all things are in me, who am

everlasting. I am undecayable, ever enduring, the receptacle of the spirit of the supreme. Brahmā is my name; the supreme soul, that is before all things, that is after the end of all."

Thus meditating, upon Vishnu as identical with his own spirit, Prahlāda became as one with him, and finally regarded himself as the divinity. He forgot entirely his own individuality, and was conscious of nothing else than his being the inexhaustible, eternal, supreme soul; and in consequence of the efficacy of this conviction of identity, the imperishable Vishnu, whose essence is wisdom, became present in his heart, which was wholly purified from sin. As soon as, through the force of his contemplation, Prahlāda had become one with Vishnu, the bonds with which he was bound burst instantly asunder; the ocean was violently uplifted; and the monsters of the deep were alarmed. Earth and all her forests and mountains trembled; and the prince, putting aside the rocks which the demons had piled upon him, came forth from out the main. When he beheld the outer world again, and contemplated earth and heaven, he remembered who he was, and recognized himself to be Prahlāda; and again he hymned Purushottama, who is without beginning or end; his mind being steadily and undeviatingly addressed to the object of his prayers, and his speech, thoughts, and acts being firmly under control.

"*OM!* Glory to the end of all: to thee, lord, who art subtle and substantial, mutable and immutable, perceptible and imperceptible, divisible and indivisible, indefinable and definable, the subject of attributes and void of attributes, abiding in qualities, though they abide not in thee, morphous and amorphous, minute and vast, visible and invisible, hideousness and beauty, ignorance and wisdom, cause and effect, existence and non-existence, comprehending all that is good and evil, essence of perishable and imperishable elements, asylum of undeveloped rudiments. Oh thou who art both one and many, Vasudeva, first cause of all; glory be unto thee. Oh thou who art large and small, manifest and hidden; who art all beings and art not all beings; and from whom although distinct from universal cause, the universe proceeds: to thee, Purushottama, be all glory!"

While with mind intent on Vishnu, he thus pronounced his praises, the divinity, clad in yellow robes, suddenly appeared before him. Startled at the sight, with hesitating speech Prahlāda pronounced repeated salutations to Vishnu, and said, "Oh thou, who removest all worldly grief, Kesava, be propitious unto me; again sanctify me, Achyuta, by thy sight."

THE BOON

The deity replied, "I am pleased with the faithful attachment thou hast shown to me: demand from me, Prahlāda, whatever thou desirest."

Prahlāda replied, "In all the thousand births through which I may be doomed to pass, may my faith in thee, Achyuta, never know decay; may passion, as fixed as that which the worldly-minded feel for sensual pleasures, ever animate my heart, always devoted unto thee."

Bhagavān answered, "Thou hast already devotion to me, and ever shall have it: Now choose some boon, whatever is in thy wish."

Prahlāda then said, "I have been hated because I assiduously proclaimed thy praise: Do thou oh lord, pardon in my father this sin that he has committed. Weapons have been hurled against me; I have been thrown into the flames; I have been bitten by venomous snakes, and poison has been mixed with my food; I have been bound and cast into the sea; and heavy rocks have been heaped upon me: but all this, and whatever ill beside, has been wrought against me, whatever wickedness has been done to me, because I put my faith in thee; all, through thy mercy, has been suffered by me unharmed. Do thou therefore free my father from this iniquity."

To this application Vishnu replied, "All this shall be unto thee through my favor. But I will give thee another boon: demand it, son of the Asura."

Prahlāda answered and said, "All my desires, oh lord, have been fulfilled by the boon that thou hast granted, that my faith in thee shall never know decay. Wealth, virtue, love, are as nothing; for even liberation is in reach whose faith is firm in thee, root of the universal world."

Vishnu said, "Since thy heart is filled immovably with trust in me, thou shalt, through my blessing, attain freedom from existence." Thus saying, Vishnu vanished from his sight; and Prahlāda repaired to his father and bowed down before him. His father kissed him on the forehead and embraced him, and shed tears, and said, "Do you still live, my son?" And the great Asura repented of his former cruelty, and treated him with kindness: and Prahlāda, fulfilling his duties like any other youth, continued diligent in the service of his preceptor and his father. After his father had been put to death by Vishnu in the form of a man-lion, Prahlāda became the sovereign of the Dāityas; and possessing the splendors of royalty consequent upon his piety, exercised extensive sway, and was blessed with numerous progeny. At the expiration of an authority which was the reward of his meritorious acts, he was freed from the consequences of moral merit or demerit, and obtained, through meditation on the deity, final exemption from existence.

Such, Maitreya, was the Dāitya, Prahlāda, the wise and faithful worshipper of Vishnu, of whom you wished to hear; and such was his miraculous power. Whoever listens to the history of Prahlāda is immediately cleansed from his sins; the iniquities that he commits, by night or by day, shall be expiated by once hearing, or once reading, the history of Prahlāda. The perusal of this history on the day of full moon, of new moon, or on the eighth or twelfth day of the lunation, shall yield fruit equal to the donation of a cow. (Since this gift would also involve gold and costly ornaments, this would be a very substantial donation.) As Vishnu protected Prahlāda in all the calamities to which he was exposed, so shall the deity protect him who listens constantly to this tale.

COMMENTARY

VALUES: PROXIMATE AND ULTIMATE (PAGE 68)

THERE IS A CHARACTERISTIC integration in Hindu thought which is achieved, not so much by reduction to some one central principle as by exhibition of the interrelations of different ideas so that one idea leads naturally through another and another and finally reflects back upon itself. The Sanskrit term "*dharma*" leads into such a complex, interrelated chain of terms. *Dharma* has many meanings: sometimes "religion" or "religious law," sometimes "duty" (e.g. caste duty), or "custom," "element," "the inner truth." In this sentence, "People are by nature drawn to *dharma*, wealth and enjoyment," the *dharma* refers to a fundamental value which could perhaps be understood as "character" or "integrity." As we have noted, Hindus are aware of many good things in life, and they believe that our propensity to desire these good things—happiness, joy, wealth, and good reputation or sound character—is a natural propensity which most people share. People do not have to be taught to want to be happy, or to want to be secure, or to want the respect and admiration of their friends and associates—though they often may need instruction on how to secure these things. Deeper Hindu thinking suggests, however, that there is also a natural progression of these values, so that one should grow toward more fundamental interests. This movement toward more enduring and satisfying values has been institutionalized in the understanding of the four stages of life or *āshramas*. No mention of this is found as early as the *Rig Veda*, but the idea is developed in the *Upanishads* and then clarified, modified somewhat and thoroughly institutionalized in the *Laws of Manu* and *Dharmashāstra*. Originally the upper-caste fathers were expected to act as teachers for their sons, but gradually this came to be taken over by the Brahmins so that sons of Brahmins, Kshatriyas, and wealthy Vāishyas would live and study with Brahmins for several years (eventually regularized at twelve years, usually from age 10–12 to the early twenties). The boys worked for their teacher in home and fields, tending the sacred fires, herding the teacher's cattle, and begging on behalf of the teacher in the town. Following this apprenticeship in discipline, different decisions might be made. Some boys would leave the teacher's house, marry and carry on the traditions of their families. Others might remain in the teacher's house, others would retreat to the forest and practice austerities, and some, putting aside all that they had, would undertake the wandering, beggar's life of the *Saṁnyāsin* or *bhikshu*. Ultimately these stages were clarified and made successive. The three stages of student (*brahmacārin*), householder and founder of a family (*grihastha*), and hermit in the woods devoted to austerities (*vānaprastha*) were set in contrast to the "men who know the *ātman*" (*saṁnyāsin*) but eventually the "knowers" became the fourth stage in the same development. The primary obligations of the student stage are the support of the *guru* and the study of *Veda*. The obligations of the householder are to raise up a son, to fulfill the six duties of teaching and learning (sacrifice as the head of the household, and through the agency of a Brahmin, giving alms and receiving gifts, to satisfy the rishis by studying the Veda, the fathers by the funeral rites, and to feed men and animals). The *vānaprastha* or forest dweller's stage was at first seen as an alternative to the life of the householder but gradually became a stage in its own right. Its primary characteristic is the systematic effort to detach oneself from the remnants of worldly ego-concern. It is a stage of purification for more favorable rebirth or for preparation for the life of the true knower of *ātman,* the *samnyāsin* stage which may follow. These standards which were established in the *Laws of Manu* and in the *Mahābhārata* have continued to develop and change. Alongside this recognition of the values of the various stages is also a kind of practical psychology which recognizes various attitudes and interests characteristic of the various stages of life. A person's earliest years are characterized by play and enjoyment. The joys of childhood are simple, innocent joys, and children naturally respond as though joy, delight, happiness, fun are all that life is for. The child has been exempted to some extent from the costs of his own happiness. So gradually fun loses some of its innocence, but even as one develops the appreciation of the lessons of the teacher, he learns that joy has its costs and hazards and begins to accept the responsibilities of adulthood. The student days are over. One moves ahead to fulfill the responsibility not to break the thread of the family, that is to rear a son, to provide security for parents, wife and children, and these necessities dominate one's life. Just as some people may be distracted by enjoyment and seem never to grow beyond a kind of perennial adolescence, so some become fixated in the adult obsession for wealth and security. They remain unsatisfied, self- and security-centered. For others, however, there may come a further mood and quality of character. They wish not merely to be happy and secure, but to move beyond this and to be true to the inner spirit of their humanity—to fulfill their role as fully *human* beings, responsible and respected members of a community and of a religious tradition. The conditions of more modern life have once again changed the character of the *vānaprastha.* The inner law to which persons in this stage of life feel bound is true *dharma.* No longer is this necessarily defined by retirement to the forest, but by retirement for a wider and more effective service to enduring values. The practical civic expression of this, of which one finds impressive examples in modern India, is a man who has secured his reputation and position in his vocation, but while he remains at the peak of his powers as a leader, devotes himself to the needs of the community, giving his service and often a substantial part of his wealth in public or religious service. All cultures have such persons: India recognizes and honors them as having achieved a high and important stage in the fully mature life. Dharma is the "duty" or "obligation" which such men obey. This is not a duty imposed on them by law, but by their own character and integrity.

These natural values—*kama* (enjoyment), *artha* (wealth, security), and *dharma* (responsibility) correlate to the natural stages of life—student, householder, and reflective retirement or wider service; but there is still another value which both culminates and contradicts all these others. This ultimate value is *moksha* (*mukti, nirvāṇa*). Later selections will discuss this topic directly, but for the moment we will define this value of the *saṁnyāsin* as the absolute and perfect fulfillment which involves elimination of all the limitations of earthly existence and the perfection of the knowledge of god.

PRASĀDA—SHARING OF HOLY FOOD (PAGE 68)

This passage. . . . ("By listening to their stories . . . taking the remains of their food . . . and by service to them. . . my mind became pure . . .") hints at a widespread Hindu practice and belief. In a pious Hindu household all food has been offered to the deity and ritually returned by the god to the family, so that it is the "food of god" and every meal is a kind of communion. So also that food which has been offered by means of proper Brahmin rituals before the temple deities and then used for temple purposes, both for the feeding of the Brahmins and for the greeting of devoted worshippers, establishes a kind of communion in which one shares the gifts of god and his devotees. Such a gesture has ritual and sometimes supernormal significance. It is no mere refreshment of the body, but a sensitivity to the presence of god and the refreshment of the Soul. This passage then is recommending study, communion and service as means to purification of mind, awakening of the love of God and more favorable rebirth.

CREATIONS (PAGE 71)

The pattern which is being described in this account is common in Hindu creation stories. Each creation follows the general cycle of its predecessors—a period of rest in which God (Bhagavan, Vishnu) or Brahman alone exists, the emergence of Brahmā as the creative principle, agent, intent of God, a gradual awakening of the divinity manifested as the creation of the world of apparent multiplicity, the shift from fine, invisible energies, toward gross material existences, the entrapment of soul in bodies, the teachings and ultimately even incarnations intended to help souls free themselves from embodiment, the gradual movement back toward fine matter, energy, invisibility as before. Since the cycle has often been repeated, minor inconsistencies between one account and another need not be regarded as serious. Some stories, however, (see Part III) are so different that they must represent altogether different cultural traditions.

GREAT GODS AND OTHERS (PAGE 72)

Powers, functions and relationships among the gods have not been static through Hindu history. Most of the deities which appear in the *Rig Veda* are no longer relevant to Hindu religious practice, and the great gods of modern Hinduism generally appear to have been relatively minor figures in the early Vedic period. Part of the function of the account of the birth of Brahmā may have been to help establish the proportionate relations of the Vedic Brahmā, identified with Prajāpati, the creator, and his successor, Vishnu. Vishnu is depicted as at rest, with an enormous ocean in his navel, in which the lotus bud which contains Brahmā is growing. Brahmā cannot even penetrate to the bottom of the lotus. This is not intended so much to depreciate his power (after all, he is still the creator of the world) as to magnify Vishnu beyond all capacity of imagination. In this type of legend we have a glimpse into the ancient social history of India, seeing in the various relations of dependence, superiority and mutual responsibility, as well as those of perennial hostility, some of the relationships of ancient tribes, the outcomes of ancient battles completely lost to other accounts. In this case we see the decline of the Vedic Brahmā before the increasing popularity of Vishnu in the Purāṇic period. In the *Veda*, Vishnu appears as

a sun deity, famous mainly for covering the universe in three
steps (see a later account of this in Part III). Through the
Upanishads there is an obvious decline in the significance of
the natural, cosmic, early Vedic deities in favor of the Brahman-Ātman (God-Soul) principle, and then in the subsequent
literature the great popular deities Shiva and Vishnu assume
the prominence they hold today. Our knowledge of the ancient times is so sketchy, however, that no detailed effort to
relate these stories to their historical-social meanings can be
very convincing or very soundly based. On the other hand,
new information is constantly being developed from archaeol-
ogy and philology which fills in some of these gaps and gives
substantial probability to some conjectures. In the light of
very recent evidence it seems likely that both Shiva and
Vishnu and their immediate courts were known in some form
in pre-Aryan India. The picture which increasingly seems
characteristic is of a highly developed but already declining
urban civilization along the Indus river before the arrival of
the main Aryan invasions. This culture appears to have been
overwhelmed by the invaders, but its technical requirements
were so great that a certain interaction among the Aryans
and the well-defined upper class Dravidians became necessary. These together seem to have formed the leading classes
of Indian society and "caste" is at least in part a means for
organizing the relative status of the different groups represented.[1]

Similarly the pre-Aryan deities seem (especially in the
Indo-Aryan literature) to have been overwhelmed by the Vedic deities, but gradually their power reasserted itself and
they emerged again from the secondary roles assigned to them
and took charge of the sacrifices and eventually of the culture.
Today they are the principal deities of Hindu worship. Agni
and other Vedic gods have been brought into the sanctum of
the great Vaishnavite and Shaivite temples to serve those
powerful, mysterious presiding gods. Vedic worship (distinguished from philosophy) is virtually extinct in India.

We have here a principle of Indian religious survival. The

[1] Cf. Sir Mortimer Wheeler, *The Indus Civilization* (Cambridge: at
the University Press, 3rd ed. rev., 1968).

"nationalization" of Hinduism throughout India has been made possible partly by the willingness of Hinduism to accept any local deities, relate them to the system as a whole, and offer them even as forms of the absolute and ultimate itself. Snake, monkey, cow worship, etc. are through various accounts brought into the Vaishnavite and Shaivite traditions. The local deities of villages and titular deities of important families find relationships with the cosmic deities of the whole tradition. The character of almost any major god reveals this tendency by its composite character. Shiva is a good example. He is *Mahāyogi,* the great ascetic: the Lord of Ghosts (Bhūtas) who haunts cremation grounds. He is mountain god in the Himalayas (especially Mt. Kailāsa). He is also the dancer, Nāṭarāja, who spins the world off as an act of sport. He is terrible, a destroyer; and also beloved, the access to the knowledge of Brahman-Ātman, and yet the object of the total affection of his devotees. He is masculine, par excellence, but his Shakti, his power, is feminine, and he is often pictured in hermaphodite form, with the right side of the masculine Shiva and the left side of the feminine Pārvatī. He is worshipped in the phallic form of the liṅgam, and sexuality is obvious in many aspects of his character, but he is also the killer of Kama, god of love, and is a practitioner of enormous austerities. The *trimurti*—three great gods, Shiva, Vishnu, Brahmā—have in general collected and coordinated the mythical backgrounds of numerous local gods, while most of the rest of the divine beings come to form various levels or rankings below these three. They are living gods because they made room for and eventually absorbed their competition. These ancient struggles are reflected indirectly in the stories of the gods and their struggles with one another.[2]

WORLDS (PAGE 75)

The significance of the Hindu understanding of the world systems lies in its capacity to make use of every tradition—

[2] Further information concerning modern hypotheses about pre-Aryan culture and religion may be found in the articles of the *Journal of Tamil Studies,* "Special Number on the Decipherment of the Mohenjodaro Script," Vol. II, No. 1 (May 1970).

astralism, animal worship, totemism, fetishism, demonology, orgiastic religion, omenology, etc., and to organize them all into the comprehensive tradition. Obviously one could make similar comments about the sense of time in this literature. This tolerance and even encouragement of variety is fundamental in the Hindu tradition as a whole. A more philosophical example of this same process in a later stage is developed in the Vedāntic philosophy of Shaṅkara, where it is taught that the system of sacrifice elaborated by the early Veda (particularly the *Brāhmanas*) is exactly correct in the actions specified in order to accomplish certain purposes. However, wisdom knows that the goals to be sought by such means are not appropriate to the seeker of liberation. Therefore he will choose not to practice what the Veda teaches because he does not desire the results which those actions will surely produce. Thus the whole sacrificial system, which seems so important to the early Vedic religion of the *Brāhmanas*, is set aside in favor of one of the paths to god through work, knowledge, experience or devotion. This method bypasses the use of the Veda without attempting to contradict one word of it. Its claim to be Vedic is based on the way it follows certain teachings of the *Upanishads*, particularly those concerned with wisdom about the true goals of life.

DECLINE (PAGE 79)

The Hindu theory of the cycles of time assumes that there is a steady decline from an original golden age which immediately succeeded creation, through several stages of dissolution to the present terrible fix. It is generally assumed that the present world is in the latter stages of the decline, and evil is about to produce the conditions which will initiate a reversal of the process and result in a disintegration of this evil age, a new period of cosmic rest, and re-establishment of a wholly new, wholly good creation. This is now man's last but also most difficult chance to be free from continued disaster. This view gives importance to religious teaching, but also serves to explain why these teachings require experts tuned in to a different cosmic order, why so many people fail to see the importance or value of *moksha,* why there is disaster, famine, warfare, and disease, why those who take religious teachings perfectly seriously must seem "to the world" to be very peculiar persons indeed.

THE CAREER OF A SOUL (PAGE 81)

To the Hindu that which lives and truly knows is Soul or Self (*jīva, ātman*). True Soul is intelligent and capable of self-reflection, though it may indeed appear to attain that capacity in the course of lifetimes below the self-reflexive level. No sharply cut line between species with Soul and without has ever been agreed among Hindus. Living systems form a continuum from the most limited "one-sense" beings to supernatural entities with nearly infinite sensitivities and powers. The important thing is that it is the *Soul* which has life: it *puts on* or possesses a body. The Soul never dies: death is the abandonment of a particular body. The Soul whose continuity of existence is not fundamentally disturbed by death will put on another appropriate body. Any particular "lifetime" then is life *en via*—in passing—and in general its end is neither to be sought nor feared. The immortal Soul will be appropriately reclothed with body. This process of "passing through" the cycles of embodiment and action is called *saṁsāra.* The ultimate source of all life is god. The determination of appropriate embodiment is based on *karma,* one's actions. Every action will have a full quota of consequences on the one who performs the act as well as upon those directly affected by it. The result to the actor will be precisely appropriate to the *moral quality* of the act (including its intentions, motivations and results). This does not require that we imagine some supreme, wise judge who hears the charges against us and the eulogy of our virtues and then metes out suitable punishment. The moral quality of an act is part of the act itself. These consequences then are also parts of the acts themselves and will occur with the same necessity that an unsupported brick will fall. The consequence is inherent in the nature of the situation.

Souls, then, are gradually (and mysteriously) differentiated from god and eventually are embodied in specific human lives. They all have one source, one task, and one ultimate outcome, but they appear to be various, authentically different individuals due to the specific careers which they have followed in their embodiment. Each action will require a career in which the exact consequence of the moral quality of the actions now performed will naturally (or occasionally supernaturally) occur. Eventually one will wish to be free from all karmic reaction (which will require the elimination of personal concern for the results of actions, thus having no actions left which could have an unfortunate moral quality for the doer). This is the message of the *Bhagavadgītā*. Practical considerations, however, suggest that one work for the *improvement* rather then the *perfection* of the soul's condition. This ultimately should lead to so superior an existence that perfection comes nearly within reach. Then the Soul absolutely knows, loves, and (in some interpretations) is god, and no karmic reaction is generated. For now, however, traditional piety, the help of the gods, the performance of those rites and services which will guarantee favorable rebirth are best to be cultivated and performed with sincere devotion. This will further the larger career of the Soul, just as study, practice and tact can further the career of the individual even though he may not be able to see the precise values of each one at the time. It is important to note that in the Hindu self-understanding every lifetime is important, valid, and in its inner essence divine. There is no reason to give great thought to one's fate in previous lifetimes, nor to worry about the placement of one's soul in any succeeding life. The problem is always just the life we now live, and to further the maturity and self-understanding of the soul within the limits now imposed upon us.

SACRIFICE SUPPORTS THE WORLD (PAGE 82)

The notion reflected in this passage is an ancient Vedic attitude. The attitude continues as a general unstated assumption which remains in Hindu thinking even though the specific Vedic sacrificial ceremonies which it supported are no longer celebrated. The fundamental attitudes are: (1) There is a vast inner rhythm or order (*rita*) exhibited through all of nature and inexorable in its operation, such that each cause must have its proper consequence. (2) The universe is a mutual consumption society in which each individual devours some aspect of its environment and in turn becomes food for some other aspect. (3) In this vast cycle of mutual fulfillment and destruction, there are two possible routes. One leads toward continuous participation in the cycle of being consumed and reborn. The other leads to escape from the world of becoming. The first requires the offering of the sacrifices in order to follow the *Way of the Ancestors*. These ancestral rites provide against non-being, by participating in the ritual structure of continuous rebirth. The smoke of the sacrifice rises to heaven carrying the faith (or devotion) which is the food of the gods. This fire-borne devotion having been fed to Indra the King becomes the Soma rain which is food (drink) for the Earth. Earth offers this food to her plants, and they grow and become food for man. Man consumes the food and drink which Earth has thus provided for him and it produces in him vitality and virility which he offers to woman. Woman receives his offering and produces the offspring which will grow to offer continued faith and devotion to the gods according to the Way of the Ancestors. Thus continues the great cycle. Should it stop at any point, dissolution and non-being would occur. The great cyclic system relates the classic gods—Agni (fire), Soma-Indra (wine, rain, lightning, authority), Parjanya-Varuṇa (rain, fertility), Bhūmi-Prithivī (Earth Mother) and all their many associates and alternative forms in an intricate and fully interconnected system. The Way of the Ancestors, of tradition, continuity, and sacrifice associates particularly with the moon, night, smoke, retirement of the sun, with mist, clouds, rain and plants, with food, drink, sex and moist vitality and fertility. The other side the Way of Escape from the world of becoming, which eventually prevailed to become the Vedāntic tradition of Hinduism, associates particularly with light, day, the bright half of the moon, the ascendancy of the sun, lightning, power, ascetic restriction of food, drink and sex, and with knowledge rather than physical vitality. We may see that these are in fact the obverse and reverse of the same symbols—

Agni as smoke and as light, Sūrya in night and in day, ascent and descent, etc. They are bounded by other divine powers such as the mist which lies between rain and dry, or dawn which is between night and day, etc.

This passage of the *Vishnu Purāṇa* enshrines one of the great achievements of Indian religion—the intricate and detailed mingling of these Aryan symbols (which may be traced also in the Hellenic and other Mediterranean traditions) and the pre-Aryan Hinduism in which Vishnu played so prominent a role. Both traditions come from and use the same symbols. They are scattered throughout the entire literature, *Vedic* and *vedāntic*. *If there were no sacrifice, the world is at an end.* This is, of course, a tragic outcome for those who live in the world and fear non-being most of all. It is an outcome devoutly to be desired by those who see the world's mutually consumptive character as one in which the cycle constantly makes us food for worms. The Way of the Ancestors is popular Hinduism. The Way of Escape is Vedāntic and yogic philosophy. Both find their symbols in the same tradition and in a way each appreciates the other as an alternative and authentic form of meaning. But they seem to go in almost opposite directions from the same starting point.

CASTE AND SPIRITUAL STATUS (PAGE 91)

We have already seen how caste is the basic pattern for Indian social organization and personal self-location. Caste, however, is not really a suitable "religious" designation. Caste controls most of the fundamental rules of life up to a certain point of religious maturity. At this point the rules of caste must be transcended. One does not change caste—it simply becomes irrelevant and does not apply to a "holy man" (or woman). There is then in addition to all the caste-ordered society a kind of religious elite no longer bound to worship in the temple, to live at home, to observe the complex daily ritual of caste tradition. These forest-wandering elitists are a *recognized exception* to caste rules. It was in this group that Buddhism and Jainism developed and emphasized their characteristic "democratic," non-caste-bound life. Of course the same attitudes were true of the more orthodox Hindu philosophers who were members of the same elite group (including the traditional Hindu teachers of the Buddha). In this early period neither Buddhists nor Jains had any thought of being responsible for a social order. To join either group was not merely to take membership in a religious sect, but to join the traditional elite itself. When Buddhism became popular and was attracting those who did not necessarily have so strong a natural propensity to devote themselves entirely to sincere religious life, that is, they were not always religiously elite, the more stable social patterns, including caste, which had always taken care of those who were not ready to dismiss the world entirely, began to strengthen and reassert themselves and paved the way for the Hindu renaissance.

In this particular story the "Mother" is from the merchant caste, but one can see how her pious devotion has lifted her beyond all considerations of caste to deserve the veneration of others and to be exempted from all routine responsibilities.

THE USES OF OPPOSITION (PAGE 96)

The main thrust of this story is sufficiently clear without elaboration, but there is a larger point for which it is only one of many examples. In Western religious traditions generally there has been a strong sense of the need for orthodoxy. Any supposed deviation from this standard might provide the occasion for controversy and the determination of authoritative criteria of the faith, after which the offending parties would be cast out and anathematized (at least). Opposition could stimulate and aid in the definition of the faith, but then it would have to be discarded as dangerous heresy. The Hindu attitude is more inclusive. Any act is complex and involves many particular circumstances to be considered. The motive and the consequence are not necesarily positively correlated. What knowledge was available to the person at the time he undertook some act? Numerous fine distinctions may be required to determine, even relatively, the "rightness" or "wrongness" of particular acts. It is possible to approve of some parts even of revolting or vicious behavior. The Hindu attitude generally seeks to preserve opposition to itself, usually by means of interpreting it as a supplement or an alternative rather than as a true contradictory. No view, attitude or action is so bad that there is nothing of value in it. You may recall, from the "Meditation on the Worlds" that God (Bhagavan) underlies the lowest Hell as well as transcends the highest heaven. This is a very basic Hindu attitude.

LIṄGAM AND SĀLAGRĀMA (PAGE 100)

A *liṅgam* is an upright pillar of almost any size which serves as an embodiment or place of manifestation of the god, Shiva. In Shaivite temples the Shiva *liṅgam* is the principal locus and apparent object of worship in the inner sanctum of the main shrine. The *liṅgam* has many associations and meanings. Its sexual significance is obvious. The *lingam* is the penis. It rises from a circular base designed to carry off the water and oils used to anoint it and called the *yoni* (vagina). It is placed in the innermost part of the main temple shrine. Standing before the *liṅgam*, then, one is in the womb of the world, where the eternal creative act transpires and is celebrated with light, fragrance, oil and sacrifice. One no longer observes the world from outside, but instead is transported within to share the secret union with the source of all creativity. Many of the Shiva myths make manifest his sexual character. In some (usually village) shrines the *liṅgam* is shaped unmistakably to resemble the phallus and is used to insure fertility, the birth of sons, the continuity of the race. Most *liṅga*, particularly those in major temples or in homes, are not shaped so as to display their phallic significance (unless one insists, for example, on seeing all the guardposts along a highway as phallic symbols). If one asks a Shaivite what the *liṅgam* means he is most often given a different cluster of meanings. It is well to respect both interpretations. In a special way the *liṅgam* is seen as both the abode of god and the god himself. It is not the stone, nor even precisely its shape, but the love and devotion of the *bhakta* (lover of god) which locates the god in the image. This is of course also represented by specific spiritual, ritual acts which have confirmed this devotion. A sacred image contains generations of devotion and reverence. The poetic outpouring of love, the overwhelming flow of gratitude, the yearning desperate pleas for fulfillment of deep needs have made the *lingam* a repository of love, hope and fear. At the same time, the formal actions of the Brahmin priests and their assistants in worship (including the appropriate deities) have consecrated the *lingam* from the standpoint of liturgical necessity. Finally, the temple or shrine as a whole embodies some meaning or event basic to human existence and exhibits that meaning in its principal myths and annual ceremonies.

One of the interpretations of the *lingam* suggests how this process would be misunderstood if thought of simply as "idol worship." Every effort to think of god at all involves some "form" in which He/It may be conceived—whether abstract terms (such as "father," "love," "creator," etc.) or concrete such as the Shiva *lingam* or an image of Vishnu. All serious theologians have recognized that the necessities of thought are likely to be misleading at this point, that our thought and talk about "God" is always suggestive, analogical, indirect or metaphorical and must not be taken in its simplest, most obvious way. Using human characteristics is most common in talk of god, but such anthropomorphizing does not mean that god is literally understood to have human form. The *lingam* is a form of god, but such an amorphous, ambiguous, undistinguished form that it approaches the formlessness of god himself. It does not tempt one so easily to misapplication as abstract, anthropomorphic language is apt to do. It can serve as the repository of devotion, the focus of religious action, the center of a sacrificial act which itself is a symbol of the inner sacrifice "from the heart." Bathing the *lingam* to cool it, anointing it with oils, decorating it with flowers, displaying the fire of devotion before it, are all symbolic gestures rendered not to the stone but to the presence which in-forms it.

In the case of Vishnu the principal object of worship in the temple is the image of the god, though in the home it is often the *sālagrāma*—a small, smooth round stone—which serves precisely as the *lingam* does, as a form for the locus of devotion.

There is an interesting sidelight on the veneration of the images in Hindu temples. In Shaivite temples the serious and sympathetic non-Hindu visitor may be invited into the very sanctum of the temple to stand before the *lingam* and receive the sacred ash upon the forehead. Very seldom will such intimate observation of the principal deity by a non-Hindu be permitted in any Vaishnavite temple. The principle involved, however, is identical. It is a basic Hindu notion called *Darshan,* that is: *To see is to worship.* As the Shaivite understands this, a sympathetic Christian or perhaps a Jew or a humanist does in fact worship Shiva, although he interprets Him through other forms (Christ, Yahweh, Truth, etc.). Therefore it is not inappropriate that he should come before the image, but he must receive the ash as indication that he has indeed worshipped Shiva (though in whatever form he chooses to conceive Him). Vishnu, however, is more specific and is not represented by the ambiguous *lingam.* If one is not prepared to worship Vishnu specifically as such, as Hindu piety and reflection interpret Him, then His devotees are not willing to have such a person in His presence. (This, of course, has nothing necessarily to do with respect and friendship for the person.) These attitudes have been much influenced by contact with conquering Muslims in earlier ages, who were often fanatic in their destruction of all images, and with Christians, particularly missionaries who regarded the images as primitive idols. Still the attitude reflected here is truly basic in Hindu thought. To see is to worship. It is also essential that there be real contact between the worshipper and his deity, that he see and be seen, and this instant of mutual contact is a major theme in Hindu literature and a profound hope in the Hindu masses. The form of the image suggests, but never fully expresses the deity.

In addition to the *lingam,* Shiva may also be represented in numerous other forms, the most famous of which is the *Nāṭa-rāja*—the Cosmic Dancer. The *Bhairava* (terrible) form recognized in the previous story is occasionally represented, the hermaphrodite form of Shiva-Pārvatī, and the ubiquitous Kali images. God has many forms. The sculptor has access to symbols of some of them, the dancer to others, the "formless-form" of the *liṅgam* or *sālagrāma* suggest still others, but the authentic reality of god will be beyond all of them.

Hindu Reflection—The Story of Prahlāda (page 116)

DEVOTIONAL KNOWLEDGE

For those who wish to understand both the style and the conceptual content of Hindu reflection, this story will repay very serious reading. In the first place, it shows the devotional character of the thought. Prahlāda gives several lectures in the course of the story in which he instructs his father, his teachers and his friends on many of the major themes of Hindu interpretation—the nature of God, the fundamental doctrines of creation of the world and the embodiment of souls, meditation, the lessons to be learned from the pains and sorrows of life, sources of knowledge, human psychology, the uses of the absolute, values to be enjoyed, karma, devotional love, political science, etc., but each of these includes, and is concluded by and finally summed up in a hymn of praise for the greatness of god. The specific ideas dealt with are treated very seriously and surprisingly systematically for such a story. But they are not developed primarily as explanations or arguments, but rather as confessions or paeans of praise. For example, on page 127, Prahlāda, in reciting his lessons on the science of government, discusses a fundamental religious attitude toward such "practical" and "scientific" knowledge. He does not attempt to refute or criticize the traditional wisdom on political science, and indicates that he has, in fact, mastered it. The point that he makes is that the whole enterprise of scientific knowing (and this is to be understood as applying to all kinds of science) depends on seeking ends which have to do with the immediate world. Scientific knowledge is always relative to such limited goals. His objection is not that it is false, but that it is directed toward the wrong ends and therefore is "tedious and unprofitable." True wisdom looks for the "sameness"— that is, the divine nature—in all things and sees the whole environment as a testimony to the glory of god. Scientific knowing looks for the differences among things. Devotional knowledge seeks the obliteration of differences. The devotional is always thought to be the superior knowledge in this tradition.

HINTS ABOUT THE ABSOLUTE

In addition to the devotional character of the thought, there is also the struggle, characteristic of a great deal of Hindu reflection, to suggest, portray, analogize, intimate a knowledge of the indescribable and indefinable. The story is certainly filled with supernatural events, but its total impact is not particularly measured by the miraculous accounts. One may see these as a kind of indirect discourse, pointing toward a deeper view of one's own existence. It is from this point of view that blows cause no pain and poison causes no injury. The point of view is not directly accessible to ordinary consciousness, so that from this standpoint its attitudes must appear in the form of miracles. One may see how this same style would be received differently by different kinds of readers. For some, the miracles would simply be evidence of the power of god to protect his devotee, for others as a form of indirect discourse, and for still others as an indication of the primitive character of the literature and the need for more serious philosophical texts.

DIDACTIC FUNCTION

Throughout the story one encounters traditional proverbs of the Hindu culture: "Youth is the season of errors." "He who has large possessions in his house is haunted." These bits of ancient wisdom, along with occasional specific references to other stories, show the didactic purpose which underlies the account. This is particularly evident in a section such as Prahlāda's lecture to the sons of the demons, in which he takes up the problem of true value. The teaching is highly condensed but both systematic and traditional. He indicates certain factors (birth, change, and death) which are known to anybody by perception. Other facts (rebirth, for example) are supported by the testimony of *shruti* (scripture, sacred texts containing revealed wisdom). Scientific or philosophical reasoning (inference) as, for example, from event to cause, is a third source of knowledge. Using these sources of knowledge, he points out that what may appear to be pleasure is often in fact the engagement in further pain, with the conclusion that escape from the cycle of injuries by the help of Vishnu is the only hope. The devices by which men postpone their own salvation until too late are then examined.

The concluding part of this episode brings the story to its climax. If one adopts the proper standpoint he will see the whole world as a manifestation of god. No longer will he be misled by the apparent, but false, multiplicity of his experience. No longer will he wish the pleasure that is really only a disguise for pain. Ultimately this will require a fourth sort of knowledge, meditative and devotional, a direct apprehension of the Truth, such as Prahlāda attained at the bottom of the ocean. This is a perception which is possible only in a different state of consciousness, which continued reflection about and praise of god will make possible. It is not an ordinary state of consciousness, but is brought about by the grace of god, when man has set the proper conditions through the disciplines of meditation, but even more importantly through the devotion of the heart. To see god, in this perspective, however, remains a direct, personal, irrefutable experience for the one to whom it occurs.

THE CONTEXT FOR THOUGHT ABOUT GOD

All religions seek to deal with the problem of death so as to enable people to face it without a devastating loss of meaning or of the power to live. Usually this is done by interpreting death in the larger context of life and the meaning of man and of god. Hinduism does this through numerous teachings and attitudes, such as rebirth, freedom, karma, etc. In the great hymn which Prahlāda sings while lying beneath the rocks at the bottom of the ocean (page 129) he identifies Vishnu with a series of objects begining with all the gods, passing from heavenly to earthly beings, to the inorganic, to elements and finally to sensory qualities, soul, time and nature. This list, which is very traditional both in its content and in its order, puts man in his place, about halfway between the gods and the basic elements (earth, air, fire, water). The terror of death is greatest when the clinging to this individual form is strongest. To understand man's life as important, but not *all* important, as good, but with a chance to be still better, is to relax the grip of terror a bit, and to see things in perspective. When one does see things in perspective, "freedom from existence" can become the goal which transcends and transforms the threat of death to a sweet promise. So some Hindus believe.

PART III

STORIES
OF THE GODS

Section I: Stories of Vishnu

IN ONE WAY or another it may be thought that the gods participate in all events which transpire in the various worlds. The forms of existence are themselves manifestations of the gods, as the gods are manifestations, individuations, personifications of ultimate Brahman. But the literature does not suggest that Hindu thinking actually expresses such an undifferentiated, unqualified pantheism. Some manifestations of god are far more indicative and significant than others. In the Vaishnavite tradition the most important of these significant presences of god in the world are called the *avatārs* of Vishnu. Traditionally there are ten of these incarnations, but this is somewhat arbitrary as slightly different lists are given, and there are many ways and times in which Vishnu is present besides these. All avatārs are important of course, but Krishna, Rāma, and the Buddha are undoubtedly the three which have caught the pious imagination of India and all Asia.

Sometimes these stories function to explain some natural event or feature—floods, ocean volcanoes, etc. At other times they are ennoblements of familiar home activities. The relationship to the life and thought of those who tell the stories is seldom much disguised. The texts always begin and end in prayer—that life may be more livable for those who read, tell or hear these stories. With that as our own prayer, let us retell some of these stories according to the general spirit of the ancient accounts.

THE TORTOISE AVATĀRA (KŪRMA)[1]

ONE TIME IN THE GREAT and continuing struggles between the devas (or divine powers) and the asuras (or demonic powers) the asuras had achieved the supremacy and were causing great havoc throughout the creation. The devas appealed to Brahmā to help them, and he in turn appealed to Vishnu to manifest himself for their aid. Having been petitioned by the other deities, Brahmā proceeded along with them to the northern shore of the sea of milk and with reverential words prayed to the supreme Hari:

"We glorify him who is all things; the Lord supreme over all; unborn, imperishable; the protector of the mighty ones of creation; the unperceived, indivisible Nārāyaṇa; the smallest of the smallest, the largest of the largest: in whom all things are, from whom all things come; who was before existence; the god who is all beings; who is the end of ultimate objects, who is beyond final spirit and is one with the supreme soul; who is contemplated as the cause of final liberation by sages anxious to be free; in whom are not the qualities of goodness, foulness, or darkness, that belong to undeveloped nature. . . . The infinite nature of Vishnu is pure, intelligent, perpetual, unborn, undecayable, inexhaustible, inscrutable, immutable; it is neither gross nor subtle nor capable of being defined: to that ever holy nature of Vishnu I bow. To him whose faculty to create the universe abides in but a part of but the ten-mil-

[1] Adapted from *The Vishnu Purāṇa* as translated by H. H. Wilson.

lionth part of Him; to him who is one with the inexhaustible supreme spirit, I bow: and to the glorious nature of the supreme Vishnu, which nor gods, nor sages, nor I, nor wisdom itself apprehend; that nature which the *yogis* after incessant effort effacing both moral merit and demerit, behold to be contemplated in the mystical monosyllable *OM:* the supreme glory of Vishnu, who is first of all; of whom only one god, the triple energy is the same with Brahmā, Vishnu and Śiva: O Lord of all, great soul of all, asylum of all, undecayable, have pity upon thy servants: O Vishnu, be manifest unto us."

Responding to Brahmā's appeal, the supreme deity, mighty holder of the conch and discus, revealed himself to them. Beholding the Lord of all gods, bearing a conch-shell, a discus and a mace, Brahmā and the other deities, their eyes moist with rapture, first paid him homage and then prayed for his help in their distress.

Hari spoke to them: "I will restore your strength with renewed energy, O gods. But you must do as I ask. Let all of you make an agreement with the asuras and together throw all sorts of medicinal herbs into the sea of milk. Then take the mountain, Mandara, for a churning paddle, and the great serpent-king, Vāsuki, for a rope, and with you on the one side and the asuras on the other, together churn the ocean for a nectar of ambrosia which will be produced, relying on my aid. To secure the assistance of the Dāityas (asuras) you must be at peace with them and agree to give them an equal portion of the fruit of your mutual toil; promising them that by drinking the *amrita* that shall be produced from the churned ocean, they shall become powerful and immortal. I will take care that the enemies of the gods shall not in fact partake of the precious draught, but shall share only in the work."

So the devas made an alliance with the demons and jointly they undertook to acquire the beverage of immortality. Together they collected many kinds of medicinal herbs and threw them into the ocean of milk, the waters of which were radiant as the shining clouds of an autumn day. They then took the mountain, Mandara, for a churning staff and the serpent Vāsuki for the cord and began to churn the ocean of milk for the *amrita.* Krishna put the gods at the tail of the great serpent while the Dāityas and the Dānavas pulled from the head and neck. This worked so that as they tugged back and forth on the great snake the asuras were repeatedly scorched by the flames emitted from his inflated hood and drenched by the floods of venom which poured from his fangs. The devas, on the other hand, were continually refreshed by the breezes of the serpent's breathing and the rotation of the great churn.

Vishnu was present in many ways. The mountain burrowed into the floor of the ocean and threatened universal flood, so Hari took the form of a great tortoise, *Kūrma*, sank to the bottom of the ocean and used his back as a pivot for the mountain. At the same time Vishnu was also present in other forms, encouraging the gods and demons in their work, sustaining the serpent-king in his ordeal, infusing vigor into the gods and steadying the top of the mountain as it turned back and forth.

From this churning by the gods and demons various things began to be produced. First to emerge was the cosmic cow, Surabhi, the fountain of milk and curds (prosperity) and she was worshipped by the gods. Even while the holy wise ones contemplated the cow, she was followed by the goddess Vāruṇī, deity of wine, with her eyes rolling with intoxication. Next from the whirlpool of the deep sprang the celestial Pārijāta tree, delight of heavenly nymphs and which perfumes the world with its blossoms. Hosts of *apsaras*, lovely nymphs of heaven, endowed with beauty and good taste, were then produced. The cool-rayed crescent moon, Soma, rose next, and was immediately taken by Mahādeva (Śiva) and placed upon his forehead. Then poison was engendered by the sea and taken by the *Nāgas* (snake gods).[2]

Finally Dhanvantari emerged, robed in white and bearing in his hands the cup of *amrita*. All the churners were delighted, and while they watched in ecstatic joy, the radiant and lovely goddess Shrī (or Lakshmī) rose from the waves

[2] There are several versions of this story. The account here follows *The Vishnu Purāṇa*, but in other accounts the poison is engendered either first (by the sea) or by the tugging and hauling on Vāsuki, the great serpent. To save the world from this flood of venom, Shiva drank it and it turned his throat purple or dark blue. This convention is widely followed in pictures of Shiva which identify him in part by a dark throat or face.

seated on a full blown lotus, holding a water-lily in her hand. The great sages and devas were enraptured and sang songs dedicated to her praise. Heavenly choirs joined in and the celestial nymphs (*apsaras*) danced before her. Goddess Gaṅgā and other holy rivers attended for her ablutions, and the elephants of the skies, taking up the pure water in golden vases, poured them over the goddess, Queen of the universal worlds. The Sea of Milk in person garlanded her with a wreath of unfading flowers and the artist of the gods, Viswakarma, decorated her with heavenly ornaments. Thus bathed, attired and adorned, the goddess, in view of the celestials, cast herself upon the breast of Hari, and reclining there turned her enraptured eyes upon the deities. The asuras, however, were filled with indignation and turning away they were abandoned by Vishnu and by Lakshmī, the goddess of prosperity.

The powerful and indignant Dāityas (*asuras*) forcibly seized the cup of *amrita* from the hands of Dhanvantari, but Vishnu, assuming a seductive, female form, fascinated and distracted them, so that he was able to recover the *amrita* and deliver it to the gods.

The incensed asuras grasped their weapons and attacked the devas, but the ambrosia had infused the devas with new vigor and they put the hosts of the asuras to flight. The gods then celebrated their victory, did homage to the holder of the discus and the mace, and resumed their appropriate reigns in heaven. The sun shone with renovated splendor and the planets circled in their respective orbits, fire blazed aloft in beauty [stars?], and the minds of all beings were animated by devotion. The three worlds were happy and prosperous and Indra was restored to power. They eulogized Vishnu and Shrī, the Mother of all beings. In the incarnations of Vishnu, she is incarnated also for the benefit and prosperity of the world.

THE FISH AVATĀRA (MATSYA)[1]

AT THE END of the last world-age the minor dissolution which
occurs as the end of a day of Brahmā took place and the three
lower worlds were submerged in water. Brahmā felt very
drowsy and was falling asleep. He sighed and breathed out the
Veda, which a powerful *asura* named Hayagriva grasped and
carried away.

In that kalpa there was a great and devout king who was
meditating on Bhagavan and doing *tapas* (austerity) by living
on only water. One day King Satyavrata was standing in the
stream making a water offering. He picked up water cupped
in both his hands, but he discovered a little fish in the water
intended for his offering and immediately dropped it back
into the stream. The little fish cried out to him, "I am afraid
that other fish will kill me and sought refuge with you. Why do
you abandon me? Have you no mercy?

The king decided to protect the fish, put it into a vessel and
took it home. In that one night the fish grew and filled the
vessel. The next day it asked the king for a larger and more
comfortable place. Satyavrata put it into a tub, but in a
muhūrta (48 minutes) it had filled the tub and again com-
plained. The king took it and put it into a reservoir. Again the
fish grew and the same episode was repeated for larger and
larger tanks until finally it was necessary to put the great fish

[1] Following the *Bhāgavata Purāṇa*, the *Matsya Purāṇa and the Mahābhārata*.

into the ocean. When this was being done the fish protested that in the ocean it would surely be devoured by powerful fish. The king, beginning to suspect a god behind these strange changes, asked who it was that confounded him in the shape of a fish, and sang a hymn of praise to the fish-god.

Bhagavan, who wished to amuse himself in the ocean of dissolution and to reward his devotee, responded to the king: "In seven days there will be a great flood in which all three worlds, beginning with earth, will be submerged. When that happens a large ship sent by me will come to you. Take the seven *rishis,* specimens of all vegetables and their seeds, large and small, and of all animals. You will float on the ocean. Be courageous. The darkness will be illuminated by the spirituality of the *rishis.* As the winds rise against you, I (Matsya—the Fish) will approach the ship with a large horn on my head. Using the great serpent, Vāsuki, [the *Mahābhārata* says ropes] tie the ship to my horn. I will draw you with me about the ocean until Brahmā's night comes to an end."

Vishnu then disappeared and the king awaited the time he had described. He continually meditated upon Brahman in the form of the Fish. Then one day the ocean began to overflow its banks, the earth was submerged, and torrents of rain fell. The ship mentioned by the Fish appeared and Satyavrata and the seven *rishis* boarded it with the animals and vegetables as directed. The terror of the storm frightened them but soon a golden fish appeared with a great horn on the snout to which they tied the boat by means of Vāsuki, the great serpent. Leading them about the wild ocean in the form of the golden fish, Nārāyaṇa taught them the truths about himself and received their hymns of praise. When at the end of that long night Brahmā awoke, Vishnu killed the demon Hayagriva and restored the *Veda* to Brahmā and the world. "O Bhagavan: Destroy all darkness in our hearts with the torch of your words. Make us perceive your feeling for the unfortunate."

THE BOAR AVATĀRA (VARĀHA)[1]

IN EXPLAINING the creation by Vishnu through Brahmā, Parāśara described the close of the previous kalpa in which Brahmā
had awakened and noticed the universal void. Hearing the
sound "Nārāyaṇa" (one of the names of Vishnu) which means
"Moving from the Waters," Brahmā concluded that within the
waters of the void lay the earth. In order to deliver the earth
from beneath this great flood, Vishnu created another form
for himself, just as in preceeding kalpas he had assumed the
shape of a fish or of a tortoise. This time he took the figure of
a giant Boar (Varāha). This form connotes delight in sporting in the water and also immense power, but at the same time
it is the name of a ritual ceremony of the *Vedas*. Thus, the
story suggests a raising of the world from a deluge of iniquity
by the rites of religion, and also that the earth had been
brought forth from some ancient flood.

When Vishnu appeared in the form of the great Boar, Varāha
was eulogized by appropriate saints in the realm of holy men
and was devoutly adored by the Goddess Earth as he prepared
to find the land below the sea. Prithivī (Goddess Earth) sang
her song of praise: "Hail to thee, who art all creatures, holder
of the mace and shell. Elevate me now from this dreary place,
as you have raised me up in ancient days. From thee I have
proceeded. Of thee do I consist, as do the skies and all existing things. Hail to thee, Spirit of the Supreme Spirit, soul of

[1] Adapted from *The Vishnu Purāṇa* translated by H. H. Wilson.

soul. . . . Thou art the creator of all things, their preserver and destroyer in the forms of Brahmā, Vishnu and Rudra (Shiva), at the seasons of creation, duration and dissolution. When you have ended all things you repose on the ocean that sweeps over the world, and are meditated upon by the wise. No one knows your true nature. Even the gods adore you only in forms it has pleased you to assume. Those who desire final liberation worship thee as supreme Brahman. Whatever may be apprehended by the mind, whatever may be perceived by the senses, whatever may be discerned by the intellect; all is but a form of thee. I am called Mādhavi—the Bride of Mādhava (Vishnu)—for I am upheld by thee. Supreme thou art."

The auspicious supporter of the world thus being praised by Goddess Earth, emitted a low murmuring sound, like the chanting of the *Sama Veda,* and the mighty, dark boar, with eyes like the lotus and body as vast as the mountains, thrust his ample tusks below the earth and lifted it up from the lowest regions. As Varāha reared his head, the waters which shed from his brow purified the region of the saints. Through his hoof prints the waters rushed into the lower worlds as a thundering waterfall. His heavy breathing began to scatter the saints, but they found protection in the scriptures, and inspired by delight they created hymns of praise for the stern-eyed upholder of the earth. In their hymn the *yogis* put foremost their own understanding of Vishnu as seen through the eyes of wisdom.

They sang:

Thou who art the aim of all:
There is none other than thee:
    Sovereign of the world.
This form we now behold (Varāha) is Thy Form.
It is essentially one with wisdom.
Those who have not practiced devotion
    Conceive erroneously of the nature of the world.
The ignorant, who do not perceive
    That this universe is of the nature of wisdom,
    Judging it only as an object of perception,
    Are lost in an ocean of spiritual ignorance.

Those who know true wisdom:
Those whose minds are pure
  Behold this whole world as One with Divine Knowl-
    edge,
  As One with Thee, O God. . . .
    Grant us happiness, O lotus-eyed Varāha!

Vishnu then placed the earth on the summit of the ocean, where it floats like a mighty vessel, and from its expansive surface does not sink (e.g., in space). The great god then levelled the earth with his tusks, divided it into portions by mountains, constructed again the continents, the four lower spheres and turning again to the form of Brahmā accomplished creation anew.[2]

[2] In the *Bhāgavata Purāṇa* a later story concerning an enormous battle between Hiranyāksha (father of the Rakshsas) and Vishnu in the Boar form is described. The demon was defeated by delivering a blow to Varāha, which rebounded against himself and killed him. Hiranyāksha is further explained as previously having been a doorkeeper of Vaikuṇṭha —Vishnu's world—who had tried to distinguish between different but equally sincere devotees who approached Bhagavan, to admit some of them and reject others and to subject them to tests. For his obstinancy and arrogance he had been condemned to the world of the *asuras*. There is no hint of this story in *The Vishnu Purāna*.

THE MAN-LION AVATĀRA (NARA-SIMHA)[1]

IN THE STORY of Prahlāda (see pp. 116–133) it was related how this pious son of the evil Asura King Hiranyākasipu repeatedly infuriated his father by his devotion to Vishnu. Magical charms protected each of them. Hiranyākasipu was unable to kill his son because of the boy's utter and absolute dependence upon Vishnu. He in turn was protected from all enemies by a boon from Brahmā.

In earlier years Hiranyākasipu had journeyed to the Mandara Mountain and there had done enormous *tapas* in order to be free from old age and death, to be unconquerable, sole ruler of all worlds. At the mountain he stood, touching the ground only with the toes of his feet, both hands uplifted and eyes to the sky. The inner heat of his mental concentration radiated in all directions and burned the three worlds. Rivers and oceans began to boil, earth trembled and hills shook, stars and planets fell from the sky and the ten directions blazed from the radiant heat of his austerities. The *devas* asked Brahmā to remove this trouble from them. When Brahmā searched for the cause of the great energy he was amazed to discover the great Asura, covered with a giant anthill, grass and bamboo, only a skeleton, as his skin, flesh and blood had been eaten by the ants, but still in undistracted, unyielding concentration of *tapas*. He had practiced a hundred divine years of austerities by the time Brahmā found him.

[1] Following the *Bhāgavata Purāna.*

Brahmā was so overwhelmed by the severity of these austerities that he spontaneously promised whatever boon might be asked by such a *yogi*. Sprinkling water on the skeleton, Brahmā revived the Asura from his austerities.

With so generous a promise Hiranyākasipu asked for the following boon:

"May no death come to me from any being created by you, neither inside nor outside a house, neither by day nor by night; nor by any weapon; neither on the ground nor in the sky; may no death come to me either from man or beast; from those with *prāṇa* (breath) or without *prāṇa*, from *devas*, *asuras* or *nāgas*. There should be no one to oppose me in battle. I should be the sole lord of all beings. May I have the greatness of the rulers of all the worlds, and the abnormal and imperishable powers attained by yogis."

Brahmā replied, "The boons that you ask are unattainable by anyone; yet I will grant them to you." With these words he returned to his own abode.

Having such protection and no scruples, Hiranyākasipu was both irresistible and insufferable. The only one to be able to resist his arrogance was his own son Prahlāda, who did so by means of his utter devotion to Vishnu. The devas, gods, rishis and men were required to present Hiranyākasipu with the offerings of their castes and stages of life. Only Vishnu, Shiva, and Brahmā were exempt from his commands. The oppressed ones appealed to Bhagavān (Vishnu) to relieve their distress, and he did promise to do so but required them to be patient until the great *asura* had fulfilled the conditions of his own undoing. This would require the attempt to kill an innocent devotee. The required devotee turned out to be the son of Hiranyākasipu, Prahlāda. The boy insisted on devotion to Vishnu despite all threats and punishments, but he was also immune to his father's wrath. He could not be trampled by elephants, poisoned by herbs nor by serpents, killed by natural or supernatural beings, injured by weapons, deceived by illusions, starved, frozen, exposed to fire, wind and thirst, his organs of excretion closed, thrown down from high places. The innocent Prahlāda could not be killed by any of these means. Failing to kill him by any means, his father had him bound and sunk to the bottom of the ocean beneath mountains of stone. In this retreat from distraction Prahlāda's mind was even more concentrated on the object of his devotion and he realized his identity with Vishnu. This, of course, released all bonds and he returned to the surface of the ocean, rediscovered his individuality without really losing his sense of identity with Vishnu, and received Vishnu's gifts, eternal power of his devotions, and forgiveness for his father. Prahlāda and his father were reconciled.

Prahlāda, however, insisted on continuing to teach concerning the ultimacy of Vishnu and won many converts among Hiranyākasipu's court. As they became devotees of Vishnu instead of the King the father became enraged at his son again.

Shaking with anger Hiranyākasipu confronted his son, "You foolish hypocrite! You will be the means of the destruction of our family. Relying on whose strength do you try to set aside my orders?"

Prahlāda replied that the strength is that of Bhagavān and taught his father that there is no enemy except an uncontrolled mind which may run after unworthy objects. The mention of "enemy" is a delusion.

Hiranyākasipu replied, "It is clear from what you say that you really wish to die. Those about to die often speak unconnected, meaningless words as you have done. You speak of a ruler of the universe other than me. Where is he? If he is everywhere, why isn't he seen in this pillar? I'll cut off your head! Now see if this Hari can save you!" With this he leaped up, grasped his sword, struck the pillar with his hand and was about to lunge at the boy when the pillar gave forth an enormous and terrible roar. Then out of the pillar there emerged a strange and wonderful form, a lion, but not fully a beast, a man, but not fully a man.

"His eyes were like molten gold; His hair fell down from His face; His teeth protruded from the ends of His mouth; His tongue had sharp edges like a razor, and moved to and fro; His eye-brows were knit; His ears stood upright; His mouth and nostrils were open and were like mountain caves; His body touched the sky; His neck was short and stout; His chest was broad and His waist thin; His body was covered with hair white as the moon's rays; His numerous hands spread in all directions and the nails of His fingers looked like weapons, and He was terrible to look at."

Attacking even Vishnu with his club, Hiranyākasipu advanced toward him but disappeared within his power (*tejas*) just as insects disappear in the flame that they attack. Nara-Simha, the Man-Lion, grasped the Asura King, but dropped him, the way an eagle will sometimes drop a snake with which it toys. Both the observing gods and Hiranyākasipu thought that this represented a weakness of the Man-Lion, but as he attacked Vishnu again with shield and sword, the earth passed into the twilight which was neither night nor day. In a burst of fury Nara-Simha threw down the Asura King, tore open his chest with the great nails of his paws, and throwing the corpse on the ground, the Man-Lion ascended and sat on the Asura's throne. His appearance was fearsome, as of a lion at the killing of an elephant. His face was contorted with fury, his eyes red with rage. He licked the blood off his mouth with his tongue, garlandẹd himself with the Asura's intestines. The whole existence was in danger. The *devas* and gods tried to persuade Nara-Simha to forego his anger until the end of the age. They asked Srī (Goddess Lakshmī) to approach and calm him, but she did not dare. Finally they convinced Prahlāda that because of his boon of protection he could approach the fearsome god safely, which Prahlāda did with various hymns of praise. Responding to his praise, Nara-Simha calmed his fury and said:

"Child! I am pleased with you, ask for anything that you desire, and I will give it to you; for I give whatever is sought by men. One that does not please Me cannot see Me, and one that has seen Me does not deserve to be troubled in mind."

Prahlāda replied with a smile: "Lord! Do not cheat me by promise of a boon—me who by nature am attached to sense objects. I fear attachments to them, and am disgusted with them. Desiring release I seek refuge in You. Apparently You wish to test whether I possess the marks of a servant, and ask what objects I desire. Otherwise this speech of Yours will not fit in with Your mercy. One who desires anything in return for his *bhakti* (love) is not a servant; he is a trader. He is not a master, who gives one what he desires, and gets his service in return. I love You, but not to obtain anything in return. You are my master for all time to come. Our relation is not the relation of a king to his servant; neither of us desire anything from this relationship. If You desire to give a boon, I ask for this only, that no desire should spring in my heart."

Then Bhagavan (Nara-Siṁha, Vishnu) replied, "Persons like you who love Me for Myself only, do not desire enjoyment in this or in the other worlds. Nevertheless in this *manu-antara* you shall be the lord of the *asuras* and experience the enjoyments available in that position. Hear stories of My deeds: worship Me with meditation—Me who am in you and in all beings. You will thus wear out whatever *karma* remains. Good deeds should be worked out by enjoyment; evil deeds by cheerfully undergoing suffering. Throw up your body in due course. Spread your fame till it is sung in the heaven world; and you will then reach Me freed from bondage."

Prahlāda then asked for one boon: "My father, not knowing your power (*tejas*), spoke insultingly of You from the false notion that You killed his brother, and he tried to injure me, Your beloved. May he be purified from the sin committed in both ways.

Bhagavan then replied: "Twenty-one generations, including your father, have become pure from the fact that you have been born in their family. One that loves Me, that is without desire and aversion, that looks upon all alike and that does his duties properly, purifies the country in which he resides, even though it is inhabited by impure persons."

Then Brahmā expressed his joy at the killing of the evil *asura*, who, obtaining extensive powers from himself, harassed the world, and at the release of his son from all the troubles to which he was exposed. To this Vishnu responded, "Do not in the future give such extensive powers to the *asuras*. They are cruel-minded by nature, and for them those powers have the same result as giving milk to a serpent."

THE DWARF AVATĀRA
(VĀMANA)[1]

THE GREAT ASURA KING BALI, grandson of Prahlāda, had been defeated by Indra and the devas after they had been strengthened by drinking the amrita which was produced by the churning of the Ocean of Milk. He did not grieve over his defeat, however, and having been restored to life by his guru, Sukra, Bali placed his fortune at the disposal of the teacher and asked him to secure lordship of the heaven-world for him. Under Sukra's instructions the *Viśva-jit* sacrifice was performed which secured the admiration of Brahmā and Agni who presented him with invincible weapons of war. With these great weapons Bali advanced on Indra-loka and sounded the conch given him by Brahmā. The sound of Bali's conch filled the hearts of the deva females with fear. Indra observed Bali and remarked to his guru:

"Reverend sir, this preparation of my old enemy is so great that in my opinion it cannot be opposed. By what *tejas* (power) has he become so strong? No one is able to overcome him by any means that he may adopt. He appears to drink this world with his mouth, lick the ten directions with his tongue, and to burn them with his eyes like the fire that blazes at the time of dissolution. What is the cause of this invulnerability?"

Indra was advised by the guru to abandon heaven for a time until Bali had begun his own undoing by disrespect to a

1 Following the *Bhāgavata Purāṇa*.

holy man. So heaven was abandoned by Indra and the devas and came under the control of Bali and the asuras even without a fight.

Aditi, Indra's mother, however, was very sad at the loss of all the prosperity and powers of her sons. Her husband, Kashyapa, returning from meditations, noticed her sadness and when he discovered the reason he suggested that she should worship Vishnu with the special *Pago-vrata* rituals. Accepting his advice, Aditi performed the following sacrifice to Bhagavan.

"On the new moon day in the month *Phālguna* (March to April) one should bathe in a stream, applying to his body the earth thrown up by a wild pig with its tusk, and do worship to Bhagavan, make offerings to the fire and feed not less than two Brahmins. Bhagavan's worship should be done in an image of Vishnu, on the ground, in the sun, in water, in fire, and in a guru. It consists of the following items. Praying to Him to come and be present in the place selected (a fixed prayer); giving Him a seat; washing the hands and feet (of the idol); giving Him water to sip; and giving Him a bath. This should be done with cow's milk. Then giving Him cloth, the holy thread, ornaments, sandal paste and flowers; showing incense and a light before Him; placing before Him rice cooked in milk along with ghee and sugar; going round Him and prostrating before Him; repeating the mantra of twelve syllables; singing praises; and lastly requesting Him to depart. The food, the sandal paste and flowers should be received with the head. Not less than two Brahmins should be fed with the offerings made, and with their permission the worshipper should eat the remains. This course of life should be led for the next twelve days. On the thirteenth day the worship should be done on a larger scale, including music and dancing. Then presents should be given to the guru, and to those that helped him in making the offerings. Every one that comes, including the lowest caste, should be fed and given presents. All this time the worshipper should bathe three times a day, and live on milk alone. He should abstain from sexual intercourse and lie down on bare ground. He should avoid speech to unworthy persons, and unworthy talk and enjoyment of every kind, high or low. He should not injure any one. He should regard Bhagavan as the highest goal. On the thirteenth day the bathing of the image should be done with a mixture of cow's milk, curd, ghee, urine and dung, with four helpers."

Following these instructions of her husband, Aditi performed the discipline and at its conclusion Vishnu appeared before her, wearing the yellow cloth and bearing the discus, conch and club. He spoke to her and assured her that he knew the desires of her heart, and, pleased with her devotions, he promised to be born as her son. Bhagavan then disappeared and Aditi returned to her husband filled with affection and delight. In due time Bhagavan was born to Aditi amid cosmic rejoicing and delight. At his birth, Vishnu had shown the auspicious marks of his true nature, but soon he disguised that form and began to grow not as a beautiful young man, but as a stunted dwarf (*vāmanan*). The rishis were delighted to see him in this form and conspired that as he grew through the stages of youth, his naming ceremony done, the Gāyatri mantra was taught by Sūrya (sun) himself, he received the holy thread from Brihaspati, the waist band of *muñja* grass from his father, Kashyapa, a deer-skin from Earth (Prithivī); a rod from the Moon, loin cloth from his mother, an umbrella from the Sky, a wooden bowl from the rishi, Vedagarba, *kusha* grass from the seven rishis, beads from Sarasvatī, begging bowl from the god of riches, Kubera, and initiation from Umā. Thus the dwarf grew up, recognized for his true nature only by the holy ones. Outwardly he was only a pitiable dwarf.

Hearing that the unconquerable Bali was performing a horse-sacrifice to consolidate his claim to control over all the heavenly worlds, Vāmana attended the sacrifice. Following the customary rules of such occasions, Vāmana was received graciously by Bali, made comfortable and his feet washed. Bali then welcomed him, and recognizing holy power within him praised him with flourish and offered him whatever he would require.

Vishnu was pleased that Bali had followed *dharma* and the noble traditions of his grandfather, Prahlāda, in the welcome. Then the dwarf asked for a bit of land, as much as might be. measured by him in three steps.

Bali did not think the request was adequate to his hospitality and warned that such a request could only be made once and suggested a larger demand. Vāmana responded, "All the lands in three worlds are not enough to satisfy one who has not controlled his senses. One who is not satisfied with the land of three steps, cannot be gratified by the grant of this whole island, for he will hanker after others. Rulers, even of seven worlds, desired more and found no end to their desires. One who is pleased with what comes without effort lives in peace; but one who is the reverse from lack of control over his senses will find no pleasure even if three worlds come to him. Not to be pleased with the wealth and enjoyment which rises easily and naturally leads to *samsāra*. But being pleased with whatever comes leads to release. The accomplishment of one who is pleased with his lot increases day by day, but it disappears from others as a fire is quenched by water. Therefore I ask for only three steps of land. My purpose will be satisfied with so much only, for wealth is desirable only insofar as it is really needed."

Bali laughed and promised him whatever he might require, but his guru intervened. He saw what was about to happen and tried to warn Bali that the dwarf Brahmin student would stride over so much land that there would be no place for the third step and Bali would go to hell for being unable to fulfill his promise. He pointed out that the promise necessarily implies its own conditions that make it possible to fulfill. He cannot be held to a promise he is unable to fulfill. According to Sukra, "Falsehood is not condemned in the following cases: When uttered to please a woman, in jest, to procure the marriage of a person, for means of livelihood, in times of danger to one's life and for the protection of cows and Brahmins."

Bali considered the guru's advice, but rejected it curtly, saying that he was unwilling ever to retract a promise or to fail to fulfill it so long as that is possible. He did not fear that Vishnu would trick him as Sukra had suggested, and promised to fight if he should try it. The rebuffed guru cursed him and promised the loss of his kingdom, but even this did not change his mind.

Pouring water into the hand of Vāmana, Bali symbolized the

promise he had made, followed by his washing of the dwarf's feet and sprinkling the purifying water on his head.

As he prepared to take the three steps for the land which he would claim, Vāmana's body began to grow in size till it had passed through all the three worlds. The whole sky, for example, was only his navel and all ten directions rested on his ears. Night was the closing and day the opening of his eyelids. The gods themselves worshipped the foot of Vishnu. He then stepped out. He measured the earth-world with his first step. He measured the heaven-worlds with the second step all the way to *Satya-loka* (truth-world) so that there was not a place left anywhere for the third step he had been promised.

Bali's advisors were angry, thinking that it was not fair that a dwarf who had asked for three steps of land should be in fact Vishnu and in only two steps had laid claim to all creations. They began to attack even without Bali's permission. Bhagavan's servants met them and were wreaking havoc when Bali saw what was being done and had them desist. He instructed the asura chiefs to leave the heavenly worlds and find their place in *rasatala* for a time. Garuḍa, the great eagle who attends Vishnu, bound Bali for his master's pleasure.

Vishnu then addressed Bali and said: "O Asura! You gave me land to be measured by three steps. With two of them I have measured all the worlds. Show me the land for the third step. All the land which is warmed by the sun, or on which the moon and the stars shine, and on which the rain falls belonged to you, and this was measured by me in one step. The intermediate worlds and the directions were filled by my body and the heaven world which is my property was measured with my second step, while you watched. If one does not give what he has promised, residence in hell is required. Therefore go to hell as your guru indicated. When one deceives a beggar by first offering a gift and then not carrying out the promise, his wishes become fruitless, and he falls into hell. You regarded yourself as a wealthy person and deceived me with the words, 'I will give!' You should experience the fruit of your falsehood by residence in hell for a few years."

Bali then responded that he did not fear the punishment of hell as much as the possibility of the falsehood which leads to it and asked that the third step be placed on his head. Then also the ancient Prahlāda appeared before Vishnu and pleaded for his descendant, Bali, and Bali's wife also spoke in his behalf.

The Vishnu responded to them all. "O Brahmā, I take away the wealth of those whom I bless, for it makes them intoxicated and proud and causes them to treat me and the worlds with disrespect. An *ātman* (soul) plunged in *samsāra* (cycles of existence) is born from various wombs in accordance with his *karma* being unable to prevent such a birth. Occasionally he attains a human birth. If then he is not conceited on account of his high birth, right conduct, youth, fine figure, great learning, control of many people and wealth, know that it is due to my blessing. One that regards me as the highest goal will not be deluded by high birth and the like, which lead to conceit and lack of humility and which oppose the attainment of every good. Bali will overcome the delusions of his existence and in the next age he will be reborn as Indra. In the meantime he may reside in *sutāla*, which has recently been improved by the austerities of Visvakarma so that in that world there are no physical nor mental ailments, no fatigue, indolence, heat prostration, cold or similar such troubles."

Bali praised and worshipped Bhagavan with tears in his eyes. The gratitude in his heart that Vishnu would preserve and care for even such lowly beings as asuras, much lower that the lowest of human castes, was overwhelming. He entered the *sutāla* world with a happy mind.

Bhagavan then instructed Sukra to complete his disciples' sacrifice so that there should be no defect due to a failure to complete the rites, and having restored Indra and the devas to their rightful places in the heaven-worlds, Vāmana returned to the form of Vishnu in Vaikuṇṭha. This avatāra was at the beginning of the seventh (or present) *manu-antara*.

THE AVATĀRA
AS PARASHURĀMA –
(Rāma with the Axe)[1]

THIS ACCOUNT, along with the appearance of HARI in the
Bhāgavata Purāṇa and the BUDDHA avatāra to follow, is one
of the minor avatāras. There are two basic types of avatāras.
One of these involves the direct presence of Vishnu in a form
of his own choosing (such as the Tortoise, Fish, Boar, Man-
Lion or Dwarf presented). The other kind of avatāra is the
presence of Vishnu in some other form as a kind of inspiration
or hidden presence such as we find in Parashurāma, in Rāma (of
the Rāmāyana), in the Buddha/Mahavira (Deceiver) form,
and in Sri Krishna. This account of Parashurāma probably sur-
vives as a legacy of an ancient struggle between Brahmins and
Kshatriyas, and has been preserved as a thinly veiled warning
by Brahmins that the Kshatriyas should preserve and respect
them properly because they come under the special protection
of Vishnu. The account will be presented briefly here.

A pious sage, Jamadagni, and his wife, Reṇukā, lived in
their forest hermitage with their five sons, of whom one was
named Rāma (Parashurāma—Rāma with the axe). One day
Reṇuka went to the Ganges to fetch water and there saw a
Gandharva King playing in the river with *apsara* women, and
her mind became entranced by the gay scene. Finally remembering her mission, she returned to her husband, but her distraction was evident to him and he became angry. The sons
had been out gathering fruits, but as each of them returned

[1] Following the *Mahābhārata*.

home, the father, Jamadagni, commanded him to kill the mother for her disobedience. None of the sons, except Rāma, would obey the father, so he killed each son for his disobedience. When Rāma was commanded to kill Reṇukā, he immediately picked up his axe and, following his father's wish, sliced off her head.

Pleased with his unquestioning and instant obedience, the father asked what boon Rāma would wish. The son requested the mother and brothers to be restored to life, despite their disobedience, and to have no memory of this event. This was done and all awoke as if from sleep.

On another day when the boys were absent from the hermitage, the mighty King Kritavirya [the *Bhāgavata Purāṇa* identifies the villain as his son, called Arjuna] came to the forest hermitage with his army and was received with great hospitality by Reṇukā, who was able to entertain them lavishly because of the calf and cow which they owned. This cow [Indian symbol of prosperity] was able to give every good thing in food or drink to one who would ask. The King decided to carry off this generous cow and her calf and took them by force. When Rāma returned and was told the story of the abduction of the cow of plenty he was infuriated and immediately went to slay the King with his weapons. [Bow and arrows says the *Mahābhārata*, axe say other authorities.]

A feud having started over the cow, the sons of Kritavirya waited until Rāma was away and then entered the hermitage and slew the pious and unresisting sage and his wife.

When Rāma returned and found this scene of carnage, he performed the dutiful ceremonies for his father and mother and then made a vow that he would extirpate the whole Kshatriya race from the earth.

Taking up his axe he started first with the sons of Kritavirya who had actually done the evil deed, and after this he killed any Kshatriya he encountered. Twenty-one times, as young Kshatriyas came of age, he cleared the earth of the caste. (Some, of course, were in hiding, disguise, remote regions, too old or too young and thus escaped the general elimination of the caste.) Having thus vindicated his innocent father, he was given the opportunity to see his father in heaven, and, performing a proper ceremony, the Brahmins received a gift of land (normally a possession of Kshatriyas) which had been presented to Kashyapa by Rāma who had taken it from the dead princes. The Brahmins divided this land among themselves.

Having done these things Parashurāma retired to the Mandara Mountains where he still resides (that. is, as a perpetual threat to Kshatriyas who might be tempted to mistreat Brahmins).

THE AVATĀRA AS THE BUDDHA (THE DECEIVER)[1]

THE RELATIONSHIPS between Hinduism and its rivals such as Buddhism and Jainism and other sects have, of course, been dynamic. There have been times and places where these movements could scarcely be distinguished, times of intense and bitter tension, and then a relapse into general indifference or highly technical disputation. By the tenth and eleventh centuries of our era, Brahmin religion based on caste, on acknowledgment of a certain authority to Vedic tradition and the development of devotional Vaishnava and Shaivite cults had replaced the Buddhist or Jain dominance in many regions. By the later eleventh century arguments between Buddhists and Hindus had lost much of their bite because of the more direct and obvious threat from the Moslems. It is a curious irony that in this period when we should say that Vedic religion, with its particular Vedic deities, outdoor sacrifices and close correlation between religion and rule, was virtually extinct, having been overwhelmed by Buddhist and Jain monastic orders, by devotional Hinduism of home and temple, and by Vedāntic philosophy, that the *Veda* should be promoted as a test of orthodoxy. Although different kinds of Hindus see entirely different teachings as fundamental, they each tend to assert that the attachment of their ideas to specific Vedic texts is fundamental, and that any movement unwilling to do this is misleading its followers.

[1] Following *The Vishnu Purāṇa* translated by H. H. Wilson.

In this period of the survival of old, but somewhat less bitter, antagonisms, the *Vishnu Purāṇa* identified the Buddha and somewhat more indirectly Mahavira, founder of Jainism, as *avatāras* of Vishnu. They are, however, negative forms, intended as a kind of test of faith which will separate true *Veda*-following devotees from false *Veda*-rejecting philosophers and ascetics. Remembering that this ancient account should not be taken as the primary attitude of contemporary Hindus concerning the heroes of Buddhism and Jainism, the following account will show an interesting Hindu interpretation of these ancient teachers. Even falsehood comes from the truth.

Maitreya noticed that in describing the proper performance of the ancestral rites, Parāshara had mentioned that the rites would be disturbed if they were to be seen by an apostate. He asked just what it is which would give an individual such a classification. Parāshara replied: "The *Rig, Yajur* and *Sama Vedas* constitute the triple covering of the several castes, and the sinner who throws this off is said to be naked or apostate.[2] The three *Vedas* are the raiment of all the orders of men, and when that is discarded they are left bare."

To illustrate his point, Parāshara related the following account.

In one of the many battles between the gods and the demons, the gods had been defeated and in their distress fled to the northern shore of the Ocean of Milk where they engaged in religious penance, prayer and praise to Vishnu. At the conclusion of their devotions Vishnu appeared before them, armed with his conch, discus and mace and riding on Garuḍa (his eagle mount). At his appearance the gods and devas prostrated themselves before him and prayed:

"Have compassion upon us, O Lord, and protect us, who have come to thee for relief from the Dāityas. They have seized the three worlds, and taken the offerings which are our

---

[2] This is probably a pun or at least a double meaning. The Jain monk sometimes practices complete nakedness as a kind of religious discipline, an act of merit. Not all nudity was a sign of heresy, but it is used here with the likely double meaning of having shed the protection of the *Vedas,* and having engaged in a fruitless or unprofitable ascetic practice like that of the Jains.

share, though they have taken care not to transgress the precepts of the *Veda*. Although we, as well as they, are parts of thee, of whom all beings consist, yet we behold the world impressed by the ignorance of unity, with the belief in its separate existence. Engaged in the duties of their respective orders, and following the paths prescribed by holy writ, practicing also religious penance, it is impossible for us to destroy them. Do thou, whose wisdom is immeasurable, instruct us in some device by which we may be able to exterminate these enemies of the gods."

Responding to this petition, Vishnu emitted an illusory form of himself, which he gave to the gods and told them that this deceptive vision of himself would beguile the *asuras* and that being led astray from the *Vedas* by their own willingness to believe in any illusion, they would be easy to subdue.

First the "Great Delusion" (*Mahāmaya*) proceeded to earth and visited a group of *Dāityas* who were engaged in ascetic penance on the banks of the Narmadā River. He came before them in the form of a naked ascetic,[3] a begging monk, with head shaven, carrying a bunch of peacock feathers. He spoke to them gently and offered them a revelation which would be the door to absolute bliss. He taught them that seen in different ways the same thing might be for the sake of virtue or of vice, might be or not be, might contribute to liberation or might not, might be the duty of an ascetic or of a householder. With such specious arguments, maintaining the equal truth of contradictory views, but delivered in gentle and persuasive tones, he managed easily to mislead them, until they had no firm knowledge of what they ought to believe or do.

The Dāityas followed his specious teachings and were led to disobedience of the religion (*dharma*) of the *Vedas*, and in turn became teachers of these heresies and perverted others also. Their apostasy, of course, weakened their real power in relation to the *devas*, but they were then unaware of this.

[3] The general description of the symbols such as nakedness, shaven head, peacock feathers, and the description of the views such as the seven negations indicates that the group now called Jainism is probably intended as the object of ridicule. There may have been a number of rather similar groups suggested by this heresy.

Vishnu's *Māyā* (decptive form), having completed his work with these Dāityas, put on a red (or yellow, that is, Buddhist) robe and visited other *asuras* of the same sort in this form. He said to them:

"If, mighty demons, you cherish a desire either for heaven or for final repose, desist from the iniquitous massacre of animals (for sacrifice) and hear from me what you should do. Know that all that exists is composed of discriminative knowledge. Understand my words, for they have been uttered by the wise. This world subsists without support, and engaged in the pursuit of error, which it mistakes for knowledge, as well as vitiated by passion and the rest, revolves in the straits of existence. Instead of this, 'Know!'"

And they replied, "It is known!" [This must be understood as a caricature of a Buddhist teaching tradition.] Thenceforth these Dāityas were induced by the arch deceiver to deviate from their religious duties (e.g., sacrifices, *Vedic* observances) and become Buddhists. When they had abandoned their own faith, they persuaded others to do the same, and the heresy spread, and many deserted the practices enjoined by the *Vedas* and the laws.

The delusions of the false teacher did not end with the conversion of the Dāityas to the Jain and Buddhist heresies, but with various erroneous tenets he prevailed upon others to apostasize, until many *asuras* were led astray and deserted the doctrins and observances inculcated by the three *Vedas*. Some then spoke evil of the sacred books: some blasphemed the gods: some treated sacrifices and other devotional ceremonies with scorn: and others vilified Brahmins.

"The precepts," they cried, "that lead to the injury of animal life (as in the sacrifices) are highly reprehensible. To say that casting butter into flame is productive of reward is mere childishness. If Indra, after having obtained godhead by multiplied rites, is fed upon the wood used as fuel in holy fire, he is lower than a brute, which feeds at least upon leaves. If an animal slaughtered in religious worship is thereby raised to heaven, would it not be expedient for a man who institutes a sacrifice to kill his own father for a victim? If that which is eaten by one at a Srāddha (that is, consecrated food) gives satisfaction to another, it must be unnecessary for one who resides at a distance to bring food for presentation in person."

"First, then, let it be determined what may be rationally believed by mankind and then," said the deceiver, "you will find that felicity may be expected from my instructions. The words of authority do not, mighty *asuras*, fall from heaven: the text that has reason alone is alone to be acknowledged by me and by you."

By such and similar lessons the Dāityas were perverted, so that not one of them admitted the authority of the *Vedas*.[4]

Having strayed from the path of the *Vedas*, the *asuras* were inwardly weak and the deities took courage, gathered for battle and renewed the ancient hostilities. This time the demons were defeated and slain by the gods who had adhered to the righteous path. Vishnu in his deceptive forms (Buddha and Mahavira) had exposed the inner weakness of the heretics and put them at the mercy of the devas.[5]

[4] The preceeding paragraph would not do very well either as a summary of true Buddhist teaching or as a description of modern Hindu attitudes, since some of these criticisms, particularly those relating to animal sacrifice, have come to be accepted by some orthodox Hindus. It is, however, very instructive both in content and in the sarcastic tone, as an account of the things some Hindus had come to feel their Buddhist critics were saying and doing. It should be remembered that this *Purāṇa* reflects a period well after the time in which these arguments were most vital and intense. Each element in the summary represents a Hindu view of a basic Buddhist teaching.

[5] Thus succinctly does this story account, within Hindu orthodox interpretation, for the struggle of the Hindu-Brahmin with the Buddhist-Jain traditions, and the virtual elimination of Buddhism from India. The *Vishnu Purāṇa* follows this story with several accounts all indicating the necessity for the orthodox to shun heretics, to purify themselves from accidental contact with them, and to observe the *Veda* exactly as enjoined by orthodox Brahmins. In the principal account a pious king was forced to undergo a sequence of rebirths in the states of dog, wolf, vulture, and crow, all miserable scavengers, meat eaters and polluted by death, before being reborn as peacock and then as a distinguished, princely son, all for the act of merely engaging in brief conversation with a heretic, out of politeness to a mutual acquaintance. Dealing with heretics is understood to be potentially cosmically dangerous.

THE RĀMĀYAṆA

THE *Rāmāyaṇa* IS a literature which is a national treasure of India, passionately praised, revered, used to epitomize moral character, personal virtue, and as a standard of aesthetic sensitivity. Its characters and incidents are known throughout Asia. The stories or parts of them are the basis for plays, sculpture, dances, and literary allusions from Cambodia and Indonesia through Thailand and Burma and everywhere in India.

The *Rāmāyaṇa* is a Sanskrit poem of some 24,000 *shlokas*, or rhymed, metrical couplets. It is the work of a poet and not merely a collection of traditional materials. The other major epic poem, the *Mahābhārata*, is more than four times as large and the *Purāṇas* are also massive by comparison, yet the *Rāmāyaṇa* is much longer than any *Upanishad*.

Traditional Hindu views hold that the events of the *Rāmāyaṇa* refer to a very distant past, before the beginning of the Kali Age. Using procedures such as analysis of the type of Sanskrit poetry and interrelation of references, it is usually dated as later than the major *Upanishads* (that is, after 800 B.C.E. at the earliest). It is perhaps slightly older than the central core of the *Mahābhārata*. We know that it was complete by the second century of our era. Although the date cannot be fixed with certainty, many scholars have suggested that the *Rāmāyaṇa* may have been developed about 500 B.C.E., while Buddhism and Jainism were just developing in the same geographical regions of north central and northeastern India (modern Uttar and Pradesh Bihar). It should be said that Book I, which identifies Rāma and his brothers as an *avatāra* of Vishnu, and Book VII, in which Sītā returns to Mother Earth, are generally thought to be later than the main body of the text. This emphasis upon the human appearance of Vishnu, overlaid on a familiar epic account, would correlate with the Hindu rennaisance in this area so heavily influenced by Buddhism. Rāma and the Buddha were interpreted as fellow manifestations of Vishnu from different eras and for different needs.

The story the *Rāmāyaṇa* tells may be interpreted in various ways. Perhaps it represents a popularization and development of an old Vedic myth concerning Indra and Sītā, a goddess of the Ploughed Furrow, and of Indra's conflict with Vitra, in which Hanuman represents the son of the Wind God (Maruti) of the earlier legend. There may also be allusions to the intrigues of an ancient Kosala queen to have her son enthroned, but it is hardly possible that the story as it stands represents an actual historical conflict. In any case, the artist has woven his materials together into a coherent story, neither history nor purely legend, which is a poetic enactment of the fundamental values and attitudes of ancient Indian culture. The portrayal is based not on an intimate knowledge of the peoples or geography of South India or Ceylon, but on the most intimate sensitivity to what India admired in a man, a king, a wife, a brother, a friend, a warrior, and to the emotional response to the human drama and to the loveliness available in many of the places of India and many of its alternative ways of life.

To abbreviate the account for our purposes we have provided a prose paraphrase of a part of the main story line, interspersed with selections from Romesh Dutt's poetic translation, to give some feel for the poetic quality of the work. All the poetic sections are his translations. Such commentary as may be needed has generally been worked into the text.

There is an interesting legend concerning the origin of the poem in the mind of Vālmikī. The Sage-Deity Nārada had appeared in the *āshrama* of Vālmikī and told briefly the story of Rāma in response to a question about virtue and wisdom. Some while later Vālmikī was walking along a river bank and observed two birds singing for the joy of life and love. Suddenly the male bird was shot down by a hunter's arrow and the female cried piteously. Vālmiki was enraged and burst into a curse,

O hunter, as you have killed one of these love-intoxicated birds,
You will wander homeless all your long years.

Almost at once the sage recovered himself and wondered why he had been so overcome by anger. "What right had I to curse the hunter? Why was I deceived by my feelings?"

Thinking of the words of his curse, the Rishi noticed the rhythm and style of the phrases. He discovered his pity had taken shape in a beautiful *shloka*. He thought that this must be part of the mysterious *līlā* (play, creativity) of God, and began meditation. In his meditation, Brahmā appeared to him and said: "Be not afraid. These things have happened to impell you to tell the story of Rāma. From sorrow (*soka*) sprang verse (*shloka*), and in this meter and rhythm the story should be told. And you shall sing it, with my blessings, for the benefit of the world. As long as mountains stand and rivers flow, so long shall the *Rāmāyaṇa* be cherished among men and save them from sin."

BOOK I

AYODHYĀ

North of the Ganges, in the fertile plain of the river Sarayu, lay the city of Ayodhyā ("Unconquerable") capital of the great kingdom of Kosala. King of the city was Dasaratha, and his fame was spread through the three worlds. His city was magnificent and well-protected, and his people happy, contented and virtuous. It was a prosperous and noble kingdom. Dasaratha's only disappointment was that he had no son. He determined to have the proper ceremony (*yajña*) performed as enjoined in the Brahmanic *shāstras*, in order to secure a son.

At this time also, the hard pressed *devas* met in heaven and appealed to Brahmā for relief from the depredations of the wicked Rakshasa, Rāvaṇa, who had been protected by Brahmā's boon from every kind of enemy except man. The heavenly forces appealed to Vishnu, and he agreed to be born as four sons of King Dasaratha in order to defeat Rāvaṇa. Appearing at the ceremony of King Dasaratha's sacrifice, the divinities gave him a bowl of divine beverage for his wives. He gave this to the three wives with instructions that Kausalya, the chief Queen, was to drink half, then Queen Sumitra half of what remained, than Kaikeyi, the young, beautiful wife, half of what yet remained, and finally Sumitra was again to have the final sip. The queens followed these instructions and in due course four sons were born.

Queen Kausalya, blessed with virtue, true and righteous Rama bore,
Queen Kaikeyi, young and beauteous, bore him Bharat, rich in lore,
Queen Sumitra bore the bright twins, Lakshman and Satrughna bold,
Four brave princes served their father in the happy days of old!

When they were young men, the fabled sage Viśwāmitra appeared in their father's court and requested that Rāma and Lakshmana accompany him to his remote hermitage in order to kill two demons who were disrupting a lengthy sacrifice he was attempting to perform. On this hazardous journey Viśwāmitra taught Rāma and Lakshmana the use of the supernatural, magical weapons and curses needed to defeat the devious power of the demonic forces they had been born to destroy. They demonstrated their attentiveness and courage in clearing Viśwāmitra's sacrifice of the interfering demons.

MITHILA

On the return Viśwāmitra took the young warriors to Mithila, capital of Videha, where a contest was to be held for the hand of King Janak's daughter, the beautiful princess Sītā. The trial was to shoot Shiva's bow which belonged to the palace museum. With grace and modesty Rāma asked to try the great bow, which had never been strung by man. He snapped the heavy string in place, drew the cord and broke the bow in two! The company rejoiced at the feat and the prospect of the marriage of the two great houses.

SĪTĀ AND THE WEDDING

Sītā was the adopted daughter of King Janak. Having no heir, Janak had prepared a sacrifice for the birth of a child, but as he personally ploughed the earth in preparation of the sacrificial ground, he found there in the ploughed earth a lovely baby girl. Accepting this child as the gift of the gods in answer to his wish, he took the baby home and reared her as his daughter. As she grew she became an extraordinarily beautiful young woman, cultivated in every grace and lovely beyond comparison. Janak was delighted that he would be able to offer her in marriage to the eldest son of his old friend, King Dasaratha, and in the auspicious signs connected with the marriage. Many Kosala men arranged to marry Videha daughters that day.

Dasaratha and his party undertook the four-day journey from Ayodhyā to Videha, and were received there with courteous and generous welcome by their hosts. After the exchange of gifts, appropriate preparations were made for the wedding, including the proper sacrifices, the *Kāutuka* rite of investiture with the nuptial cord, the preparation of the site, presentation of the flames and the recitation of the sacred *mantra* (hymns). The ritual and vows of the wedding of Rāma and Sītā are still repeated in many Hindu weddings. The ceremony was under the general direction of the sage Vaisishṭha, from Dasaratha's court.

Sage Vaisishtha skilled in duty placed Videha's honoured king,
Viswamitra, Satananda, all within the sacred ring,
And he raised the holy altar as the ancient writs ordain,
Decked and graced with scented garlands, grateful unto gods and
        men.

And he set the golden ladles, vases pierced by artists skilled,
Sanka bowls and shining salvers, *arghya* (offering) plates for
        honored guest,
Parched rice arranged in dishes, corn unhusked that filled the rest,
And with careful hand Vaisishtha grass around the altar flung,
Offered gift to lighted AGNI and the sacred *mantra* sung!

Softly came the sweet-eyed Sita—bridal blush upon her brow—
Rama in his manly beauty came to take the sacred vow,
Janak placed his beauteous daughter facing Dasaratha's son,
Spoke with father's fond emotion and the holy rite was done:

"This is Sita, child of Janak, dearer unto him than life,
Henceforth sharer of thy virtue, be she, Prince, thy faithful wife,
Of thy weal and woe partaker, be she thine in every land,
Cherish her in joy and sorrow, clasp her hand within thy hand,
As the shadow to the substance, to her lord is faithful wife,
And my Sita, best of women, follows thee in death or life!"

Tears bedew his ancient bosom, gods and men his wishes share,
And he sprinkles holy water on the blest and wedded pair.
Next he turned to Sita's sister, Urmila of beauty rare,
And to Lakshman, young and valiant, spoke in accents soft and fair:

"Lakshman, dauntless in thy duty, loved of men and Gods above,
Take my dear, devoted daughter, Urmila of stainless love,
Lakshman, fearless in thy virtue, take thy true and faithful wife,
Clasp her hand within thy fingers, be she thine in death or life!"

To his brother's child, Mandavi, Janak turned with father's love,
Yielded her to righteous Bharat, prayed for blessing from above:
"Bharat, take the fair Mandavi, be she thine in death or life,
Clasp her hand within thy fingers as thy true and faithful wife!"

Last of all was Srutakriti, fair in form and fair in face,
And her gentle name was honored for her acts of righteous grace,
"Take her by the hand, Satrughna, be she thine in death or life,
As the shadow to the substance, to her lord is faithful wife!"

Then the princes held the maidens, hand embraced in loving hand,
And Vaisishtha spoke the *mantra*, holiest priest in all the land,
And as ancient rite ordaineth, and as sacred laws require,
Stepped each bride and princely bridegroom round the altar's
          lighted fire,
Round Videha's ancient monarch, round the holy rishis all,
Lightly stepped the gentle maidens, proudly stepped the princes
          tall.
And a rain of flowers descended from the sky serene and fair,
And a soft celestial music filled the fresh and fragrant air,
Bright *Gandharvas*, skilled in music, waked the sweet celestial song,
Fair *Apsaras* in their beauty on the greensward tripped along!
As the flowery rain descended and the music rose in pride.

Thrice around the lighted altar every bridegroom led his bride,
And the nuptial rites were ended, princes took their brides away,
Janak followed with his courtiers, and the town was proud and gay!

Soon the party returned to joyous welcome in Ayodhyā,
where the Queens graciously and happily greeted their new
daughters and made them welcome in their new estate.

Shortly after their return Bharat and Satrughna responded
to the invitation of Queen Kaikeyi's brother and went back
with him to visit and stay with their grandfather. Rāma and
Lakshmana remained in Ayodhyā to perform their duties as
the sons of King Dasaratha.

BOOK II

CORONATION

Dasaratha called a consultation of all nearby chiefs and even
distant monarchs as well, entertaining all of them graciously in
Ayodhyā, and then gathering them in the Council Hall. He
spoke to them of his intention to make Rāma Regent in his
place and to retire in the traditional way to the forest to prepare himself for the more distant future. The audience over-
whelmingly agreed, but he demanded of them reasons for their
agreement. One after another they eloquently praised the preparation and fitness of Rāma for the rule. Since they had already entered an auspicious month, Dasaratha gave orders
that the city should be prepared for the coronation festival
later in the month and called Rāma to tell him of his plans.
Rāma showed no eagerness to rule, but if it were his father's
wish, he would do all in his power to fulfill it. Hardly had he
managed to get back to his apartment when a special messenger from his father caught up with him and informed him
that his father wished to see him again. Rāma returned at
once and found King Dasaratha disturbed by perplexing
dreams and inauspicious signs, and anxious to perform the
ceremony in haste lest there be some slip between him and his
hopes. "The stars indicate an auspicious day tomorrow," the
King said, "I want you and Sītā to prepare yourselves for the

coronation by fasting and the appropriate rituals tonight, so that we may hold that event tomorrow." The news spread like fire and the city was in a joyous commotion of expectancy and preparations for the great festival to follow so soon.

In their own apartment Rāma and Sītā quietly performed their abultions, prayed to Vishnu, and placed offerings before the image. They spread the proper altar grass, and kept a fast and vigil. With the dawn the town burst forth in gaiety and joy and hope in the coronation of Dasaratha's noble son.

FEAR AND INTRIGUE

In the apartments of the queens, the woman companion and confidential servant of young Queen Kaikeyi, a hunchback named Manthara, had watched the preparations of the city in the evening without understanding what they were about. Approaching her mistress, she had asked what festival was to be observed. Hearing that it was to be the coronation of Rāma she was in great distress and warned her mistress, "A flood of misfortune is rising to drown and swallow you:" Manthara believed the whole event to be a plot: sending away of Bharat to a distant land, and the hasty plans for the coronation of Rāma, designed, she believed, in some way to dispose of Queen Kaikeyi and of her rightful claims and those of her son. The Queen, who was delighted at the thought of the coronation of Rāma, dismissed her words and sought to calm her. "Manthara, you have brought me good news," she said. "Is my son Rāma to be crowned tomorrow? What great joy can come to me? Here, take this. Ask me for anything else." Saying this Kaikeyi took off her necklace and gave it to Manthara after the custom of giving a present to the bearer of any important, good news.

Manthara threw the jewels aside and poured anguish and abuse upon the queen. She interpreted Rāma as devious and jealous of Bharat's rival claim upon the throne. All her own malice and mistrust she read into Rāma and his mother, and she predicted that slavery for Queen Kaikeyi, banishment or death for Bharat would be the sure result of Rāma's coronation.

Like a slow but deadly poison worked the ancient nurse's tears,
And a wife's undying impulse mingled with a mother's fears,
Deep within Kaikeyi's bosom worked a woman's jealous thought,
Speechless in her scorn and anger, mourner's dark retreat she
    sought.

That evening Dasaratha came back, pleased with the prospect of the morn, and with the beauty and gaiety of the palace. To share his joy he sought Kaikeyi in her chambers, bedroom and garden, all to no avail. Inquiring of her warder, he discovered to his surprise and dismay that she had fled to the mourner's chamber where upset Queens could cry and sulk. He followed and found her there, disheveled and weeping, upon the cold stone floor. Using the flow of soothing words with which an experienced King would appease a sullen, sulking Queen, he offered reassurance, promises and gentle flattery. But all in vain. She began to remind him of a half-forgotten day when he had been at war and gravely wounded. Finding him near death, Kaikeyi had nursed him with the tenderest care and preserved his life. For his life he had offered her two boons, but Kaikeyi had not then claimed them. Now she would request the two promises for which he owed his life. He would fulfill them or she would die the victim of his broken word.

By these rites ordained for Rama—such the news my menials bring—
Let my Bharat, and not Rama, be anointed Regent King,
Wearing skins and matted tresses, in the cave or hermit's cell,
Fourteen years in Dandak's forests let the elder Rama dwell!
These are Queen Kaikeyi's wishes, these the boons for which I pray,
I would see my son anointed, Rama banished on this day!

THE KING'S LAMENT

The King was overcome with profound dismay to hear the words. He fainted and revived, babbled, pleaded, weakened, cried, but the jealous Queen demanded his obedience to her perverted wish, because of his ancient promise to her, and he was caught between duty and desire, between promise and hope. He spent the night in agony, with fainting spells, nightmares, and feverish hopelessness.

ANNOUNCEMENT TO RĀMA

In the morning the messenger came before the King's chamber singing the glad hymn of the day and announcing that the coronation party was arriving. Dasaratha was unable to speak in his anguish, so Kaikeyi called out asking that Rāma come to his father in the chamber. This strange request disturbed those around with vague foreboding, but it was carried out at once, and soon Rāma stepped into the sulking room. Rāma was instantly shaken with fear and dismay. His father lay upon the floor, obviously in the grip of some great agony, unable to speak, save once only the name of Rāma. Acknowledging his father and Queen Kaikeyi with the obeisance of a son, he turned to her to discover the cause of his father's deep distress. She disregarded his apprehension and required that he first commit himself to follow exactly Dasaratha's mandate. She explained the circumstances of the King's promise to her, and demanded that he would indeed fulfill the father's promise. With this she threw the two demands: "Bharat shall be heir and Regent; Rāma shall be banished far!" With no sign of disappointment or dismay Rāma agreed at once.

BOOK III

SITA'S LOVE

Rāma immediately set about the preparations for his departure, dissuaded his own mother from following him and deserting the feeble King, and Lakshmaṇa from overthrowing the King at once and taking the throne for Rāma by force. He then returned to Sītā. She saw him coming, not in pomp and glory as she expected, but alone and strangely perplexed. Rāma told her the story briefly, of the vow and of his banishment, and instructed her in ways she might endure the separation. But Sītā, in love that took the form of anger, responded with what has become a classic Hindu love song, portraying the inward identity of wife and husband. Sītā:

For the faithful woman follows where her wedded lord may lead,
In the banishment of Rama, Sita's exile is decreed,
Sire nor son nor loving brother rules the wedded woman's state,
With her lord she falls or rises, with her consort courts her fate.
If the righteous son of Raghu wends to forests dark and drear,
Sita steps before her husband, wild and thorny paths to clear.
Like the tasted refuse water cast thy timid thoughts aside,
Take me to the pathless jungle, bid me by my lord abide.
Car and steed and gilded palace, vain are these to woman's life,
Dearer is her husband's shadow to the loved and loving wife!
For my mother often taught me and my father often spake,
That her home the wedded woman doth beside her husband make,
As the shadow to the substance, to her lord is faithful wife,
And she parts not from her consort till she parts with fleeting life!

Therefore, bid me seek the jungle and in pathless forests roam,
Where the wild deer freely ranges and the tiger makes his home.
Happier than in father's mansions in the woods will Sita rove,
Waste no thought on home or kindred, nestling in her husband's
    love!
World-renowned is Rama's valour, fearless by her Rama's side,
Sita will still live and wander with a faithful woman's pride,
And the wild fruit she will gather from the fresh and fragrant wood,
And the food by Rama tasted shall be Sita's cherished food.
Bid me seek thy sylvan greenwoods, wooded hills and plateaus high,
Limpid rills and crystal rivulets as they softly ripple by,
And where in the lake of lotus tuneful ducks their plumage lave,
Let me with my loving Rama skim the cool translucent wave!

Years will pass in happy union—happiest lot to woman given—
Sita seeks not throne or empire, nor the brighter joys of heaven,
Heaven conceals not brighter mansions in the sunny fields of pride,
Where without her lord and husband faithful Sita would reside!
Therefore let me seek the jungle where the jungle-rangers rove,
Dearer than the royal palace, where I share my husband's love,
And my heart in sweet communion shall my Rama's wishes share,
And my wifely toil shall lighten Rama's load of woe and care!

THE DEPARTURE

Lakshmaṇa joined Rāma and Sītā for the exile and at once
they prepared to leave for the forest. The sadness of the mothers, the babbling old King wavering on the brink of sanity, the

mingled resolve and anticipated tinges of loneliness, the dismay of citizens and friends strain the poet's power to express.

All the sites mentioned in a poem some 2,500 years old have become holy places, where still today barefoot pilgrims follow the well-worn path of Rāma and Sītā, following where the poet says they went, seeing what the poet says they saw—though the great forest which then lined the bank of the river is now gone.

THE FOREST HERMITAGE

The forests of India of that time were beautiful, terrifying places. Inhabited by tigers and other wild animals, the wild jungles were also interspersed with sylvan glens and forest hermitages (*āshrams*) of ancient sages, who there meditated and conversed with disciples and friends. Such hermits live the simplest possible life; rough, plain clothes, natural, vegetarian foods and quiet contemplation. The hospitality of the *āshrams* is extended to all who come that way. All along the way the three exiles were often guests in such hermitages.

After a time Lakshmaṇa built them a forest cottage and they had their own *āshram* beside the river Mālyavatī on the slope of Chitrakuta Hill. There they played in the sun and river, and sang songs of joy in the peace and beauty of the place.

BOOK IV

DEATH OF THE KING

Meanwhile, at Ayodhyā, the aged, senile King remembered a careless deed of his youth to which he attributed his present misfortune. Finding there the cause of his distress, he saw his death as its fulfillment. That night King Dasaratha died. Bharat returned to discover what had happened, disowned his mother's jealous act, performed the necessary ceremonies for the dead king, and tried to restore Rāma to the throne. However Rāma insisted on fulfilling the father's vow, by remaining in the forest for the fourteen years. Bharat then took Rāma's sandals, placed them on the throne, and ruled as regent in Rāma's absence, but lived as a hermit in the palace.

BOOK V

ON THE BANKS OF THE GODAVARI

For a time Rāma, Sītā and Lakshmaṅa lived in a hermitage they built near that of the fabled sage Agastya, at the source of the Godāvari River. There they spent a winter, in which nostalgic memory often wavered back and forth between the crisp loveliness of the place and thoughts of Ayodhyā.

BOOK VI

SĪTĀ LOST

Wandering about Dandaka forest the three were entertained as guests in the āshrams of the forest hermits. They were received most graciously by the ascetic sages, the greatest of whom, of course, knew by supernatural insight of their divine origin and mission. Rāma, Sītā and Lakshmaṅa learned that the forest was also inhabited by many Rakshas, vicious, superhuman creatures, able to change their forms at will, and many of which enjoyed sages as their favorite diet. These creatures had created a terror for the defenseless ascetics, and continually interrupted and polluted their austerities and ceremonies. Rāma and Lakshmaṇa responded to their appeal and promised to defend them from their enemies and to subdue the malicious Rakshas.

The calm, peaceful life of the rishis was gradually restored as their more malignant enemies were driven off or killed by the two protectors. So passed more than ten years of the exile in the forest of Dandaka.

THE VISIT OF ŚŪRPAṆAKHĀ

Lounging at their Pañchavati retreat, Rāma, Sītā and Lakshmaṇa enjoyed the beauty of the woods, the cool fresh water, the visits of passing hermits and their increasingly fond memories of home in Ayodhyā. While in the midst of such a pleasant recollection the three were visited by a Rakshasa female, Śūrpaṇakhā, who having seen Rāma from a distance had instantly fallen in love with him. She appeared before them and crudely demanded to know who they were. Rāma answered candidly and similarly asked who she was. They learned that she was sister of the Raksha King, Rāvaṇa. In her inimitable crudity and coarseness she immediately proposed that Rāma leave with her and she would eat the "pale, misshapen Sītā." Rāma treated her as a joke and proposed that she should be interested in Lakshmaṇa instead. Lakshmaṇa entered the banter with Rāma.

Śūrpaṇakhā became furious and stunned Sītā with a glance. Rāma realized that they had erred in trying to joke with her. Lakshmaṇa in instant wrath cut off her nose and both her ears and sent her screaming through the wood.

Soon Śūrpaṇakhā brought support of the armies of her brothers and of friends, but Rāma and Lakshmaṇa with powerful weapons defeated all of them.

REPORT TO RĀVAṆA

Śūrpaṇakhā and Akampaṇa, one of the few Rakshas to have survived the great slaughter at Pañchavati, fled to Laṅkā (Ceylon) to report to Rāvaṇa, the Rakshas' King. Knowing that it is dangerous to carry unpleasant news to tyrants, Akampaṇa demanded his protection before making his report. When Rāvaṇa learned what had happened, he exploded in rage and demanded to know which of the gods had done this to his forces and brothers. When he heard that it was Rāma alone who had done this, he was perplexed and determined to seek revenge at once. Akampaṇa, however, advised that he could not kill Rāma directly and suggested that if he would abduct the beautiful Sītā, the separation would kill Rāma more effectively than weapons. Hearing of Sītā's beauty, Rāvaṇa thought that in addition to the destruction of his enemy, he would be able to have another beautiful queen, and accepted the advice. At once he visited Marīcha and they made up a plot to abduct

Sītā. Marīcha took the form of a beautiful golden deer, and he
and Rāvaṇa travelled to the forest near the hermitage.
In the form of the lustrous, golden deer, Marīcha aroused
the interest and desire of Sītā. Warned by Rāma and Lakshmaṇa that it was probably some kind of trick, Sītā became
more determined than ever to have the deer as a pet or rug.
She demanded that Rāma should catch or shoot it for her. In
this way he was led off into the woods to try to capture it, but
could not. Finally, he was compelled to shoot the illusive deer,
but as it fell under his arrow, the Raksha imitated Rāma's
voice in a great cry of anguish. Hearing this cry from a distance, Sītā was terrified and asked Lakshmaṇa to desert her
and help Rāma. When he refused, she accused him of wanting
her himself. He was dismayed by her angry accusation and
went to find Rāma.

THE ABDUCTION

At once Rāvaṇa, who had been watching Sītā from hiding,
approached her in the form of a Brahmin, and engaged in flattering conversation. Overcome by lust and hope he soon revealed his true form, and when Sītā refused his proposal to be
his queen, he grabbed her and threw her in his flying chariot.
As they flew over the forests Sītā tried to drop fragments of
her jewels and clothes as traces of their path, and old Jatayu,
aged King of Eagles, attacked the chariot valiantly to defend
her, but though he fought with vigor, Rāvaṇa finally slashed
off his wings and the pathetic old bird was mortally wounded.

BOOK VII

KISHKINDA

Rāma rejoined Lakshmaṇa, but their frantic search for Sītā
was fruitless. Rāma was consumed by despair and frantic concern. He was convinced that Sītā had been killed and eaten by
some Raksha, and he was unconsolable. Gradually, however,
he and Lakshmaṇa began to find evidence of the flight, flowers
from Sītā's hair, broken bits of her jewels, wreckage from the
chariot caused by the fight with old Jatayu, and finally the

feeble old bird himself, who could only report that Rāvaṇa had flown southward with her. The valiant bird then died, and was buried as a father by the two warriors. In his dying, Jatayu had assured Rāma that he would still find Sītā and return her to his palace. Sustained by this hope, Rāma and Lakshmaṇa continued southward seeking aid in their quest for Sītā.

SUGRĪVA AND HANUMAN

(Note: In the imagery of this poem various peoples are called or described as monkeys, bears, elephants, birds, etc. Different interpretations are offered for this, ranging from those who understand this to be early Indian anthropology concerning distant and unknown tribes, to those who see it as a kind of political cartoon, as we might refer in short to the "Russian Bear," "British Bull," "Chinese Dragon," or "American Eagle." In any case, Surgrīva, King of the Vanar people, and his even more famous general, Hanuman, are always described as monkeys and pictured in religious art as monkey-men, though this does not detract from their heroic—even divine—stature.)

Moving steadily southward Rāma and Lakshmaṇa encountered Sugrīva and his General, Hanuman, leaders of the Vanar (Monkey) people, but living in a forest cave. In their conversation they found the common bond of mutual misery. Sugrīva had been robbed of wife and kingdom by his tyrant brother, Bali. Rama and Lakshmaṇa agreed to help recover his kingdom, if they could then count on help to rescue Sītā. They returned to Kishkinda and Rāma did help Sugrīva defeat Bali, even though it took his shot almost from ambush to do so.

Monsoons were just setting in. Rāma went impatiently to the Nilgiri hills to pass the time in fulfillment of the original vow, while Sugrīva revelled in the pleasures of wine and women in his recovered palace.

THE QUEST RESUMED

As the rains let up, and Rāma's impatience increased, Hanuman acted on behalf of the indulgent king and sent word for the chiefs to assemble with their forces at the first good weather. Sending Lakshmaṇa to press the demand, Rāma insisted that they seek for Sītā at once. With some difficulty Sugrīva was sobered up, the armies assembled and divided into four groups, each instructed to search and report back in one month.

The party moving south, led by Hanuman, were badly delayed and had not completed their mission in the month. Convinced that they would be killed if they did return late with no report, they prepared to die right there. While waiting they entered into conversation with the vultures who were waiting for their deaths. From the vultures they learned that Sītā was a prisoner in Laṅkā.

With this knowledge it was essential for one of them to visit Sītā in Laṅkā, to deliver Rāma's ring and to learn from her the circumstances of her captivity. Assuming a gigantic size, Hanuman placed his foot firmly upon the earth and leaped across the ninety-mile strait. As he flew over the water he was tested by a mountain which rose up from the ocean and offered him rest, by a demon which sought to swallow and destroy him, and by a trickster which slowed him down by dragging on his shadow. Hanuman was not distracted and passed all these texts with flying colors. He landed in Laṅkā and assumed the shape and size of a normal monkey.

HANUMAN IN LAṄKĀ

Hanuman scouted about the city. He was amazed at its size and beauty. Finally he came upon the most magnificent buildings of all, Rāvaṇa's palace, and in the inner chambers a scene of seductively sleeping maidens in dishabille. Reluctantly he called his mind back to the task at hand, but nowhere could he find Sītā. In despair, he returned to all the places he had searched previously, but to no avail. At the depths of his despair he discovered a small park with high walls near the palace and entered it—hopeful that he would soon find Sītā herself.

The garden Hanuman entered was exquisitely lovely on this

early spring night. Hiding in the trees above, he surveyed the garden, until he spied a frail and lovely figure, glowing like a streak of moon, but bathed in tears of despair. While Hanuman studied how he might best approach the wan and wary Sītā, Rāvaṇa himself came into the garden. Hiding in the tree above, Hanuman heard Rāvaṇa's final appeal and command. Though Rāvaṇa could have possessed Sītā by force alone, he had determined that she should consent to marry him. He offered her every gift and pleasure, a world to rule for her father, a household of lesser wives for herself to govern. He appealed for her love and pity in strange condescension for so magnificent and powerful a king. Sītā rejected him derisively, instructed him concerning happiness and warned him of the inevitable approach of his doom at Rāma's hand.

Rāvaṇa replied in anger that only two months of choice remained to her—or she would become a meal cooked in his kitchen. Sītā wavered between brave confidence and the utter gloom of secret fear. She struggled between hope and dark despair, flashing up in hope and the certainty of Rāma's return, lost in fear that he had turned to a life of penance, or that he had forgotten her. She contemplated suicide.

Hanuman, watching from above, was beset by a new problem. He had found all that he needed for the report of a spy, but somehow he needed also to strengthen Sītā's courage and confidence. He had to speak to Sītā, but of course she would be suspicious, and it would have to be done without waking her guards. Quietly singing a song of praise for Rāma so as to allay her fears or suspicions, he began to descend from the trees. Soon she heard the gentle song and responded to the hope that this was a messenger of Rāma. Then her mind retreated in the fear that it was Rāvaṇa with one of his tricks. Finally Hanuman was able to identify himself and to deliver his message and Rāma's ring. He told her to expect the swift return of Rāma, Lakshmaṇa, Sugrīva and the whole Vanara army. She was of course ecstatic with new hope.

Giving Hanuman delicate and personal memories of her days with Rāma and one of her wedding jewels as token, she finally reluctantly said goodby, and he reassured her of their swift return. Since he could not both carry her over the strait and fight off the pursuit of her captors, she would have to await the sure return of Rāma with the army.

TAKING LEAVE OF LAÑKĀ

As he prepared to leave Laṅkā, Hanuman thought that he should leave some memento of his visit which might give confidence to Sītā and fear to Rāvaṇa and his cohorts. He swelled to immense size and began to tear up trees and devastate the park. The sleepy Rakshas reacted slowly. Tearing off the iron gate, he used it as a weapon on the guards who sought to stop him. Hearing of the commotion in the garden and that the guards had been slain, Rāvaṇa sent greater warriors to kill Hanuman. Hanuman swelled to even larger size, tore apart the temple and used its pillars to smash the sentries and the warriors. Being wounded only increased his power and fierceness. Hanuman, with supreme ferocity, scattered and killed those sent to capture him. For the first time in his career the chill fear of the possibility of defeat struck Rāvaṇa. Even one of his sons was killed in the effort to take Hanuman. Finally Rāvaṇa sent his other son, Indrajit, the conqueror of Indra, master of all the supernatural weapons through his austerities. The battle raged furiously as the two were about equal in power. Eventually Indrajit released the Brahmastra which he had obtained as a boon from Brahmā. But Hanuman too had secured a boon from Brahmā—that the bonds of the Brahmastra could hold him only for one muhurta (48 minutes). He lay down—bound by the Brahmastra and apparently helpless. The aids of Indrajit, not knowing the secrets of the supernatural weapons, bound him also with ropes and dragged him before Rāvaṇa.

In a way Hanuman admired the resplendent and powerful Rāvaṇa, who might have been incomparably great if he had not taken his fabulous powers and swerved from the path of dharma. As he was questioned, Hanuman responded as the messenger of King Surgrīva and of Rāma, and in the name of these Kings requested the return of Sītā and to dharma. Since custom forbade killing a messenger, his captors proposed torture. The soldiers wrapped his tail in oil-soaked rags and set fire to it and began to drag him through the streets. Relying on Sītā's prayers to Agni, the god of fire, the flames were cool to him. In an instant he slipped his bonds, assumed his gigantic size, and leaped from building to building using his tail as a torch; he soon had the whole city afire. He had a moment of panic when he thought that his intemperate rage had endangered Sītā as well as Rāvaṇa's city, but he found that the gods had protected her garden and it was cool, fragrant and pleasant there. He returned for her permission to leave Laṅkā and then flew straight back with a great roar of victory. He landed near the Vanara army assembled on the beach.

REPORT TO RĀMA

(This is a deeply devotional literature in which there are frequent repetitions and summaries of events already described. When Hanuman returned to the army he repeated to them the entire account of his experiences in Laṅkā, and then again when they returned to Kishkinda and reported to Rāma, Lakshmaṇa and Sugrīva, he went through the whole account twice more in order to respond to Rāma's insatiable desire to hear about Sītā. In devotional usages these variations make possible reflection of the most detailed sort on feelings, hopes, and events from several different perspectives. None of these recapitulations have been provided here.)

In Kishkinda Rāma and Lakshmaṇa waited with Sugrīva in despair and dejection. No hopeful report had been received and the southern army had even failed to report its failure! The only hope was the pathetic sort which comes from not yet knowing the worst. Suddenly there were reports that the southern army had returned and were plundering a pleasure garden near the capital. Knowing this to be a sign of a victorious report, the king sent at once for Hanuman. There he modestly reported all that he had learned—of Sītā's dejection and ecstatic hope, of Rāvaṇa's purposes and military capacities, of the notice he had given of their coming, of his having given Rāvaṇa the required opportunity to deal with them according to dharma. Rāma fainted for joy at the good news of Sītā, but soon they were all at work in a council of war. The star of triumph began to shine the next night and under its good influence they began the march at noon.

The army travelled rapidly and with growing fury. While they moved southward the leaders planned how they might assault the well-defended city.

BOOK IX

RĀVAŅA'S COUNCIL

In Laṅkā Rāvaṇa had been thoroughly disturbed by Hanuman's exploits. His powerful and well-defended city had been penetrated and great sections of it destroyed by this single enemy. Many of his leading warriors had been killed. He did not dare to underestimate his enemy. To fulfill the ancient way he called a council and demanded straightforward speech of his advisors. Several of them boasted vainly and asked for permission to go ahead and destroy Rāma and his forces singlehandedly or with a small expedition before they tried to cross the sea. Bibhishan, Rāvaṇa's youngest brother, alone stood up and pointed out that the cause of the difficulty was the improper abduction of Rāma's wife, and proposed that she should be restored to Rāma. Rāvaṇa, in a rage, dismissed Bibhishan as a coward and rejected his advice.

Bibhishan left in dignity and appealed to Rāma for sanctuary. Though others were suspicious and vengeful, Rāma received him graciously and promised to make him king of Laṅkā when they had taken it with his help.

(Those who read this account as the incarnation of Vishnu find this passage pregnant with meaning concerning the grace of god toward any person who will surrender himself to god, regardless of his state of merit or sin. Even the enemies of god will be accepted. A similar teaching is found also in the *Bhagavadgītā*.)

BOOK X

THE WAR IN LAŅKĀ

The first great problem faced by Rāma and Sugrīva was to transport the Vanara army of monkeys and bears across the sea to Laṅkā. With the help of the god of the sea, the ocean floor rose up at points, and the Vanara army threw rocks on the high spots creating a series of piers for a great bridge from the mainland to Laṅkā. Running and leaping from section to section, they quickly passed over to the island. There Rāma and Sugrīva divided their troops for several attacks and kept a large force in reserve. Rāvaṇa also prepared carefully for the battle and held much of his force in reserve.

Vālmīki tells the story of the battles in terms of a series of single combats between great warriors, all arranged in specific ranks. Best warriors of all and nearly evenly matched were Rāma and Rāvaṇa. At the next rank were Lakshmaṇa and Kumbhakarṇa, the brothers of the two great warriors. Then Hanuman and Indrajit, Rāvaṇa's son, though Indrajit is especially dangerous because of his possession of magical, supernatural weapons. Beyond these great warriors were other well-matched foes—and the two massive armies. The Vanaras fought with great trees and stones as their principal weapons—perhaps consistent with their description as bears and monkeys. The Rakshas and men fought with armor, swords and arrows. The warriors on both sides were brave, fearless and skilled, and though great numbers of them died, they earned respect of their foes and of the reader.

THE FIRST BATTLES

The first day's battle was so fierce that contrary to custom it did not end at nightfall, but continued unabated into the night. Finally Indrajit, using his magical power to keep himself invisible, attacked Rāma and Lakshmaṇa with supernatural poisoned snake arrows which rendered the heroes unconscious and bound, but not actually dead. Soon Garuḍa, the great eagle of Vishnu, and enemy of all snakes, flew over the stunned warriors. His shadow so terrified the snakes that they fled to their holes and the men gradually recovered.

Later Rāvaṇa and Rāma began to fight directly together. Although the fight was very even, gradually Rāma succeeded

in shooting away all of Rāvaṇa's weapons, but instead of killing him there, sent him back in humiliation to fight another
day.

KUMBHAKARṆA

Kumbhakarṇa, the immense brother of Rāvaṇa, used to
sleep for months at a time. It happened that he had just fallen
asleep following the council, a few days before the battle had
begun. Although he knew both the difficulties and the dangers
of awakening Kumbhakarṇa before he had had his rest, Rāvaṇa decided that he needed the help of the gigantic warrior.
The ministers sent to awaken Kumbhakarṇa first piled the
room high with his favorite foods—for he always awakened
with a ravenous appetite and would eat the messengers if his
appetite were not appeased by some tastier morsel. Then they
set about waking him. It was a considerable task. They brought
in conch-shell horns and drums, trumpets and bugles and
shouting troops. They marched elephants across his mighty
chest. Finally he began to stir, sleepily stretched, and seeing
only the food began to devour it. After the worst of his hunger
had been mitigated, the ministers sought to explain why he
had been awakened so soon. With a roar he rose up and joined
Rāvaṇa, where he was received gratefully and sent forth to
kill Rāma and Lakshmaṇa.

Kumbhakarṇa caused great carnage among both soldiers
and their leaders. Finally he fought with Rāma himself. They
were worthy foes. After a long indecisive struggle Rāma was
able to sever Kumbhakarṇa's throat with a well-placed arrow.
The giant Kumbhakarṇa was dead.

DEATH OF INDRAJIT

With this unanticipated setback Rāvaṇa turned again to the
supernatural weapons of Indrajit. His *Brahmastra* struck down
both Rāma and Lakshmaṇa and brought them both near
.leath. Old Jāmbhavan asked Hanuman to bring some magical
herbs from the Himalayas. Hanuman leaped prodigiously all
the way to the Himalayas, but fearing he might not recognize

the herbs tore off the top of the mountain and leaped back. Even as he approached the stricken warriors with the mountaintop in his arms, they began to feel the healing power of the herbs, and soon after the administration of the drug they grew strong and stood up.

Indrajit tried to demoralize Rāma by creating an illusion of Sītā and slaying her before him, but instead he was defeated by Lakshmana using a weapon from Indra and bearing Rāma's name.

THE END OF RĀVANA

Hearing of the death of his son, Rāvana was so distraught that he rushed forth for a final sally. Rousing his forces they attacked the Vanars with renewed ferocity. Eventually Rāvana came before Lakshmana, the slayer of his son, but Lakshmana was helped by Bibhishan. Together they fought Rāvana off for a time, but his anger at the slaying of Indrajit was so consuming that he struck through their defense and his *shakti* struck Lakshmana unconscious. Rāma saw this and came over and drove Rāvana off, and revived Lakshmana, with many memories of their days together.

Rāvana had retreated to get a new chariot, and soon returned more resplendent and vengeful than ever. The gods were watching the great battle, and Indra sent his chariot and driver to Rāma for the final confrontation.

Gods and mortals watched the contest and the heroes of the war,
Ravan speeding on his chariot, Rama on the heavenly car.
And a fiercer form the warriors in their fiery frenzy wore,
And a deeper weight of hatred on their anguished bosoms bore.
Clouds of dread and deathful arrows hid the radiant face of sky,
Darker grew the day of combat, fiercer grew the contest high!

Pierced by Ravan's pointed weapons, bleeding Rama owned no pain,
Rama's arrows keen and piercing sought his foeman's life in vain.
Long and dubious battle lasted, and with fury wilder fraught,
Wounded, faint, and still unyielding, blind with wrath the rivals
    fought.
Pike and club and mace and trident scaped from Ravan's vengeful
    hand.
Spear and arrows Rama wielded, and his bright and flaming brand!

Long and dubious battle lasted, shook the ocean, hill and dale,
Winds were hushed in voiceless terror and the livid sun was pale.
Still the dubious battle lasted, until Rama in his ire
Wielded Brahma's deathful weapon flaming with celestial fire!
Weapon which the Saint Agastya had unto the hero given,
Winged as lightning dart of Indra, fatal as the bolt of heaven.

Wrapped in smoke and flaming flashes, speeding from the circled
   bow,
Pierced the iron heart of Ravan, laid the lifeless hero low!
And a cry of pain and terror from the Raksha ranks arose,
And a shout from joyous Vanars as they smote their fleeing foes!
Heavenly flowers in rain descended on the red and gory plain,
And from unseen harps and timbrels rose a soft celestial strain.

And the ocean heaved in gladness, brighter shone the sunlit sky.
Soft the cool and gentle zephyrs through the forest murmured by.
Sweetest scent and fragrant odours wafted from celestial trees,
Fell upon the earth and ocean, rode upon the laden breeze!
Voice of blessing from the bright sky fell on Raghu's valiant son—
"Champion of the true and righteous! Now thy noble task is done!"

AFTERMATH OF WAR

 Rāma ordered heroes' funerals for all, the slain Vanar and
Rakshasa alike, and Bibhishan was installed as Laṅkā's new
King. Rāma unstrung his bows and laid aside the arms of war.

BOOK XI

SĪTĀ

 Rāma sent Hanuman to carry the news of their victory to
Sītā. He went to the Asoka grove and there found Sītā speechless with joy and gratitude. Hanuman wished to slay the female Rakshas who had troubled her, but Sītā responded, "No,
my son. Who in the world is blameless? It is the part of noble
souls to be compassionate towards all—sinners as well as good
people." Hanuman asked what he should say to Rāma. "That I
am eager to be in his presence!" responded Sītā.
 When Hanuman returned to Rāma and gave his account,

Rāma's face darkened, his eyes lost their luster and he seemed distracted and gave no immediate answer. A little later he ordered Bibhishan to ask Sītā to bathe and bedeck herself with jewels and fine clothes and be brought before him. When she heard the message, Sītā wished instead to go at once, but was persuaded to follow his request. The Vanars pressed close upon her palanquin to see the radiant woman for whom they had fought so valiantly, as she was carried to Rāma.

As the palanquin bearing Sītā was brought before Rāma his face showed a strange transformation of mind and purpose. She greeted him with a word of endearing love, but he was cold, dark and formal. She had lived in Rāvaṇa's keeping. It would be presumed by all that she was no longer fit to be Ayodhyā's Queen!

In shock and disappointment Sītā asked Lakshmaṇa to prepare for her a funeral pyre. Rāma coldly consented and the fire was set. With a vow of her true fidelity and calling the gods and fire to witness, she stepped into the circle of roaring flame.

Slow the red flames rolled asunder, God of Fire incarnate came,
Holding in his radiant bosom fair Videha's sinless dame,
Not a curl upon her tresses, not a blossom on her brow,
Not a fiber of her mantle did with tarnished luster glow!
Witness of our sins and virtues, God of Fire incarnate spake,
Bade the sorrow-stricken Rama back his sinless wife to take.
Rama's forehead was unclouded and a radiance lit his eye,
And his bosom heaved in gladness as he spoke in accents high:
"Never from the time I saw her in her maiden days of youth,
Have I doubted Sita's virtue, Sita's fixed and changeless truth.
I have known her ever sinless—let the world her virtue know,
For the God of Fire is witness to her true and changeless vow!"

RETURN

In the original poem the return to Ayodyhā by means of Rāvaṇa's great flying chariot provides an opportunity for a recapitulation of the main lines of the story, the sight of Laṅkā from the air, the great bridge built by the monkeys and the bears, the place where old Jatayu fell, Kishkinda and the kingdom of Sugrīva, and then the places which Rāma and Sītā had enjoyed together, until finally they approached Ayodhyā itself.

As word was sent to Bharat of the returning Rāma and his party, he immediately gave orders for a joyous reception, music in the shrines and temples, bright colors on display, gay and festive costumes, recital of the sacred *mantras*. He ordered the city swept and cleaned. The royal family went out to meet the arrival of Rāma, Sītā, Lakshmaṇa and their friends.

Bharat took with him the sandals of Rāma which had occupied the throne during all his absence, and presented them back to Rāma as tokens of the kingdom returned to Rāma to rule.

Joy! Joy! In bright Ayodhya gladness filled the hearts of all!
Joy! Joy! A lofty music sounded in the royal hall.
Fourteen years of woe were ended. Rama now assumed his own,
And they placed the weary wand'rer on his father's ancient throne.

And 'tis told by ancient sages, during Rama's happy reign,
Death untimely, dire diseases came not to his subject men,
Widows wept not in their sorrow for their lords untimely lost.
Mothers wailed not in their anguish for their babes by Yama crost.
Robbers, cheats, and gay deceivers tempted not with lying word.
Neighbor loved his righteous neighbor and the people loved their
        lord!
Trees their ample produce yielded as returning seasons went,
And the earth in grateful gladness never failing harvest lent.
Rains descended in their season, never came the blighting gale.
Rich in crop and rich in pasture was each soft and smiling vale.
Loom and anvil gave their produce and the tilled and fertile soil,
And the nation lived rejoicing in their old ancestral toil.

BOOK XII

SUPPLEMENTAL

Apparently the epic originally ended at this point, but in some ancient time a supplement was added which gives a curious and pathetic turn to the story. The false rumors and stories of Sītā's unfaithfulness persisted and spread among the people until many felt the kingdom tainted by her presence.

The trial by fire through which she had passed and her exemplary life scarcely retarded the vicious imaginations of the rumormongers. Finally Rāma, feeling that his responsibilities as king and judge required it, dismissed Sītā again, to the forest hermitage of Vālmīki. There, unknown to him, she gave birth to Rāma's twin sons, Lava and Kusa. The boys grew up as forest dwellers rather than as young princes. Vālmīki put Sītā's story into the epic poem and the two boys memorized the whole account as a song. Singing twenty cantos a day, a recital of the epic took twenty-five days.

Late in his reign Rāma decided to perform the traditional *Ashvameda*, Horse-Sacrifice Ceremony, as the symbol of his imperial power. For this ceremony, which requires two years and great wealth to perform, large groups gathered for ceremonies and appropriate public entertainment.

Vālmīki brought the two hermit-boys to the ceremonies and had them sing twenty cantos of the song one morning. The audience was delighted, remarked on how the boys reminded them of young Rāma and asked to hear the whole song. So the boys came back daily and sang until the poem was completed. Before the song was fully over, Rāma had recognized the boys as his own sons whom he had never seen, and this recognition opened the floodgates of his loneliness and unforgotten love for Sītā. He sent for her to restore her as his Queen.

Vālmīki brought Sītā to the auspicious gathering. All his tenderness awakened by the sight of her, Rāma pleaded for pardon of Sītā and of the gods for having put her aside out of fear, for the people's sake, though he knew her to be innocent of their malicious charges.

Sītā, however, torn by sorrow, love, disappointment and injustice, having seen her sons recognized and restored to Rāma, asked the Goddess Earth to receive her as the ultimate proof of her virtue:

"If unstained in thought and action I have lived from day of birth,
Spare a daughter's shame and anguish and receive her, Mother
        Earth!
If in duty and devotion I have labored undefiled,
Mother Earth, who bore this woman, once again receive thy child!

If in truth unto my husband I have proved a faithful wife,
Mother Earth! relieve thy Sita from the burden of this life!"

Then the earth was rent and parted, and a golden throne arose,
Held aloft by jewelled *Nagas* as the leaves enfold the rose,
And the Mother in embraces held her spotless, sinless Child,
Saintly Janak's saintly daughter, pure and true and undefiled.
Gods and men proclaim her virtue! But fair Sita is no more,
Lone is Rama's loveless bosom and his days of bliss are o'er!

The End

COMMENT

The interpretation of this concluding section is unusually difficult. The exile of Sītā, even the trial by fire on charges which Rāma presumably knows to be false, seem inconsistent with his character. The wives of great men are always subject to calumny regardless of their actual deeds, and it would seem the part of a strong and righteous king to make his rulings based on the truth he knows, whatever the people may think. To bow to their popular demands in a course he knows to be unjust, would seem to deprive him of his virtue, and ultimately even of his kingdom. It is indeed difficult, not only for us but for Indian writers as well, to understand this passage.

Some emphasize that this part does not appear to be Vālmīki's doing, but is a later "cover story" designed to suggest how the original poem came to be preserved. The story is then designed to emphasize the authenticity of the main account, since it was Sītā herself who told it directly to Vālmīki, and he who taught the royal sons to memorize it. Another interpretation, though often several are offered together, is that the career of Rāma as the incarnation (*avatar*) of Vishnu ended with the defeat of Rāvaṇa, for which purpose he had chosen this incarnation, and that the events of the trial by fire and afterward represent the actions of merely an Ishvaku king according to the customs of the time. The great Indian patriot, Sri C. Rajagopalachari, suggests that this ending of the story reflects the agony and sorrow-laden voice of Indian womanhood. It grows out of what they know of life—misjudgment, mistreatment, misery and injustice.

At the end of the Rāmāyaṇa, as at the end of most of the important bits of Indian literature, is the colophon which assures the reader of his merit and joy in having read, recited or meditated upon this account of Rāma and Sītā. So may it always be. One feels that he has been in touch with man and woman, not as they really are, in India or anywhere else, but as Indian imagination thought they ought to be. No wonder that this is so much a literature of the home, a story told to children that they may learn to admire, and as much as possible to become "Little Rāma," "Little Sītā," Vishnu and Lakshmī here on earth.

THE AVATĀRA AS SHRI KRISHNA

THE CYCLE OF STORIES concerned with the descent of Vishnu
in the form of Krishna is even more complex though not so
consistent as the story told by the Rāmāyana. The *Bhāgavata
Purāṇa, Mahābhārata* and *Vishnu Purāṇa* are the principal ancient sources for the stories. It is beyond the scope of the present collection to attempt to retell the whole cycle of Krishna
stories, but a general outline will be provided which may help
to account for references to Krishna which one will encounter
elsewhere.

These stories may be divided into three series of episodes—
those connected with Krishna's birth and infancy, those concerning his life as a youth and young man primarily in the
pastoral setting and concluding with his return to Mathura,
and finally those of the warrior-prince through the battle of
Kurukshetra and to the end of the age. In this account we will
outline some of the events from each cycle, and tell a few of
the Krishna stories from each.

In these stories there are possible difficulties for the unwary
reader. Generally they follow the usual conventions in which
the reader knows from the outset the true nature of Krishna
and his mission, but in which most of the characters in the
stories themselves do not. In some cases there is even an apparent contrast beween Krishna's role in the legend—as a
spoiled and demanding child, for example—and his real character as an embodiment of *dharma*. In one case—his seduction

of the wives of the cowherds—the contrast is so severe that an explanation is required in the story itself. Some of the actions attributed to him are so prodigious that it requires a considerable literary concession to allow that those around him could not have known his true nature. At a few places the characters are given direct and unequivocal opportunity to know his real nature, but these are usually saints and close associates. Conveniently, these instances have been forgotten by the time the next incident develops. All in all these stories demonstrate that ordinary rules of perception and inference do not necessarily apply when one deals with a divine intervention. There is also throughout these stories the basic conviction that if a story serves the purpose of increasing devotion to Vishnu, many other flaws may be forgiven. Relying on this assurance let us turn to the stories of Shri Krishna.

Birth and Infancy of Shri Krishna

In a time when the earth was troubled by the weight of the armies of the *asuras* and their pollution of its beauty and character, Vishnu gave word that he would be born as the eighth son of Vāsudeva, in order to take action to destroy the control of the *asuras*. This birth was foretold to Kaṁsa, the Asura Prince, who learned that this child would kill him. At the time Kaṁsa was driving the bridal chariot for Vāsudeva and his bride, Devakī. Learning of this prophecy, Kaṁsa stopped the chariot, grasped Devakī by the hair, and unsheathed his sword to kill her. Vāsudeva leaped to her defense and showed Kaṁsa that Devakī was not his enemy, but because they were cousins, she should be treated like a sister. Only her eighth son could constitute a danger according to the prophecy. Kaṁsa agreed to spare her life, but only on the condition that each of the children to be born of Devakī would be delivered to him. The first son so presented to Kaṁsa, he returned to the parents, but, by the time the second child was born, Kaṁsa's evil propensities were fully in the ascendancy, and he killed each child as it was born. By the time of the birth of the sixth son, Kaṁsa had also imprisoned Vāsudeva and Devakī, and even his own father whose throne he had usurped. Knowing the danger of Kaṁsa's wrath, when Devakī became pregnant with her seventh son, Vishnu had the embryo transferred to another of Vāsudeva's wives, Rohiṇī, who had fled from the capital and was living in a nomadic, pastoral village (called a *vraja*) under the care of Nanda, Vāsudeva's brother. This son when born was known as Balarāma (or more often simply as Rāma, but not to be confused with the hero of the *Rāmāyana*). Though Balarāma was in fact conceived as the child of Vāsudeva and Devakī, this was not known to Kaṁsa, so he did not realize that her seventh son had been born. Finally, in the fullness of time, Vishnu made himself infinitely small and placed himself inside the body of Vāsudeva, from which in due course he was delivered to the womb of Devakī. Though the radiance of her divine maternity was imprisoned and of no use immediately to increase the joy of mankind, it did not escape Kaṁsa's notice that she lighted up the prison room. He struggled with himself whether to kill her immediately, but finally chose to wait until the birth of the child itself. Hatred for the unborn child grew daily in his mind.

At the moment of Shri Krishna's birth all nature blossomed with surpassing loveliness to welcome the author and source of all existence. Peace and gladness prevailed. The sun and stars were auspicious. The directions were clear. The stars shone brightly, and everywhere on earth—in cities, villages and shepherd tents—hearts were unaccountably filled with gladness. The waters in the rivers were clear; the jungle trees blossomed with flowers, birds sang and bees hummed. Breezes were gentle and fragrant and fires burned brightly. In the heaven-worlds also gladness was felt and praise was sung.

At the moment of the deepest darkness of the night, Vishnu came forth from Devakī in his full form, though very small. He was a marvelous child, blue like a dark cloud, with four hands, and eyes like a lotus flower. He wore a gold-colored cloth and bore the conch, the club, the discus and the gem. He displayed his ancient marks and wore the ancient jewels. His hair was curly, dark and lustrous, and he wore the jeweled crown upon his head. His presence lighted up the room. Vāsudeva and Devakī were overwhelmed with joy to know that the source of the universe had been born as their son, but soon began to fear that this child-god might fall into the hands of Kaṁsa, who sought for him. Vishnu explained to them how he had been born to them previously in their earlier forms (as Vāmana, for one) and then he assumed the form of an ordinary, but beautiful, newborn child.

At the same moment in which Krishna had been born in the prison cell, he had also been born, in the form of Māyā, to Yashodā, wife of Nanda, in the village of the cowherds. Following the instructions of Bhagavan, Vāsudeva took the infant Krishna, walked out of the prison, whose gates mysteriously stood open for them and whose guards remained asleep. Covered and protected from the torrential rain by the thousand-headed serpent, they crossed the flood-swollen Yumna River, which provided a dry pathway for them. Soon Vāsudeva, carrying his divine son, arrived at the hut of Nanda and Yashodā, who had fallen asleep from exhaustion, without knowing whether their new infant was a boy or a girl. Vāsudeva exchanged the babies without waking anyone and returned quickly to the prison with the baby daughter, Māyā. As he placed this baby beside his wife, the doors of the prison closed and locked themselves. The baby cried, the guards woke up and sent a message to Kaṁsa, who came running to the cell. Despite Devakī's pleas, he grasped the baby by the feet to dash her against the stone floor, but the child slipped from his hands, rose and appeared in the air in her true, divine form, condemned Kaṁsa to his certain death, and disappeared. In astonishment and fear he released Vāsudeva and Devakī, but later consulting with his advisors he determined to kill all children who might be his enemy.

In the village of the cowherds the joyous word was spread that a son had been born to Nanda and Yashodā. Houses were swept and washed. The streets were adorned. Animals were decorated. The people all dressed in their very best and brought gifts of various kinds in honor of the beautiful child. Music, stories and songs were heard, and gifts were liberally presented to the poor. The shepherd camp was too poor and insignificant to be noticed at first by Kaṁsa, so the people there were happily unaware of the way in which the tyrant king sought to kill all newborn boys.

A short while later it was necessary for Nanda to travel to Mathura, the capital, to pay his annual tax-tribute to Kaṁsa. Vāsudeva met him there and congratulated him on his new son, inquired about his wife, Rohiṇī, and their son, Balarāma, and then advised him to return promptly after the payment of the tax, as he could foresee trouble at the camp.

Kaṁsa in the meantime had realized that he needed to be more systematic in his execution of infants and had engaged an evil Rakshasi, called Putana, to visit the more remote places and kill the infant boys there. One day she came to Nanda's *Gokula*, where she concealed her natural form in that of an incredibly beautiful woman. When she saw Krishna, she did not know that he was death for wicked persons, but he knew her true nature. She took the baby and placed him on her lap. Neither Yashodā nor Rohiṇī interfered because they could see in her only a beautiful and gentle woman. Putana uncovered her breast, filled with a deadly poison, and gave it to the baby. Krishna held her with his hands and drank her milk, and without stopping sucked the life right out of her as well. She gave an anguished cry so loud that the worlds shook and people fell down in the streets. Her body returned to its natural form with long teeth, wild hair and huge bulk. The fall of her body reduced trees to powder for fifty miles around. Krishna was quickly taken away and a Rakshasa ceremony was performed by servants and friends to protect him from any evil influences of the Rakshasi. Nanda returning from Mathura wondered at the huge corpse, which was cut to pieces with axes, taken far away and burned. Because Krishna had taken her evil poison upon himself, however, her evil deeds had been absorbed and the burning of her body was a fragrant smell. She reached the same goal reached by worthy men. If even Putana could reach this goal by His grace, can we not be certain of success, if we trust Him?

On another occasion, the ceremony of first leaving the house was being performed for Krishna. By midday the baby was drowsy and Yashodā placed him in a cradle which she put in the shade underneath a cart. Unknown to her, an evil asura was hiding in that cart. A bit later the baby awakened and wanted to be fed. His mother, who was busy with her guests, did not hear, and so the baby began to kick and squall. His tiny feet struck the cart above and shattered it to pieces, killing the hidden asura. Again the people were amazed and performed the protection ceremony, but they would not believe the story of the children who stood about and said that the kicking of the baby had destroyed the cart.

Still another time a great asura tried to steal Krishna when his mother had put him down on the ground. The asura stirred up a great whirlwind of dust to mask the escape. As he carried the baby Krishna away, however, the child began to get heavier and heavier and heavier until the asura discovered that he was trying to carry the whole weight of the universe. But when he tried to let go, the baby was clinging too tightly around his neck. The great asura fell and his body was shattered upon the rocks, but the baby was unhurt. The people did not understand, but believed that the baby must have been killed and reborn on the spot to survive such a fall from the top of the whirlwind.

An incident of a different sort occurred one day. While Yashodā was churning, the baby Krishna took hold of the churning rod and prevented it from moving. The gentle mother took him on her lap and gave him her breast, but before the infant was finished, she had to lay him down and get up to put cold water on some milk she was scalding. This made him angry, and he broke the pot of curd with a stone, took some of the butter and crawled inside to eat. When Yashodā came back she found the broken pot and, thinking that he must have done it, went to find him. As she approached him with a cane in her hand, the remembrance of his theft made him fearful and he began to cry, streaking the eye make-up which his mother had put on him in the morning. Seeing that he was sufficiently afraid, Yashodā threw the cane away, but to keep him out of further trouble tied him to the heavy mortar-stone where he was playing. A few moments later he crawled outside dragging the mortar behind him. He came to a place where two *Arjuna* trees grew side by side and crawled between them. Behind the baby the mortar jammed against the two trees, but still he crawled forward and soon the two trees were uprooted and came crashing to the ground. As the trees shattered, two beings stepped out of them, blessed the baby Krishna and thanked him for having released them from the ancient curse which had turned them into trees. Once again the parents and friends found the story, told by children who had watched the baby pull down the trees, amusing but beyond serious belief.

In the village of the cowherds Krishna and Balarāma grew up together, enjoying every kind of childish play and prank, making their mothers and the other women of the village (*Gopīs*) happy with their joyful presence. Some of his pranks when reported to his mother were a bit destructive or bothersome, but her love for him was so great that she did not wish to chide or chastise him.

At an appropriate time Vāsudeva sent the great priest-guru' of the divine beings to Nanda's *vraja*. At the request of Nanda the great guru was persuaded to perform a secret naming ceremony (*samskāras*) for the two boys, Krishna and Rāma. At this ceremony Nanda learned for the first time that the boy was really the son of his brother, Vāsudeva, and of Devakī, and that great expectations were in store for both the boys.

Youth in the Brindāvan Hills

Believing that various events had warned them sufficiently of the dangers, Nanda moved his clan and herds to the fertile pastures and lovely forests of Brindāvana (the Brindāvan Hills). Soon Rāma and Krishna were entrusted with small herds and joined the other lads who tended calves. To destroy evil (one of the functions of an *avatāra*), Krishna once discovered an asura hidden in the herd, disguised as a calf. He sneaked up on it, grasped the false calf by the hind legs and tail, whirled it around and threw it so prodigiously that the asura's head was dashed against the top of a distant tree. Another time the boys were drinking from the river after having watered their herd, when a colossal crane swallowed young Krishna. The other boys all fainted, but Krishna made himself very hot, so that the crane spit him out of its beak and tried to peck him to pieces. Krishna then grasped the slashing beak and ripped the crane in two from top to bottom. On a third occasion an asura took the form of a giant serpent and lay on the path to the pasture with his mouth open. The serpent was so large, about ten miles long, and occupied all the space from the ground to the clouds, fangs like mountaintops, so that its tongue was merely like a long path. The unwary boys walked in the mouth without noticing. Krishna paused, wanting to kill the snake, but without harm to his friends. Finally he stepped inside the mouth, but then immediately began to grow in size inside the asura's throat until the blocked breath caused the serpent to explode. Krishna lifted out and revived his friends who had fainted.

There were many idyllic moments in Brindhāvan among the cowherds, picnics in the forest glens, listening to Krishna's flute, taking pleasure in shared meals and in play. Once Brahmā tested Krishna's resourcefulness and took all the calves and hid them. When Krishna went to find the calves, Brahmā took all the other boys. Soon Krishna realized what had happened. To save Brahmā from the humiliation of having his trick disclosed, Krishna made himself into all of the calves and all of the boys, so perfect an imitation that neither the cows nor the mothers could tell the difference. This farce went on for a year. During this time the love of the mothers for their sons (as forms of Shri Krishna) had constantly increased, and love, prosperity and gentleness had grown throughout the village. At the end of the year Brahmā returned dumbfounded and returned the boys and the calves, completely unaware of the fact that they had been gone for a year, which, of course, was only a moment with him. Life with Shri Krishna was delightful, free, happy, foolishness; the bliss and innocence of true childhood was an absolute delight. For all his greatness the bliss of his presence was accessible to all, particularly to the humble and lowly.

The great snake, Kaliya, lived at the bottom of a pool in the Yumna River. He was so vile that the water boiled with the fire of his poison. In the burning summer heat the cows came to the river and drank, but so much poison was mixed in the water that they all keeled over. Krishna working alone discovered the tragic scene and at once revived the cows, but wishing to get at the source of the trouble, climbed a tall tree leaning over the river and dove directly into the pool of Kaliya. Hearing him thrashing about at the surface, the snake came up and attacked Krishna. The onlookers thought that he had been destroyed and were in utter dismay of grief and fear. Krishna lay still in the coils of the great snake for about a muhūrta (48 minutes), then he enlarged himself sharply, breaking the coils, freed himself from the embrace of the snake, feinted back and forth with the snake until Kaliya struck at him. Krishna dodged and leaped upon the hood of the snake. There he began to dance, whirling, leaping, posturing, as the greatest artist of the dance. Hoods smoked and were beaten under the fire of Krishna's dancing feet, but Kaliya had a hundred hoods. Finally Krishna's dance had crushed all the hoods. The snake lay in great distress and near death. His wives appeared before Krishna appealing for his life. Knowing that snakes cherish their anger and are wicked by nature, yet Krishna also knew them to be part of his creation. So he sent Kaliya and all his brood away to the ocean, and the Yumna became clear and its water sweet and wholesome. Krishna was received back with joy by the people.

On another occasion Nanda, Krishna's foster-father, was about to offer a ceremony in honor of Indra, when Krishna, wanting to teach Indra humility, persuaded his father to withhold the ceremony. Krishna was actually teaching a lesson concerning the inevitability of karmic consequences and the irrelevance of special actions designed to "please" the individual gods, who cannot modify the karmic necessities in any case, but this was not realized at the time. Nanda followed Krishna's advice and the ceremony prepared for Indra was used to worship cows, Brahmins, and the Govardhana Hill near which they dwelt.

As Krishna had expected, Indra was angry and jealous and sent his clouds to deluge the village with torrential rains. It was as though the whole earth had passed under water. The raindrops came down hard like stones. Krishna knew this to be the work of Indra, so he tore up the whole hill, Govardhana, and held it over the village like an umbrella. The villagers and their cattle were safe and dry under the hill. Krishna held it over them for seven continuous days and nights without fatigue. Indra realized that this power was far beyond his own, called off the storm, and learned his lesson. Krishna put the hill back.

Krishna was also praised by the great, divine cow, Kāmendhenu, bathed in her milk, and then called Govinda, protector of cows.

One hot day the girls and young women of the village had gone down to a pool to cool and refresh themselves. They left their clothes on the bank and were splashing about in the water when Krishna came up and stole their saris. He retreated a short distance and leaned against a tree watching their play. Soon enough one of them noticed him, but when they pleaded with him to return their clothes, he laughed and told them that each one would have to come up and get her own from him. They protested and promised to tell on him, but finally, both their affection for him and their desire to secure their clothes overcame them, and one at a time they came before him. They tried to cover themselves with hands and arms, but he made each one put her palms together above her head and bow before him. The intense love of each girl for him overcame her modesty and shame, and each approached him. He promised to marry all of them.

After the heat of summer came the rainy season, and then the rains lifted, the earth was fresh and fragrant, the moon was full and reddish. Krishna took his flute, slipped off to the forest glen and began to play. In the village each woman heard it, and her love was excited. She dropped whatever she was doing, and, oblivious to the presence of others, slipped off to the forest to join the young man with the singing flute. In their haste and stealth they even failed to dress and adorn themselves properly. No matter what husbands, fathers or brothers did, the women could not be prevented from joining the one they loved. When they arrived with him, however, he encouraged them to return to their homes, and chided their thoughts of infidelity. Nothing he said, however, sent them back, though they did cry and pleaded with him to be received by him who had stolen their hearts. They protested that it was impossible for them not to love him. His love had set them on fire and they asked him to receive and play with them, and for their sake, he did.

Because Krishna had received their love, some of the *gopis* began to be conceited. To correct this fault one night, Krishna disappeared in the midst of the festivities. They were frantic with the loss and inquired of him everywhere. Later they began to act out the events of his life—the killing of Putana, the whirlwind, and all. These acts became the village plays, the dramatic enactment of these stories which are carried out in festivals, plays, songs and dance in India, even to this day. On some of these nights of delight in the forest, Krishna and the *gopis* would dance the *rasa*. They formed a circle with Krishna between each two *gopis*. [Two explanations are offered by the commentators: (1) that he multiplied his forms so as to be with each of them, or (2) that he appeared with each one momentarily and she was so enchanted by her love for him that the girls paired off with each other, each under the illusion that she was with Krishna himself. The dance may be performed either way—that is with many Krishna parts, or only one.] They danced in a circle with arms about one another's neck and the women sang praises of Krishna.[1]

For two months the nightly sport in the forests continued. When the women finally turned reluctantly home, their husbands and fathers were not jealous or angry, however, because Krishna had provided each with the illusion of his wife or daughter while they had been gone.

Return to Mathura

Kaṁsa finally learned where Krishna was and his anger was renewed. He had Vāsudeva and Devakī bound with chains and sent the demon Kesin to the *vraja* to kill Rāma and Krishna.

---

[1] All of these stories, but particularly this incident, have become especially important to a substantial number of devotionally oriented Hindus, some Vaishnavite, some even Shaivite, and have been organized into worship and into festival activities. A fascinating discussion of many of the dimensions of this is available in *Krishna: Myths, Rites, and Attitudes*, ed. by Milton Singer (Honolulu: East-West Center Press), 1966.

Kesin came in the form of a wild stallion, but Krishna killed him by thrusting his arm into the horse's throat and enlarging his arm until the horse suffocated. Then Kaṁsa arranged a wrestling match. At the gate of the amphitheater a huge elephant with a club in its trunk was to be stationed to beat Krishna and Rāma to death. If this failed, they would be challenged by the kingdom's greatest wrestlers. Kaṁsa thought that in this way he would be ridding the world of what he regarded as its two most troublesome elements. Kaṁsa then sent Akūra to invite the two young men to the city. He did this and they consented to come to Mathura. The women of the *vraja* were almost inconsolable. They tried to stop him but could not. He did, however, promise to come back. The chariot reached Mathura about evening, and Krishna and Rāma were invited to stay with Akūra. They agreed to do so, but first they wished to see the city. Krishna, Rāma and the other cowherders decided to go into the city that very evening. They found it large, well-defended and neat. The city had a joyous appearance. They began to have adventures almost immediately. Seeing the king's *dhobie* (washerman) with a large supply of clean clothes, they asked for some. The dhobie-man was arrogant and rude, so Krishna snapped off his head, and they took what they wished. Coming to a bent-over crippled girl carrying sandal wood paste, they received from her a gift of the paste which had been made for the king. In turn, Krishna stepped on her toes, and placing his fingers under her chin, lifted her head and straightened her deformity. She had previously a very pretty face and was now beautiful in every way. She was so enchanted with him that she invited him home with her. Declining, however, Rāma and Krishna moved on and knowing of Indra's bow, which was kept in the city archives, they found the place, where, over the protests of the guards, Krishna took the bow, strung it, and snapped the string so hard that the bow was broken in two. The sound of the twang alerted Kaṁsa, who sent a detachment of his army to kill them, but Rāma and Krishna, each using part of the broken bow as a club, made an end of all of them. They continued to inspect the city for a time, but it was soon time for them to return, wash, eat and rest.

Kaṁsa was disturbed by reports of their actions. All kinds of bad omens attended him, but he continued with his plans. The amphitheater was prepared: the drums and musical instruments sounded; the wrestlers paraded. The crowd gathered: as Rāma and Krishna approached the theater, the elephant blocked their way. Krishna demanded that the elephant driver move the beast to give them passage. The mahout would not, and charged Krishna instead. Breaking past the trunk, Krishna hid on the underside of the animal, giving it great kicks on the legs. Enraged at this attack by an invisible enemy, the elephant seized Krishna in his trunk. Krishna broke loose again, and grabbed the tail and dragged the elephant away. The feet dug trenches in the earth. Then, coming in front of the beast, Krishna feinted and struck the animal so that it gored the earth viciously with its tusks, but always missed Krishna with each charge. The elephant became so confused with his leaping about that it stumbled and fell. Holding the elephant down with his foot, Krishna wrenched off a tusk and used it to beat both elephant and driver to death.

Each one who saw Krishna saw him in a different way. To the waiting wrestlers he appeared like a thunderbolt; to ordinary men he was the finest man; to women he was their beautiful lover; to the shepherds a relative and friend; to his parents a baby; to foolish men a mere human being; to yogis the highest being; to those who know the truth the highest god; to Kaṁsa he was doom itself.

The crowd shouted for Rāma and Krishna to participate in the wrestling. Though protesting mildly their youth and inexperience, Rāma and Krishna accepted matches with the two greatest wrestlers. As the fight developed the women protested that it was unfair and unworthy to pit two young boys from the forests against such hardened and experienced wrestlers, but it was not long before both Rāma and Krishna had killed their adversaries and were receiving the adoration of the crowd—except, of course, for Kaṁsa.

In desperation Kaṁsa then sounded the drum and ordered them killed, including Vāsudeva, and his own father as well. Krishna heard this and leaped up to the King's box at the amphitheater. King Kaṁsa drew a sword and fought aggres-

sively, but Krishna was overpowering and threw him down
into the arena, jumped down and stomped the life out of him.
He then dragged the body through the dust of the arena.
Kaṁsa's eight younger brothers attacked to avenge the evil
king, but Rāma mowed them down with his mace.

Krishna ordered appropriate ceremonies for the dead, freed
the prisoners, including his parents, to whom he gave the joy
of knowing him as a son. The proper kingdom of Ugrasena was
re-established. It was then possible for the proper and open
upanāyana ceremony to be performed for Rāma and Krishna
and they were initiated into *yoga*. To pay their *guru*, they returned his son who had been drowned, and in the process
Krishna found the conch shell, *Pāñchajanya*, in the stomach of
an *asura* he had killed. This conch remained one of his major
instruments of warfare. He sent reassuring messages back to
Nārada and the *gopīs* in the shepherd village. The *gopīs* were
both peeved and eager to hear of him. At first they teased and
chided about their fickle lover, but then they listened intently
as the messenger explained how it is that one is never truly
separated from him who is all things.

For a time Krishna with Rāma at his side was involved with
his responsibilities at Mathura. He returned to Trivakra, the
deformed girl whom he had straightened, and in embracing
him her suffering was released. Krishna and Rāma also returned to Akūra and asked him to go on a mission to Hastinā-
pura, to carry a message of good will, and to return with a
careful report. He carried out this delicate mission well, bringing comfort to Kuntī, the mother of the Pāṇḍavas, and pre-
senting Krishna's hope to Dhritarāshtra that he would be fair
and impartial both to his own and to his brother's sons. Dhritarāshtra recognized the good teachings, but also confessed his
prejudice in favor of his own sons. This failure to follow the
dharma offered by the mission of Krishna at an early time
eventually resulted in the great battle of Kurukshetra between the sons of Dhritarāshtra (led by Duryodhana) and the
sons of Pāndu led by Yudishṭira.

At Mathura two of the former queens of Kaṁsa persuaded
their fathers to attack Krishna. Krishna determined to destroy
the army, but preserved their leader so that he might attack

again and again, until the destruction of the enemies of the
devas would be even more complete. One of these leaders of
the *asuras* was Jarasandha, the king of Magadha. The battles
were fierce, but with Krishna's bow covering the enemy army
with arrows and Rāma's club blasting them out of their char-
iots and off their elephants, the army was soon destroyed. They
captured, but released, Jarasandha. At first Jarasandha wanted
to retire to a monastery, but then was persuaded to gather
another army and return to the attack. He did this eighteen
times, and on the final occasion even brought in hordes of
foreign allies. Krishna felt that for so violent a battle, it would
be best to have the people removed, so he selected an island
near Gujarat, and had his city built upon it. By his power Shri
Krishna caused all the *Yadava* (his own clan) inhabitants to
be carried to the new city from Mathura. The new city of
Krishna was Dvārakā.

Having secured the safety of the people, Krishna returned
to Mathura, and appeared before it to defend it, without his
armament. But when the enemy approached him, he ran, staying just out of reach. Their taunts did not influence him, but
he led the army into a cave. There the leader saw a sleeping
person and thinking it to be Krishna, kicked it, but it turned
out to be a protector of *devas*, Muchukunda, who reduced the
intruders to ashes in an instant. Krishna thanked him for the
help and offered him the opportunity to be free from *samsāra*
itself. Krishna and Rāma then finished the annihilation of the
foreign armies, confiscated the enemy's wealth, and eventually
returned to Dvārakā to be with their people.

Soon Krishna entered into several marriages, which created
alliances among the kingdoms of that region. One of these
brides was Rukminī. She and her parents thought the match
eminently suitable, but her older brother hated Krishna and
chose another man for her instead. Hearing of this, she sent a
messenger to Krishna to inform him of her brother's plan.
Krishna left at once, and Rāma, hearing of the problem, set
out the next day with a large force. Arrangements for the
wedding were already far advanced so that when Krishna arrived the wedding was planned for the next day. Finally, as
Rukminī was walking slowly from the shrine to the place for

the marriage, Krishna intervened and placed her in his chariot. Having expected some kind of showdown, the groom's aides attacked Krishna in force, but he laughed away their shower of arrows and called for the army provided by Rāma to destroy them. The army routed, Rukminī's brother himself attacked, but each weapon which he sought to use Krishna destroyed. Krishna planned to kill him, but his sister pleaded for his life. Krishna agreed, but tied him up and shaved off most of his hair and moustache. Rāma protested. A near relation should not be killed nor deformed. He had already been killed by his evil deed. It should not be necessary to do it again. Thus he gently chided Krishna and reassured Rukminī. Krishna and she returned to Dvārakā and were married with great festivities.

One of Krishna's citizens owned a gem which had been given by the sun, and was intensely bright and beautiful. Krishna asked for it, but was refused. A little later the brother of the owner of the gem wore it on a hunting expedition from which he never returned. The surviving brother spread rumors that Krishna had killed his brother and stolen the gem. To refute these rumors Krishna and some citizens undertook an investigation. They found that the hunter had been killed by a lion, which in turn had been killed by a bear, and the gem had been given as a toy to the bear's club. After fighting with the bear over a long period, finally Krishna was able to explain his purpose, and the bear and he made peace. The bear gave Krishna the gem and also his daughter, Jāmbhavati, in marriage. With his return to Dvārakā, where it was believed that he had been killed in the cave with the bear, Krishna sent for Satrajit, the owner of the gem, and returned it to him. The man was ashamed for his part in the incident and resolved to give his daughter to Krishna in marriage. Shri Krishna agreed to marry the daughter, Satyabhāmā, but left the gem with her father.

Krishna also married Kalindi, who had done great *tupas* in order to secure him as her husband. Another wife was Mitravinda, who loved him but was under the control of Duryodhana. Krishna abducted her by force, which helped to incense Duryodhana later when Krishna tried to help to prevent

the great war of Kurukshetra. The wife Satya was secured by
the feat of subduing seven wild bulls for the king of the Ko-
salas, her father. He also married Bhadrā and Lakṣmaṇi which
allied his kingdom with most of the forces of western and central India. Besides these eight principal wives, he also married
sixteen thousand girls whom he freed from capture by the
asura, Bhauma. He married all of them at the same moment,
sent each to Dvārakā in different palanquins, provided each
with a separate house and took as many forms as there were
brides. Some time later the sage Nārada was reported to have
some doubts about Krishna's ability to keep so many wives
happy and secure, but when he visited and inquired, he found
Krishna in each place where he turned, and in each being
served with the most tender and genuine devotion and affection by a wife who believed herself to be his only consort. All
of the pleasures of the householder were being enjoyed by him
and his wives in their many homes. God may be served in
many ways.

The Closing Years

Gradually Krishna and Rāma subdued the *asura* kings of
western India. Many of these evil kings had secured boons of
one sort or another from Shiva (Rudra), but Krishna was
able to find ways to evade these protections without any direct
battle developing between himself and Shiva. Several of his
battles had to do with finding suitable wives for his sons and
grandsons. On several occasions Krishna and his party visited
their cousins, the Pāṇḍavas and the Kurus, at their capital,
Indraprastha. Krishna helped Yudishṭira perform the *rājasūya*
sacrifice which required the symbols of loyalty from all the
other kings of the area. All were glad to send these gifts, except Jarasandha alone. He had desisted from his attacks upon
Krishna, but had never abandoned his jealousy of him.
Krishna, Rāma and Bhīma (one of the five Pāṇḍava brothers)
put on disguises as Brahmins and went to Jarasandha, where
they flattered him and asked for a gift. He noticed their powerful arms and the marks of the bowstrings on their wrists,
and was quite sure that they were in fact Kshatriyas rather

than Brahmins, but decided to offer them the gift anyway. When the gift they requested was a fight, he laughed and selected the huge Bhīma as the most appropriate opponent. It was a terrible fight, lasting twenty-seven days without a winner. Finally Krishna hinted to Bhīma how he should dispose of his opponent by taking a forked twig and splitting the two branches apart. Understanding the hint, Bhīma threw Jarasandha down, stepped on one of his legs and grasping the other in his hands, split him in two.

In one curious incident, it happened that an old friend of Krishna's, who had been a fellow student with him many years before, had married and lived the life of a householder. His mind, however, was truly pure and he had no particular desires. He lived only on what chanced to come to him, and had a serene mind, contemplating the love of Bhagavān. His nickname was Kuchela, "poor man." One day his wife asked him to visit Krishna and request some gifts so that they might live a little more comfortably. He did make the trip to Dvārakā carrying only four handfuls of fried rice which she had begged and tied up in a bit of rag. Krishna saw him coming and rose to greet and welcome him. He showed the "poor man" every mark of respect, which rather surprised those around the palace that he should so greet a dirty Brahmin, clothed in rags and thin from starvation. Krishna, however, paid no attention to them, and engaged in vivacious conversation with Kuchela, remembering their days with the *guru*, and being brought up to date on what had happened since then. They revived together many happy memories. Soon Krishna saw that he had come only to please his wife and Krishna secretly planned to give him all the wealth he might use. When Krishna asked about their exchange of gifts, Kuchela hung his head in shame because he had nothing. Undaunted, Krishna spied the rice and took a handful with the comment, "What you have brought gives me the greatest pleasure!"

On his way home the next day Kuchela was ashamed that he had not received any wealth as his wife had wished, but he had to admit that he had not asked for it. He was still enjoying the welcome of friendship which he had received. He approached his old home but did not recognize it, for his humble cottage had been converted virtually into a fine palace. Just as rain comes without being asked and gives wealth while the farmer is sleeping, so Krishna had rewarded his devotee. He and his wife used the gifts of Krishna without much longing for them, and his love for the Lord was rewarded by that freedom from *karma* and attainment of the goal which all good men ultimately win.

Krishna was also able to show his mother, Devakī, how she had played a part in the destruction of the *asuras*. Knowing that Kaṁsa was going to destroy each of the children, Bhagavān had arranged for these children of Devakī to be the rebirth of great *asuras*, so that in thinking he was destroying his enemies Kaṁsa was actually destroying his own support. Having thus been destroyed, however, they were freed from their evil *karma*. Krishna visited and returned from hell with his six brothers in the form of babies, who being received and nursed by Devakī, were made fit immediately to live in the heaven-worlds.

Arjuna, the great bowman, was a particular favorite of Krishna and Rāma and visited them often. While on one of these visits Arjuna fell in love with Subhadra, Krishna's sister. She was committed by arrangement to marry Arjuna's cousin, Duryodhana. Adopting the disguise of a Saṁnyāsin, Arjuna was able to woo her and arranged to abduct her. These arrangements were agreed to by Krishna and her parents, but Rāma had helped to make the original agreement with the father of Duryodhana. On a festival day Arjuna leaped into her chariot and carried her away. Rāma was furious, but Krishna pleaded with him to accept the arrangement, and he was calmed down. This incident was one more reason for the ill feelings between Duryodhana and Arjuna and Krishna.

The tensions between the Kurus and the Pāṇḍavas had heightened continuously until general warfare seemed to be the only solution. In fact Krishna (as Vishnu) had arranged that Duryodhana and the forces of the Kurus were embodiments of most of the evil *asuras* left in existence. Rāma wished to remain strictly neutral in this encounter and so departed on a pilgrimage away from the scene of the battle. When it came to war, both Arjuna and Duryodhana rushed to Krishna to

secure his aid in the conflict. Duryodhana arrived first and
Arjuna second, but Krishna was asleep. As they stood near
his bed waiting for him to awaken he saw Arjuna first and
Duryodhana second. Kshatriya honor required that he become the ally of whomever should ask him first, but in this
perplexing situation Krishna offered a choice. One of them
could have his army and all the forces committed to him. The
other could have himself, except that he would not participate as a combatant himself, but only as advisor and friend.
Duryodhana instantly chose the army, while Arjuna chose
Krishna himself and asked him to be his chariot driver. Thus
for the great war at Kurukshetra, Krishna was friend and ally
of the Pāṇḍavas, advising them in many ways and serving to
drive the chariot for Arjuna.

On the eve of the battle, as the two armies prepared for
war the following day, with almost all the warriors of India
drawn up on one side or the other, Arjuna asked Krishna to
take him in the chariot to the middle ground between the two
armies. There in the twilight before the battle, his heart grew
faint at the thought of a war in which he would be the enemy
of his friends, cousins, teachers and associates. He could see
no possible winner of such a holocaust. There Krishna talked
with him and gave him that lesson and view of himself which
is preserved in the *Bhagavadgītā*. Arjuna returned strengthened in his sense of what his *dharma* required at that tragic
moment, and fought bravely, relying often on Krishna's aid
throughout the battle.

The end of the battle at Kurukshetra which virtually destroyed all armies, had eliminated the *asuras* whom Krishna
had been born to help destroy. The only ones not fully destroyed were Krishna's own clan, the *Yadavas*. Since they were
guarded by himself from their enemies, it comprised a special
problem for him.

Some old sages went to a holy bathing place near Dvārakā
while some *yadava* boys were playing at the place. The young
rascals dressed one of the boys as a woman and confronted
the sages, saying, "This woman is pregnant and desires to
know what child she will have, but is too shy to ask you herself."

The sages were not amused with the joke and replied irritably, "She will bring forth a pestle, which will bring ruin to your family." This frightened them and all who heard about it because they knew that the sage's curse must come true. Uncovering the costumed boy, they discovered an iron pestle under the sari. They took it and returned home and explained what had happened. The king was worried, but had the iron pestle ground to powder and thrown in the ocean. One bit of it, however, chipped off and fell in the ocean unpowdered and was swallowed by a fish. The iron powder, on the other hand, was washed up by the waves and thrown on the bank, and from it grew a weed called *airākas*. The fish who had eaten the iron piece was caught and sold, and a huntsman finding the bit of iron used it as the tip for an arrow.

A little later Krishna, reading evil portents in many omens, proposed a general pilgrimage to the waters of Prabhāsa, and the *yadavas* receiving this instruction also prepared to go. He sent the women, children and old folk one way, while the *yadava* men went another. As their boats reached Prabhāsa, they found that the airākas weeds growing there produced a sweet, powerful liquor, which they began to drink. Soon they were very intoxicated and it was not long before a quarrel began. Gradually the fight enlarged in viciousness and in the weapons used until finally they had used everything they had. Then they pulled up the reeds growing on the seashore and found that as soon as they were seized they became as hard as iron clubs, and so they used them to strike each other. Krishna and Rāma tried to prevent them, but they were attacked also, so they retreated and sat aside while the anger of the *yadavas* consumed them.

When this work of self-destruction was complete, Krishna announced that the burden of the earth had been removed. Rāma decided to leave the world, sat down and meditating on Bhagavan united himself with him and abandoned the form of a human being. Krishna went over to a peepul tree and sat on the ground at its foot. He sat in silence with his left foot on his right thigh. In the distance a hunter, named Jari, saw only Krishna's red-painted foot and thinking that it was the hide of a deer, he shot his arrow directly at it—the arrow tipped with the iron piece from the stomach of the fish. Jari came up, and when he realized his mistake pleaded to be forgiven and killed. Krishna comforted him, and explained that what had happened he himself desired, and granted him to go to the heaven world of good men.

The charioteer found the dying Krishna and was struck with dismay, but Krishna asked him to have the city of Dvārakā abandoned because it would soon disappear in the sea, and to put his wives under the protection of Arjuna. Suddenly from the heavens praises were sung and Krishna disappeared as a flash of lightning disappears. When the news of his death was carried back to Dvārakā many of the widows threw themselves on funeral pyres, but Arjuna took those who wished to escape back with him to Indraprastha. In the old capital Vajra, the grandson of Krishna, was anointed king and both Arjuna and Yudishṭira, finding life in this world hollow and meaningless, wandered into the forest on the search for the life that matters, in total devotion to Bhagavan.

Two streams are capable of destroying the evil deeds of the three worlds—one consisting of the stories of His noble deeds, and the other rising from the actual contact with his person. Those that take the trouble to attain purity resort to both streams, for ultimately the stream of hearing runs into the other, the stream of being. So may it be for us, who have listened to the stories of Shri Krishna.

KALKI—THE END OF THE
KALI AGE

Parāśara had described and interpreted to Maitreya the meaning of all those events which had disclosed Vishnu's activities in creation of and upon the earth, but to make the story complete he also set about to describe the future events and rulers, even to the age in which we now live. He was granted the wisdom of those unbound by time, whether past or present or future, and laid before Maitreya the names of families and happenings yet to be.

In Magadha, he said, a sovereign named Vishvaphātika will permit outside people to rule. He will set aside the Kshatriyas and elevate fishermen, barbarian foreigners, incompetent Brahmins to power. Strange tribes will control many of the kingdoms, will recognize no dharma, no common bonds, no *Veda*. These kings will rule jealously, and be of churlish spirit, violent temper, addicted to falsehood and wickedness. They will kill women, children and cows, and seize the properties of their subjects. In those days kings will be of limited power, subject to many tottering alliances, and for the most part will rapidly rise and fall. Their lives will be short, their desires insatiable, and they will show little piety. The mixing of the states and races, adopting of barbaric institutions and customs, continuing in disorder and neglecting the purity of caste will destroy the people. True wealth and piety will decrease daily. Then property alone will confer rank. Wealth will be the only source of hope. Passion and sensuality will be the sole relation between the sexes. Falsehood will be the main means of success. Women will be merely objects of sensual gratification. The veneration of the earth will be only for the sake of its mineral wealth: there will be no particular places held sacred and made the objects of devotional pilgrimage. The thread alone—not his character—will identify the Brahmin, and external symbols such as the staff or the red cloth will be the only distinctions among the orders of men. Dishonesty will be the universal means of subsistence. Weakness will cause dependence. Threats and arrogance will substitute for teaching and learning. Gifts will be only repayments and ablutions only handwashing. Marriage will be only a convenient agreement. Men will be measured by their clothes. Obscure things will be called holy, simply because they are not well understood.

The right to rule will be determined merely by strength, and the people will flee from their sovereign and take refuge in the mountains and forests, living precariously on the wild honey, herbs, roots, fruits, flowers and leaves. No man will be able to count on a life longer than twenty-three years. In this way, in the Kali Age, decay shall constantly proceed until the human race approaches its own annihilation.

When the practices taught by the *Vedas* and the institutes of *dharma* shall nearly have ceased, and the close of the Kali Age shall be near, then a portion of that divine being who exists of his own spiritual nature, takes the character of Brahmā, who is the beginning and the end, and comprehends all things, shall descend upon the earth. He will be born in the family of the Vishnuyashas, an eminent Brahmin, in the Sambhala village, to be named Kalki and endowed with eight superhuman faculties. By his irresistible might he will destroy all foreigners and thieves, and all whose minds are devoted to iniquity. He will reestablish righteousnes upon the earth, and the minds of those who are still alive at the end of the Kali Age shall be awakened and as clear as crystal. The men whose minds and characters are thus changed by virtue of that peculiar time at the end of the age shall enter the ensuing *pralaya*, as it were, as the dormant seeds of the human beings who will rise as the race which will follow the laws in the succeeding Krita Age of purity. And when the sun and the moon and the lunar astarism Tishya and the planet Jupiter are in one mansion, the Krita Age shall return.

With the departure of Krishna the Kali Age began. When the first two stars of the Seven Rishis (Great Bear constellation) rise in the heaven, and a lunar astarism is seen at their midpoint, and the constellation continues stationary in that conjunction for hundreds of human years, the decay of the Kali Age will be far advanced. But the family of Ikṣwāku, through the force of their devotions, continues alive through all the four ages, living in the village of Kalapu, and will return at the beginning of the Krita Age to give origin to the Kshatriya dynasties.

Whoever shall listen reverently and in faith to this narrative shall be purified for all his sins, and will live in perfect possession of all his faculties, in unequaled affluence and prosperity. Does not thinking about all these races, these great and valiant men, who now exist only as though they were legends, set a man free from inordinate and selfish desires? Powerful kings or not, they were all subject to the same fate. Since we may be aware of this, a wise man would never be influenced by the desire for personal possession, and will regard whatever role and task is his as a transient and temporary trust, and will not consider them to be his own, and will not be bound by them. At the end of the age, Kalki will make all who survive so wise, and thus prepare for the golden age which shall surely come again.

Section II: Stories of Shiva

Several of the accounts of devotion which were developed in Part II have to do primarily with devotion to Shiva and the other deities associated with him. In this part we have only two of the many cycles of stories of Shiva. One is a Westernized retelling of the most familiar of all Shiva stories. The dance by itself and the variations of accounts is the subject of a whole body of literature. The telling here has picked up some, but not all, of the variations and has adapted the whole in a modernized version. Some Indian stories have the same light sarcasm which this telling suggests. Some pick up and interpret specifically, not only the elements mentioned here, but in much greater detail—positions of the feet, glaze of the eyes, position of fingers, etc. This account gives the whole main story line only. The second story cycle has to do with Ganapathi (Ganesha) and represents a particular interest of the student of Hinduism in having his blindness and ignorance removed so that he would be equipped to come into the presence of Truth. It makes a good place to end a "natural approach to Hinduism," with the god who stands guard at the doorway of the inner sanctum of the knowledge which goes beyond all that we have known, and removes the obstacles from before all serious and devoted inquirers.

SHIVA NĀṬARAJA
A PARABLE IN SCULPTURE

A GOD DOES NOT have to be professed in order to be a god. That One can exist in supreme indifference to the honor which men would like to confer by their belief. It matters not to god. Even when ten thousand heretic sages agreed to refuse to believe in the gods, the gods were undisturbed. Still, since a god has all the time there is with which to play, he can afford to take a moment to render clear to obstinate and clouded minds his real Presence and his Power. So Shiva, though tranquil, let his overflowing love and grace impel him to the gesture of visiting the skeptical sages in their forest hermitage to show them the truth. A gracious god will spare the time to step forth and clear up cloudy points.

On his arrival at the forest glen, Shiva was received with the violent reactions of men who face a fact that doesn't fit their orthodoxies. They discovered, however, that neither disbelief nor disbelief in a louder voice augmented by curses could dislodge a simple fact. Shiva smiled.

When vehemence had failed to justify their ignorance, they summoned brute force to authenticate the just reasonableness of their claim and unleashed a ferocious tiger at the god. The only god who would be frightened by a tiger would be just the kind of god these sages could imagine and reject. It was no such puny god, nor god for puny men, who stood before them. Calmly and deftly Shiva stripped the tiger of its skin and slipped the tiger-skin around his waist, a gesture of propriety toward man.

With their power countered and graciously transformed to modesty, as gently as their vicious curses had echoed back from the real Presence, the faithful champions of skepticism released their next defense, a strategy of craftiness. A hideous, venomous snake coiled silently in the grass and slowly raised its head, spread out its hood and bared its dripping fangs. Shiva bent down and gently stroked the outspread hood, then sliding a hand down to smooth the coils, he cast the snake around his neck as adornment for his mighty chest.

The sage lovers of the Truth, armed with an infinity of their disbelief, were furious with the truth which stood before them. Their curses had no sting; their power hung on the opponent as a garment; their craftiness adorned him as a necklace. They decided to admit half of what they did not believe, in order to avoid believing in the other half. From out of the dim, occult region of their misformed faith they called forth a supernatural demon to wield his club against the threatening truth. He came forth with power, hideous and vile as their intentions, but dwarfed as if in mimicry of their half-formed faith. Shiva pressed the demon to the ground, set a foot upon his back and paused.

Somewhere within the soul of that great god a faint strumming of uncertain sound began to stir. So faintly it began that he turned his whole mind inward and distinguished a slow and stately rhythm rising from his overflowing grace. A hand which held a drum began to tap it in the slow and even cadence of a pulsing heart. His supple body responded to the invitation and the movement of his legs picked up the rhythm. The sound welled forth; the cadence cleared and strengthened with a more insistent throb. The drum he stroked began to beat an intricate rhythm. Crescendos of joy poured forth in the sound and movement of a dancing god. The fire in his left hand traced the gestures of the accelerating tempo. Graceful arms and hands declared the motion of his ecstasy. Surging legs lifted in ascending leaps of unpremeditated joy. Shiva was absorbed in the rapture of his own expression. He danced. Once swept up and captivated by its inward throb, the rhythms and the mood began to soar. His body glistened and then glowed with dazzling splendor as he danced.

The heretic sages prostrated themselves to be his dancing floor. The gods came down from their heavens to watch the joyful dance. As Shiva moved with stately grace and gay abandon, as only a Shiva could do, mist began to form in the outer reaches of the universe. The torch he waved aloft flared forth in pulsing rhythms of the dance, and stars expired before its dazzling brilliance. All that was not Shiva dancing began to fall apart, disintegrate, evaporate into the thin vapors of apparent nothingness. The dance of joy became *Tāṇḍava*, the Dance of Eternity, a dance of universal death and joy.

At the climax of the nothingness, when only the audience of gods remained to contemplate his grace and power, Shiva paused, and then began again—as slowly as before. His was to be a dance of the full measure of grace. He had danced the worlds out, now he danced them in again, flinging stars into their heavens, evoking life upon the earth, a kinesthesis of overflowing grace and love. So Shiva danced a new world and a new age into being, and had himself a day of lovely sport and playful joy. The world is here because Shiva danced, but can we know, because the world is here, that Shiva has been dancing?

When he brought the world very near to where we stand, the dance closed quietly and he slipped back to the cosmic fellowship. After all, it matters not to god to dance a world out or in, or whether wise men will believe in him or not. He danced. It was enough.

GANESHA:
THE ELEPHANT-HEADED GOD

ONE OF THE MORE interesting and animated cycles of stories
of the gods has to do with Ganesha (Ganapati), the elephant-
headed son of Pārvatī and Shiva. There are frequently several
different accounts of each incident. The following stories are
mainly from the *Shiva Purāṇa*, the *Ganapati Upanishad*, *Mahābhārata* and Karapātrī's *Śri Bhagavat tattva*.

With his characteristic indifference to propriety Shiva frequently entered the room while Pārvatī was engaged in her
bath. She was disturbed by these interruptions and determined
to have a proper guard at her door to ward off any intruder.
Taking some of the scurf of her body and mixing it with dust
and oils she shaped a handsome, young man and gave him
life with waters from the Ganges. This son, Ganesha, was stationed at the door to guard her privacy.

Soon Shiva came bursting in, but was stopped by the stub-
born new guard, who even struck Shiva in protecting the door.
Shiva called upon his demon devotees to slay the rash fellow,
but the powerful Ganesha held them all in check. To prevent
frustration of the will of the dangerous god, Vishnu sent his
voluptuous Māyā to pass before Ganesha, which distracted him
for a moment, and one of the assailants slashed off his head.

Pārvatī was furious at the killing of her son, and threatened
enormous destruction in her rage. To placate her, Shiva prom-

ised to restore Gaṇesha to life, and sent his troops to bring the first head they could find. It was the head of an elephant, which Shiva used to restore life for Gaṇesha and peace at home. He was delighted with his young son and made him chief of his troops (though later Subrahmaṇya seems to have taken over this role). In particular Gaṇesha became the remover of all obstacles to one's truest purposes. His mount is a rat, a former demon which he had subdued, but which knows no obstacle on the way to the granary.

Among the characteristics of Gaṇesha are his pot belly and enormous appetite. The story is told that one day there had been an unusually generous offering of sacrificial cakes, and Gaṇesha had eaten every one, till he was stuffed to the teeth. At evening he mounted his rat to ride home and was moving sleepily along when suddenly the steed spied a giant snake on the path ahead. Instinctively the rat bolted, throwing his overstuffed rider to the ground, where his distended stomach burst open and let cakes roll out upon the ground. Gaṇesha got up and instantly grabbed for every single spilled cake and stuffed all of them back into his paunch. To keep them from falling out anew, he seized the snake which had begun the mischief and wound and tied it around himself to hold the slit together. He then continued on his way.

In one account it is even said that the laughing of the moon and his constellation of wives caused Gaṇesha to break off a tusk and throw it at the moon, along with the curse which causes it still to lapse into darkness a part of every month.

In another account, however, he was guarding the privacy of Shiva and Pārvatī when Krishna arrived to return Shiva's axe. Krishna was impatient when his way was blocked by Gaṇesha and threw the axe at his head. Gaṇesha might easily have dodged the blow but was not willing to have his father's weapon be thought useless, so he permitted it to slice off one of his tusks.

Gaṇesha is the god of intelligence. This trait was shown when Shiva and Pārvatī called Gaṇesha and Subrahmaṇya, his younger brother, before themselves. The divine couple had determined to arrange a marriage for whichever one of their sons could go around the world most quickly. Subrahmaṇya took off like an arrow, but Gaṇeśa stepped back, bowed respectfully, and circled his parents from left to right, saying: "You are the universe in all its forms. The son who honors his parents with the rite of circumambulation has as much merit as he who goes around the world." (This last purports to be a quote from *Veda*.) His apt wit won him two wives, Buddhi (Wisdom) and Siddhi (Success).

This god is popular throughout India and has many philosophical as well as mythical meanings. He is the Lord of Categories (Gaṇapati), the visible form of the principle of principles. In different sects he is variously identified, but especially with Brihaspati, the teacher of the gods. His elephant head suggests his wisdom and power, his curved trunk the eternal *OM* and *svastika,* and his power, wisdom and cleverness make him able to remove all obstacles which threaten the achievement of the goals of life. He guards the door of Shiva shrines and is worshipped and venerated by each entering pilgrim to remove the obstacles which might in any way interfere with the true worship of the god who rises within. He is patron deity of students, teachers, and all who live by intellectual activity. "O Gaṇesha, prepare for us the way: remove for us the obstructions in life's true path."

COMMENTARY

Stories of the Gods

WHAT DO HINDUS MEAN by "god" or the "gods"? This question is not easy to answer because there are different kinds of answers. One type of answer would trace the historical development of the concepts of the gods from the Vedic to the modern period. Indra, the thunderbolt-wielding King of the devas, Varuṇa, deity of the sky, Vāyu, the wind god, Sūrya, the Sun—and a whole cluster of deities associated in one way or another with sun, light, and weather—would have to be interpreted both in direct traditional descriptions from the Vedas and also in their functional social, psychic and historical roles. The priests among the gods, Agni, Soma, Brihaspati, Brahmā, would have to be distinguished from the beings (both men and devas) whom they served. In time these associates of the Brahmin priests endured through transitions to reemerge in the company of the great popular gods and their ranks of associates and consorts. A third stage in this evolution from Vedic to modern would be the emergence of the particular forms of god which are the special objects of popular devotion. The stories and deeds which lead Krishna, Rāma, the dancing Shiva, for example, to be venerated as forms of deity and also as lovers, teachers, and helpers of mankind, reflect this development. One might wish to develop a "history of the gods" to interpret their Hindu meaning.[1]

Another way of dealing with the question would be to follow the Vedāntic lead and treat the question of the meaning of god as a philosophical inquiry. In this approach one would ask whether Hinduism is or is not polytheism, dualism, monism, and in what sense one understands any such answer. The Vedāntic monist answer that all gods, and all else as well, are but forms of God is one such Hindu view. It is almost inevitable that this kind of analysis will follow in some respects Shankara's view that the nature of the concept follows the capacities of the thinker, so that differences in concepts of the "gods" actually reflect differences in human capacities for understanding. The supreme viewpoint holds that the many are but one, but not everyone knows or can know that supreme viewpoint.[2]

Thirdly, one can follow the various cycles of the stories of the gods, not so much to establish historic precedence and sequence or to achieve philosophical clarity (though both are worthy goals) but to attain some functional sense of what god has become for the Hindu, of the emotional and structural service performed by these ideas.[3]

[1] Several studies of this sort are available including: Carpenter, Joseph E., *Theism in Medieval India* (Oxford Univ. Press, 1915); Elmore, Wilber T., *Dravidian Gods in Modern Hinduism* (Nebraska Univ. Publications, 1915); Keith, Arthur B., *The Religion and Philosophy of the Veda and Upanishads* (Cambridge: Harvard University Press, 1925); Manicol, Nicol, *Indian Theism from the Vedic to the Muhammadan Period* (London: Norgate and Williams, 1921).

[2] For examples of this approach see: Deussen, Paul, *Outline of the Vedanta System of Philosophy* (New York: Grafton Press, 1906); Kumarappa, Bharatan, *The Hindu Conception of Deity as Culminating in Ramanuja* (London: Luzac Publishing Co., 1934); Mahadevan, T. M. P., *The Philosophy of Advaita* (Madras, 1938); Sastri, Suryanarayana, "The Philosophy of Saivism," in *Cultural Heritage of India*, Bhattacharya, Haridas (ed.), (Calcutta: The Ramakrishna Mission Institute of Culture, 1956), Vol. IV; Zimmer, Heinrich, *Philosophies of India* (New York: Pantheon Books, 1951); and Danielou, Alain, *Hindu Polytheism* (New York: Pantheon Books, 1964).

[3] The major sources for this approach are: Zimmer, Heinrich, *Myth and Symbols in Indian Art and Civilization* (New York: Pantheon Books,

The most striking fact which would emerge from any collection of the stories of the gods is that they are primarily objects of devotion. In some sense they do explain things, but the explanations are often more difficult than the questions they are supposed to answer. The stories we have collected here are by no means a full representative sample of the range of the stories of the gods, but even so they reveal some of the functions of these stories, and introduce in their very content some of the ways in which Hindus think.

One of the functions provided by the stories of the gods is *to coordinate the elements of the tradition* so that change is seen as organic to the process and does not appear as a contradiction or as the introduction of novelty, but only as the necessary unfolding of earlier states and forces. For example, in *Rig Veda*, Vishnu is important chiefly as a deity who encompassed the universe in three steps. In the account we have here, the *Purāṇas* have elaborated that reference into the Vāmana *avatāra*, have found numerous devotional and inspirational values in the account, and have brought together the ancient Vedic with the later Purāṇic traditions. By identifying this event, reported in the earliest *Veda*, as only one example of a sequence of such *avatāras*, it is not merely a question of the elaboration of an earlier account. It connects all accounts of *avatāras* with *Veda* by implication.

A second function of these stories is *to provide the basis for the integration of virtually any religious movement into the larger framework of Hinduism.* Here the principle has been established that god can take any form he will, and that in numerous moments of need and amid auspicious events he has done so. Any heroic figure, therefore, who has done what an *avatāra* should do in his circumstances, must have been an *avatāra* (or at least may have been). Stories of his heroic acts can be given full credence. Such accounts in no way need to be balanced off against each other. The descendants, associates and consorts of the various deities provide adequate opportunity for appropriate ranking and placement of any local deity in relation to the great, encompassing gods of the central tradition. The existence of different birth stories for such deities, and different accounts of their feats, suggest this gradual coalescing and interrelation of the stories. The great tradition has in it the natural capacity to provide room with dignity for any smaller units which need to be included. This rule, of course, will not apply if the local tradition denies the vision of the supreme god. Christainity, for example, was not willing to accept the view that Jesus may have been merely another *avatāra* of Vishnu in a different time and place, and Islam was unwilling to believe that Allah had truly manifested Himself in such forms as Rāma and Krishna. Such groups could not be assimilated into the main stream of Hinduism. On the other hand, we can see here how some Hindus sought to absorb and transcend the Buddhist movement by reaching out to show that the Buddha (and Mahāvira) were in fact forms of Vishnu, but also clearly differentiating the false doctrines which Vishnu had presented while in those forms from the true doctrines and powers displayed in his other incarnations. One then admires the Buddha and knows why at some points his teachings have the ring of truth, but at the same time one is justified in judging his teachings from the more orthodox Vedic tradition to show that his followers have created a misleading and dangerous doctrine because of their own failures.

A third function shown in some of these stories is *to give persons more complete access to the gods*. It is above all the human *avatāras* which do this, and preeminently the stories of Rāma and Krishna (including Shaivites as well as Vaishnavites). The fantastic sweep of existence and time is so incredible that knowledge of that sort is usually beyond our capacity to appreciate. But love and delight, honor and integrity, filial obedience and family jealousy, human emotions and different ways in which any event will be interpreted by those who experience it, these are familiar and relevant. Such gods can live in imagination and in dramatic enactment; they can be sung about and enjoyed. The imagery of the accounts stimulates popular rather than only philosophical imagination and the baby Krishna, the sporting young woodland lover, the proud prince, can become emotionally and aesthetically real. It is no great wonder that this has been the direction for so much Hindu development—and even, in recent times, a stir among North Americans. Not only do these images bring god closer to man and man to god, but they also provide in their enactment devotional exercises which arouse and employ a wide range of human emotions and responses.

A fourth function of these cycles of stories is *to develop, though often more by implication, the theme of the divine līlā*. This theme is found in both Vaishnavite and Shaivite cycles. Perhaps here is one of the truly basic differences between Hindu and prevailing Western presuppositions. Most Judeo-Christian interpretations hold that creation of the world and men is serious business for God. It is not that the job is difficult for Him, but that this creative act is important to Him: it is His purpose, intention or will. The Hindu view of *līlā*, by contrast, suggests that creation is a by-product of an act which can be said to have no purpose beyond itself and its own immediacy. The principle also attaches to other achievements of the gods. Baby Krishna kicks a cart and destroys a demon. Rāma befriends an exiled king and secures the essential assistance of Hanuman. Decisive matters so often are side effects of acts for other ends. God plays and worlds are born. No justification or purpose for an act of god is required outside of the act itself. Human creativity, like divine, may sometimes be the unintended (but not rejected) by-product of self-justifying joy.

A fifth function of these stories is *to provide levels of interpretation and styles of response which appeal to the wide variation in human capacity, interest, and power of response*. The great mother goddess is always present—in the local deity of childbirth and maternity, in consorts of the gods and in the *shakti* of the great god himself. From village girl to yogic master, each can find the object of his or her devotion and concern. Hinduism has something for everyone, something which may be enjoyed for itself or followed as a path which leads to something else beyond, or even to the no-thing from which all somethings come.

Finally these stories function *to give the base to the religio-*

aesthetic cycle of the Hindu calendar. Each holy place has its stories and its days, its pilgrimmage path, its holy shrines. There is considerable variation in these cycles in different communities, but most of the major religious festivals of both country as a whole and of particular villages, revolve around such stories as these.

CONCLUSION

THERE ARE MANY WAYS in which people have attempted to identify the basic principle of Hinduism. We have not found another, but rather have followed the natural approach by which a Hindu young person would have acquired his heritage of myth and hope. No simple, single basic principle emerges. One is led to various possibilities. For some it is enough to believe that the world order in all its incredible vastness and intricacy is nevertheless an expression of the divine order, that the very life one has right here and now is divine life, to be lived, not rejected. The remote austerities and philosophies of *yogis* may be admired in a way, but in practical terms they represent only an occasional act of charity, a few *paise* for the holy man. Such life is neither sought nor feared. For the great majority the religious life is much more immediate. It consists of daily rituals in the home, occasional visits to the temple for the offer of praise and sacrifice, the vigorous celebration of holidays, rare but moving pilgrimages to some holy place to venerate its holy day. By such acts one is assured that all which needs doing is being done, that one's true destiny belongs—equally with highly placed or holy folk— to the great eternal system which pervades all. Religious life is much a matter of feeling—feelings associated with family, its daily food and growing children, feelings associated with the dark mysterious womb of the temple, where continuous devotion pours forth to Vishnu or Shiva and where acts of veneration, remembrance and hope are thought or done before other shrines. Religion is the response of surging crowds to the presence of the deities in procession along the temple streets. It is the remembrance of ecstatic songs of love. It is much besides the philosopher and his books.

Beyond these popular stories lie other stories with more philosophical tone and content, and then the sacred texts themselves. But beyond all these is the religion which helps people feel that their fate is secure, and their way is known in the way of the Universal Truth. For village life, for the traditional learned academies, for forest-dwelling hermits and *bhaktis,* for university classes, and for popular lectures in the public halls, for each there is a way. One cannot live a life from which god is absent.

Some find the pious faith which these stories proclaim and portray is adequate. Some go farther and study the different ways of devotion. Some respect, and a few even follow, the path of the *saṁnyāsin.* Truth along these paths is harder to find and requires more help. Not merely the promises of a priest, but the teaching of a guru is required. Yet beyond even intellect is the still more difficult way of insight itself—the austerities, devotion, emancipation from fear and temptability which is for the rarest of all men, the living saint (*jīvan-mukti*).

All these are Hinduism and more besides. It is natural to follow, as children do, the teaching contained in simple stories, the truth dressed in the costume of action. It is also natural to grow beyond such childishness, to want harder lessons, and to review the easy ones with eyes to see their deeper meanings. Followed faithfully, the Indian imagination will lead beyond itself to the deeper reflection toward which it points.

SELECTED BIBLIOGRAPHY

The books listed here include those which contain further Hindu stories, serious religious texts, and others which may be of interest to beginning students of Hinduism.

Aiyar, V. Krishnaswami. *Stories from Indian Classics*. P. Sankaranarayanan (tr.). Bombay: Bharatiya Vidya Bhavan, 1966.

Basham, A. L. *The Wonder that Was India*. New York: Grove Press, 1959.

Bhandarkar, R. G. *Vaishnavism, Saivism, and Minor Religious Systems*. Varanasi: Indological Book House, 1965.

Bhattacharji, Sukumari. *The Indian Theogony*. Cambridge: Cambridge University Press, 1970.

Bhattacharyya, Haridas (ed.) *The Cultural Heritage of India*. Calcutta: The Ramakrishna Mission Institute of Culture, 1956.

Bloomfield, Maurice (tr.). *Hymns of the Atharva Veda*. Vol. XLII, *Sacred Books of the East*, Oxford: Clarendon Press, 1897.

———. *The Religion of the Veda*. New York: G. P. Putnam's Sons, 1908.

Brown, W. Norman, "The Basis for the Hindu Act of Truth," *Review of Religion*, Vol. 5 (Nov. 1940), pp. 36–45.

Carpenter, Joseph E. *Theism in Medieval India*. London: Williams and Norgate, Ltd., 1921.

Chan, Wing-tsit; Isma'il R. Faruqi, Joseph H. Kitagawa, and P. T. Raju. *The Great Asian Religions*. New York: Macmillan, 1968.

Chandradhar, Sharma. *A Critical Survey of Indian Philosophy*. London: Rider and Company, 1960.

Charria-Aguilar, O. L. (ed.). *Traditional India*. Englewood Cliffs: Prentice-Hall, 1964.

Chatterjee, Satischandra. *The Fundamentals of Hinduism*. Calcutta: DasGupta and Company, 1950.

Coomaraswamy, A. K. *The Dance of Siva*. New York: Farrar Straus and Company, 1957.

———. *Hinduism and Buddhism*. New York: Philosophical Library, 1943.

Danielou, Alain. *Hindu Polytheism*. New York: Pantheon Books, 1964.

———. *Yoga: The Method of Re-integration*. New York: University Books, 1955.

Dasgupta, S. N. *Hindu Mysticism*. New York: Ungar Press, 1927.

de Bary, William T. (ed.). *Sources of Indian Tradition*. New York: Columbia University Press, 1958.

de Bary, W. T., and A. T. Embree. *A Guide to Oriental Classics.* New York: Columbia University Press, 1964.

Deussen, Paul. *The Philosophy of the Upanishads.* Edinburgh: T. and T. Clark, 1906.

Dimcock, Edward S. and Denise Levertov (trs.). *In Praise of Krishna: Songs from the Bengali.* Garden City: Doubleday, 1964.

Dowson, John. *Classical Dictionary of Hindu Mythology.* London: Kegan Paul, 1961 (reprint of 1928 edition).

Dutt, Romesh C. (tr.). *The Ramayana and the Mahabharata: Condensed into English Verse.* New York: E. P. Dutton and Co., 1910.

Edgerton, Franklin. *The Bhagavad Gita.* New York: Harper, 1964.

———. *The Beginnings of Indian Philosophy.* Cambridge: Harvard University Press, 1965.

Eliade, Mircea. *Patterns in Comparative Religion.* Cleveland: Meridian Books, 1963.

———. *Yoga: Immortality and Freedom.* Princeton: Princeton University Press, 1969.

Eliot, Charles. *Hinduism and Buddhism: An Historical Sketch.* New York: Barnes and Noble, 1954.

Embree, Ainslie T. (ed.). *The Hindu Tradition.* New York: The Modern Library, 1966.

Farquhar, J. N. *Modern Religious Movements in India.* New York: Macmillan, 1924.

———. *An Outline of the Religious Literature of India.* London: Oxford University Press, 1920 (reprinted Delhi: Motilal Banarsidass, 1967).

Garratt, G. T. (ed.). *The Legacy of India.* London: Oxford University Press, 1937.

Ghosh, Oroon. *The Dance of Shiva and Other Tales from India.* New York: New American Library, 1965.

Gray, J. E. B. *Indian Folk-Tales and Legends.* London: Oxford University Press, 1961.

Griswold, H. D. *The Religion of the Rig Veda.* London: Oxford University Press, 1923.

Hackin, J. (et. al.). *Asiatic Mythology.* New York: Thomas Y. Crowell Co., n.d.

Hazra, R. C. *Studies in the Puranic Records on Hindu Rites and Customs.* Calcutta: University of Dacca, 1940.

Hiriyanna, M. *Outlines of Indian Philosophy.* London: Allen and Unwin, 1932.

Hopkins, Thomas J. *The Hindu Religious Tradition.* Encino (Cal.):
    Dickenson Publishing Co., 1971.
Hume, Robert E. (tr.). *Thirteen Principal Upanishads.* London:
    Oxford University Press, 1958.
Ions, Veronica. *Indian Mythology.* London: Paul Hamlyn, 1967.
Keith, Arthur B. *The Religion and Philosophy of the Veda and
    Upanishads.* Cambridge: Harvard University Press, 1925.
Kingsbury, F. and G. E. Phillip (trs.). *Hymns of the Tamil Śaivite
    Saints.* New York: Association Press, 1921.
Kitagawa, Joseph M. *Religions of the East.* Philadelphia: West-
    minster Press, 1968.
Kosambi, D. D. *Ancient India.* New York: Pantheon Books, 1965.
Lemaitre, Solange. *Hinduism.* New York: Hawthorne Books, 1959.
Lewis, Oscar. *Village Life in North India.* Urbana: University of
    Illinois Press, 1958.
MacDonell, A. A. *Hymns from the Rigveda.* London: Association
    Press, 1922.
––––––. *The Vedic Mythology.* Varanasi: Indological Book House,
    1963 (reprint of the 1897 edition).
Macnicol, Nicol. *Indian Theism from the Vedic to the Muham-
    medan Period.* London: Oxford University Press, 1915.
––––––. *Hindu Scriptures.* London: J. M. Dent, 1963.
Mahadevan, T. M. P. *Outlines of Hinduism.* Bombay: Chetana
    Press, 1956.
Majundar, R. C. and A. D. Pulsaker (eds.). *The History and Cul-
    ture of the Indian People.* Bombay: Bharatiya Vidya
    Bhavan, 5 vols., 1953.
Mascaro, Juan (tr.). *The Upanishads.* Baltimore: Penguin Books,
    1965.
Morgan, Kenneth W. (ed.). *The Religion of the Hindus.* New York:
    The Ronald Press Company, 1953.
McKim, Marriott (ed.). *Village India: Studies in the Little Com-
    munity.* Chicago: University of Chicago Press, 1955.
Nikhilananda, Swami. *Hinduism: Its Meaning for the Liberation
    of the Spirit.* New York: Harper and Row, 1958.
O'Malley, L. S. S. *Popular Hinduism.* Cambridge: Cambridge Uni-
    versity Press, 1935.
Piggott, Stuart. *Prehistoric India.* Baltimore: Penguin Books, 1961.
Radhakrishnan, Sarvepalli. *The Hindu View of Life.* New York:
    The Macmillan Company, 1968 (reprinted from 1927).
––––––. *Indian Philosophy.* 2 vols., New York: Macmillan, 1923,
    1927.

———. *The Principal Upaniṣads.* London: George Allen and Unwin, 1953.

———, and Charles A. Moore (eds.). *A Source Book in Indian Philosophy.* Princeton: Princeton University Press, 1967.

Rajagopalachari, C. *Mahabharata.* Bombay: Bharatiya Vidya Bhavan, 1966.

———. *Ramayana.* Bombay: Bharatiya Vidya Bhavan, 1965.

Raju, P. T. *Idealistic Thought of India.* London: Allen and Unwin, 1953.

Rao, P. Nagaraja. *Introduction to Vedanta.* Bombay: Bharatiya Vidya Bhavan, 1966

Renou, Louis. *Hinduism.* New York: Brazillier, 1961.

———. *Religions of Ancient India.* New York: Schocken Books, 1968.

Sarma, D. S. *Renascent Hinduism.* Bombay: Bharatiya Vidya Bhavan, 1960.

Seeger, Elizabeth (ed.). *The Five Sons of King Pandu; The Story of The Mahabharata.* New York: William R. Scott, Inc., 1967.

Sen, K. M. *Hinduism.* Baltimore: Pelican Books, 1962.

Singer, Milton (ed.). *Krishna: Myths, Rites and Attitudes.* Chicago: University of Chicago Press, 1968.

"Special Number on the Decipherment of the Mohenjodaro Script," *Journal of Tamil Studies,* Vol. II, No. 1 (May 1970).

Stevenson, Mrs. Sinclair. *The Rites of the Twice-born.* London: Oxford University Press, 1920.

Van Buitenen, J. A. B. *Tales of Ancient India.* Chicago: University of Chicago Press, 1959.

Verrier, Elwin. *The Myths of Middle India.* London: Oxford University Press, 1949.

Wheeler, Sir Mortimer. *Civilizations of the Indus Valley and Beyond.* New York: McGraw-Hill, 1966.

———. *The Indus Civilization.* Cambridge: Cambridge University Press, 3rd. ed. rev., 1968.

Whitehead, Henry. *The Village Gods of South India.* Calcutta: Association Press, 1921.

Wilson, H. H. *The Viṣṇu Purāṇa.* Calcutta: Punthi Pustak, 1961 (reprint of the 1840 edition).

Zaehner, R. C. *Hinduism.* London: Oxford University Press, 1962.

———. *Hindu Scriptures.* New York: Dutton, 1966.

Zimmer, Heinrich. *Myths and Symbols in Indian Art and Civilization.* New York: Harper, 1946.

———. (Joseph Campbell, ed.). *Philosophies of India.* New York: Pantheon Books, 1951.

GLOSSARY AND PRONUNCIATION GUIDE
TO HINDU TERMS

This text has used a simplification of Sanskrit forms and diacritical marks. The Ś, Ṣ, and Ç of Sanskrit have been uniformly rendered as Sh, the vowel Ṛ as Ri, Â as Ā. Where Anglicized or Americanized forms exist they have been followed. Accent marks have not been introduced. Commonly, accents fall on the first syllable of two syllable words, and in longer words on the next to last syllable when it is long, otherwise on the preceding syllable. A syllable is long if it contains a long vowel (ā, e, ī, o, ū or any dipthong), or if its vowel is followed by more than one consonant (except *h*). An *h* following a consonant is pronounced as an aspiration of the consonant (e.g., boat*h*ouse, ab*h*or).

In using Sanskrit words in English sentences it has become common to form plurals by adding *s*, although this is not the Sanskrit plural. This pattern has been adopted here where a singular form was especially awkward. The form and spelling of Sanskrit transliterations in the various stories follow those used by the original translator in most cases, though we have tried to reduce the variety where possible. Diacritical markings follow the pattern used by Alain Danielou in *Hindu Polytheism*, with the exceptions noted above. For purposes of pronunciation some approximate English equivalents are given below.

Pronunciation

VOWELS		CONSONANTS	
a	p*a*rt	g	*go*
ā	f*a*ther	ṇ	si*ng*
i	p*i*t	ñ	si*ng*e
ī	*e*ve	c	ch as in *ch*uckle
u	f*u*ll	ṭ	*t*rue
ū	r*u*de	ḍ	*d*rum
ṛ(ri)	merr*i*ly	th	boat*h*ouse
e	*ay* in s*ay*	dh	ma*dh*ouse
ai	*ai*sle	ṡ	*s*ure
au (ou)	h*ou*se	s	*sh*ine
o	g*o*	s	*s*it

Glossary

Aditi most ancient of all the goddesses; the primordial vastness; mother of Vishnu in the Vāmana incarnation

Āgamas ancient myths and rituals of the Shaivite cults, texts

Agni the Vedic god-priest; Fire; mediator between men and gods; witness of all actions

260

amrita   the elixir produced by churning the Ocean of Milk; source of life and immortality

anavam (Tamil)   ignorance

annaprāshana   a domestic ceremony of the first feeding of solid food to an infant

apsaras   heavenly nymphs and courtesans; unmanifest potentialities

Āranyakas   the forest books; a third class of Vedic literature

arghya   presentation of delicacies to welcome a guest

artha   aim, advantage, wealth, property; that for which one goes

āshrama   a forest hermitage; a remote dwelling for ascetic sages

āshramas   the stages of life; student, householder, hermit and beggar

Āshraya Bhagavan   that God on whom everything rests—He who offers support, protection, refuge (Vishnu)

ashvattha   the sacred fig tree

asura   an enemy of the devas (gods); powerful being wrongly inclined

Atharva Veda   the fourth of the principal Vedic Samhitās, primarily composed of prayers, charms and incantations associated with health and good fortune

ātman   Self, Soul, Spirit; the inner essence of life and feeling; also Soul of the Universe (Brāhman)

avatāra   a descent or appearance of a god in the universe, especially appearance or incarnation of Vishnu

Ayodhyā   capital city of the Kosala kingdom in the Rāmāyana

Bādarāyana   a name for Vyāsa, reputed author of Purānas, etc.

Bali   King of the Asuras (defeated by Vishnu in the dwarf avatāra)

Bhagavadgītā   "The Lord's Song," famous episode from the Mahābhārata in which Krishna explains Hindu philosophy to Arjuna

Bhagavan   a devotional name; "All Powerful"; the presiding deity

Bhāgavata Purāna   one of the mythical histories of the gods and ancient men, especially dedicated to Vishnu in His many forms

Bhairava   the god Shiva (Rudra) in his most destructive aspect and terrifying form, as a naked ascetic who takes pleasure in destruction

bhakta   a devotee

bhakti   devotion, attachment, love, worship

Bharat(a)   half-brother of Rāma, who ruled in his place while Rāma was in exile; also an Indian name for India

bhikkshu (bhikku-Pali)   beggar; a monk in the fourth stage of life

Bhu   the Earth, usually as a goddess; That-Which-Became

Bhūmi-Prithivī   names for earth goddesses

bhūtas   (1) ghosts associated with Shiva; (2) the basic elements (earth, water, fire, air, ether)

bhuvas   the heaven-worlds between the earth and the sun

Brahmā   "The Immense Being," the god who creates the universe, also known as Prajāpati and Hiraṇyagarbha; rides a swan or goose, sits or stands on a lotus, residence is the universe, has four heads and arms; not the object of cult worship, but is respected and venerated in all traditions

brahmacārin   religious studentship, the first stage of life of holiness

Brahman   the impersonal spirit that pervades the universe, the ultimate principle of reality

Brāhmaṇas   Vedic writings containing the dicta of priests on matters of faith and cult

Brahmāstra   a supernatural weapon, possessed by Brahmā and given to Indrajit

Brahmin (Brāhmaṇa)   a member of the priestly caste; highborn

Brahmopadesha   ceremony of the assignment of a boy to his Brahmin teacher

Brihaspati   teacher and priest of the Vedic gods, essential to ritual sacrifice

Bru   the Earth, usually as a goddess; That-Which-Became

Buddha   in Hinduism, the principle of awakened intellect; title of the deceiver

chakra   the discus of Vishnu; a wheel

Chārvāka   a form of Indian philosophy generally identified as materialism and strict empiricism

chatur yuga   a sequence of four ages (Krita, Treta, Dvapara and Kali)

Dāitya and Dānava   Asura, opponents of the Aryan gods; genii

Deccan   a large triangular plateau covering most of peninsular India south of the Godavari River

deva   deity; the shining one

Devī   the Shakti or power of Shiva as "Resplendent One"

dharma   a very complex Hindu term; religious law, duty, order, teachings

Dharmashāstra   authoritative or canonical compend of laws

dharmātma   having virtue as one's nature

Durgā   consort of Shiva, also Kālī; "Fearsome"; "Beyond Reach"

Gandharva   celestial musician, often consort of the apsara

Ganesha   Elephant-headed god; son of Shiva and Pāruatī

Gaṅgā (Ganges)   Goddess; the Purifier; river Ganges; the heavenly river (Milky Way), underworld river and earthly river which cross at the City of Shiva (Banaras, Varanasi)

Garuḍa   the great Eagle which is the mount of Vishnu

Gāyatrī Mantra   the most important of the mystic chanted Vedic formulas; praise to the sun

ghee   clarified butter; a gift in hospitality and an essential in many religious ceremonies

Goloka   "Cow Heaven"; the paradise presided over by Surabhi, the cosmic cow of plenty

Gopīs   the "Cow Maidens" who were lovers of Krishna

grihastha   a householder, the second stage of the life of a twice-born Hindu

guṇa   quality, virtue or nature of a thing; "a single thread"

Guru   the religious teacher; god incarnate in the teacher

Hanuman   the monkey-god companion and aide for Rāma; son of the wind-god

Hari   one of the names of Vishnu—the Remover of Ignorance and Sorrow

Indra   King of the gods in the Vedic tradition, ruler of the sky-world, wields the thunderbolt, rides the elephant, represents the East, is often drunk and lustful, dispenses rain

Jainism   the name of one of a series of religious reform movements apparently in the sixth century before our era; an ascetic approach to the religious life

jātakarma   domestic religious birth ceremony

jīva   Soul or Self; may mean ātman with its karmic burden

jñāna   knowledge, wisdom, especially of religion and philosophy

Kailās (Kailāsa)   the mythical pleasure-mountain of Shiva in the Himalayas

kālakāla   an occasional name for Shiva, conqueror of Time

kālakūta   name of the poison drunk by Shiva to save the world

Kālī   goddess, shakti of Shiva, destructivity; naked, tongue lolling, she stands on the dead universe, wears a garland of skulls of children, holds a blood-dripping head and sword

kali yuga   the "black" age, the fourth and last in the devolution of the universe; the current age; time of lawlessness

Kalki   the Fulfiller, the avatāra yet to come, riding a white horse and with a sword blazing like a comet

kalpa   a day of Brahma, a period of 1,000 yugas, used somewhat like "age" or "eon"; duration of one world system

kāma   wish, desire, longing, love, pleasure

Kapālinī   One of the consorts of Shiva; "Adorned with Skulls"

karman (karma)   deed, work, action, sacred act or rite; the Law of Karma refers to the idea of an invariable connection between the performance of any act and the enjoyment or suffering due to the performance of that act

Kashyapa   "Vision," the husband of Aditi and father of the twelve sovereign principles; perhaps a pre-Aryan deity

kathā   story, tale, fable or discussion (literally, "telling the how")

krita yuga   the golden age; name of the first yuga; lucky number

kriyā   an action or performance, especially a religious act or rite
Kshatriya   the princely (second) caste, or one who belongs to it; a ruler, prince or warrior
Kubera   the God of Riches, regent of the North, chief of yakshas, half-brother of Rāvana
Kūrma   the name of Vishnu in the Tortoise avatāra
kusha (kāśā)   sacred grass essential to Vedic rituals
Lakshmī (Shrī)   principal consort of Vishnu; Goddess of Fortune, beauty, power of multiplicity
līlā   play, effortless action; also a basic Hindu teaching of god's creation/destruction as merely "play" for him
liṅga (liṅgam)   the object of worship in a Shiva shrine; a phallic symbol associated with the generative powers of the universe
loka   open space, place, the world; used in compounds to identify different world-systems
Mādhavi   bride of Vishnu as God of Knowledge
Mahābhārata   a great epic compendium which enshrines much of the legendary tradition of India; generally tells the story of the struggles between the Pandavas and the Kurus
mahat   transcendent principle of intellect; principle of manifestation, intellect, analytical consciousness
Mahāvīra   the great one; a title, usually for one of the founders of Jainism
Mahāyogi   the Great Contemplative; one of the names of Shiva
Maitreya   "Friendliness," one of the ten divine sons of Brahmā's mind; tells the story of the Buddha avatāra
Mandara   "Slow Mountain," the great mountain used to churn the Ocean of Milk
mantra   sacred utterances used in worship; a thought-form involving sounds and images designed to "realize" the object
Manu   first man, the Lawgiver; born in each creation to perform sacrifices and give man laws and traditions; the reign of a Manu is a manvantara and lasts about four and one third million human years
Matsya   the name of the Fish avatāra of Vishnu
Māyā (māyā)   the power of illusion, appearance of motion, change, difference, the world from the empirical standpoint; a form of Vishnu; source of the cosmos and of the consciousness perceiving it
moksha   liberation from transmigration and limitation; the ultimate goal of the Hindu; also mukti (mutti), nirvāṇa
muhūrta   a measure of time equal to forty-eight minutes of English time; thirty muhurtas equal one (twenty-four-hour) day
mukti   relief of souls from the bondage of karma; also moksha
Muni   sage, seer or ascetic
nāga (Nāga)   snake, divine power of the underworld, dan-

gerous but sometimes helpful to men; Kings of the Nāga include Sesha, Takshaka and Vāsuki

nāmakarma   domestic religious ceremony in which the first personal name is given to a child on the eleventh day after birth

Nandi   "The Joyful," the bull which is the mount of Shiva and devotee and protector of Shiva shrines; embodiment of sex impulse

Nara-Simha   the name of Vishnu in the form of the Man-Lion Avatāra

Nārāyaṇa   a name of Vishnu, meaning "Moving on the Waters" and "Abode of Man"; may refer to the rest of Vishnu on Sesha

Nāṭarāja   King of the Dance; name of the dancing Shiva

nirvāṇa   Buddhist term for the ultimate liberation, freedom from all limitations and suffering, the Absolute

Om-garam   the great symbol *OM* (sounds A–U–M), said to include all language and meaning; indestructible sound; the "Immensity"

padya   ritual presentation of water for the foot washing of a guest

Pāñchajanya   Vishnu's conch shell horn

Pañchatāntra   a collection of Indian fables from very ancient times, probably before the second century B.C.E.

pañchāyat   leaders of a village or of a caste

Parāshara   means "Crusher," teacher or father of Vyāsa, compiler of the scriptures

Parashurāma   the name of Vishnu in the Avatāra of Rāma with the Axe

Pārijāta   the celestial tree emerging from the Ocean of Milk, later carried off by Krishna

Parjanya-Vāruṇa   Vedic god(s) of rain and Lord of the Waters of earth and sky; Vāruṇa is the Binder, later Law of the Gods

Pārvatī   Daughter of the Mountain, principal consort of Shiva (Shakti); the yoni or female emblem which embraces the liṅga in the sanctuary; the coiled energy of consciousness (Kuṇḍalinī)

Pitri   the Ancestor, first progenitor of the human race; immortal and equal to the gods; object of homage (Shraddha)

Prajāpati   Lord of Progeny, the creative impulse which creates the gods (devas), world and men; later called Brahmā

prakriti   Nature; the original form; that which one presupposes

pralaya   dissolution and rest of the universe

Prithivī   Earth (as Goddess) after it was raised to the surface of the cosmic ocean by Vishnu as Varāha; the Extended One

pūjā   worship by an individual which may be done in the home, temple or universe

Pumsavana (pum̐s-savana)   a domestic religious ceremony designed to secure a son, held on a mother's first perception of signs of living conception

punyashetras   auspicious or virtuous places which are objects of pilgrimage

Purāṇas   a class of Hindu literature containing traditional accounts of the gods, creation, first man, etc.; Purāṇas are considered edifying but do not have the scriptural status of Vedas

rāga   coloring, affection, feeling, passion; often used in an aesthetic sense

Rāja (rājan)   King, Prince, powerful

rajas   the second of the three major qualities; soul darkening passion, activity, movement, change, ambition; originally atmosphere, vapor, gloom, darkness; sometimes associated with passion

Rākshasa   Night Wanderer (of various sorts); generally they devour human beings, disturb sacrifices, haunt nights, can assume various forms at will; Rāvaṇa was Rākshasa King of Lanka

Rāma   Rāmachandra—Rāma the Charming, the avatāra of Vishnu in the form of the Iksvaku King; Rāma, hero of the Rāmāyaṇa

Rāmāyaṇa   a major epic poem written by Vālmīki, telling the story of Rāma and Sita

rasa   feeling, sensibility; here a specific tradition of dance which imitates the account of Krishna with the Gopis

rasatala   one of the lower, demonic worlds; hell

Rāvaṇa   the demon (Rākshasa) King of Lanka (Ceylon), half-brother of Kubera, Lord of Riches, abductor of Sītā

Rig Veda (Ṛg Veda)   Ṛg Veda Saṁhitā—a collection of 1,028 ancient hymns comprising the oldest literary source of Indian religion

Rishi (ṛṣi)   an author of sacred hymns, an old saint; a pious man, especially an anchorite

rita   Vedic concept of the absolute cosmic order, inner reality and higher truth which all things exhibit; source of Karma

Rudra   the Vedic name of Shiva (meaning obscure); "Howler," "Weeper," Lord of Tears

sādhu   one who follows a straight path to the goal; generally means ascetic holy man

Sālagrāma   "Black pebbles"—the smooth, round, black stone sometimes used as a symbol of Vishnu

Sāma Veda   second of the major Vedic Saṁhitās; chants containing texts primarily concerned with the Soma sacrifice

samādhi   the state of contemplation of ultimate reality

saṁnayāsin   one who has abandoned all worldly affections; a man of the fourth order, final stage of life; an ascetic

samsāra   the passing through of existence; wandering of the soul from one existence to another; transmigration or reincarnation

samskāra   a preparation or purification; domestic religious ceremony for receiving the proper name of one's deity

Sāṅkhya   a school of Indian philosophy which stressed a dualistic metaphysics

Sarasvatī   "The Flowing One," Goddess of knowledge, daughter and consort of Brahmā; associated with speech, song, music, lute or vina, fertility and the famous river

sat   being, real, genuine, true or good

sattva   condition of being; beingness, existence; being good; the highest of the qualities; strong, real, good; first guṇa

satyakriyā   an act of truth or reality

Satyaloka   all the heavens over which Vishnu stepped in the Dwarf avatāra

satyavratá   a vow of truthfulness; to make or keep such a vow

secmanta (sīmanta)   a domestic religious ceremony which involves puiling of the hair on the head with a view to providing easy delivery of a child

Shaivite   an individual who belongs to one of the sects of worshippers of Shiva as the principal god

shakti   the energy or creative (or destructive) power of a god, usually visualized as a goddess, consort, or feminine aspect of the deity

Shaṅkara (Shaṅkarachārya)   eighth-century Hindu holy man, philosopher and devotee; developed Advaita philosophy of unqualified monism

shāstra   instructions, rules; a scientific or canonical work or directions

Shūtapatha Brāhmaṇa   the most important of the collections of priestly, ritualistic documents following the earliest Vedic literature

Shiva (Shiva)   the great god (Mahashvara); one of the most important Indian deities; in the Vedas called Rudra; Shiva means "Auspicious"; He is Lord of Sleep, Tears, Anger, Deadly Fire, Ghosts; associated with cremation grounds and with the "way of knowledge"; lives on Kailāsa (or wanders), rides Nandi the Bull.

Shivabhakta   lover or devotee of Shiva.

shloka   the thing heard (sound); a strophe, particularly of an epic poem

Shraddhā   homage, the rituals through which the ancestors are fed

Shrī   Lakshmī; Goddess, consort of Vishna

Shrī Bhāgavata   a devotional name for the Bhāgavata Purāṇa

Shrī Krishna (Kṛṣṇa)   one of the human avatāras of Vishnu, at the onset of the Kālī Age to reduce the powers of the asuras shruti   the hearing, a sacred utterance handed down by tradition; a sacred text; Veda, the most important religious texts

Shūdra   a man of the fourth caste; servant, laborer

siddhānta   the perfection of reasoning and attainment

Siddhi   perfection, that is of magic power; magician

Sītā   consort of Rāma in the Rāmāyaṇa; "Nature"; also Lakshmī

skandhas   ramifications, branches, used in the Buddhist sense to mean the elements of personality forming the empirical individual

soka   sorrow, pity

Soma   Vedic deity of the sacrifice, the offering, fuel, cold, moon, food, victim, sperm, wine, cool inward breath, night, dark blue, rain; one of the priestly divinities

Surabhī   "Fragrant Earth," the cow of plenty; the Earth Goddess in the form of the cow who nourishes all things

Sūrya   the god of the sun; the fiery principle

sutāla   one of the lower worlds, just below the quality of earth; a rather bland kind of hell with neither pain nor pleasure

svarga   generally heaven; the realm between the sun and the pole star

svastika   the cross with arms, symbol of Gaṇesha; the two directions of the bent arms can indicate both right- and left-hand tantra

Takshaka   one of the three kings of the great snakes (nāgas)

tamas   darkness, third and lowest of the three qualities (guṇas); spiritual darkness, infatuation, inertia, indolence

Tāṇḍava   Shiva's dance of destruction

tapas   usually austerities, ascetic devotions, voluntary suffering; also heat, fire

tejas   the power of fire that is thought

Tiruvāçagam   an extensive Tamil poem in praise of Shiva, written by Māṇikkavāçagar in perhaps the seventh or eighth century

treta yuga   the third age in the cycle of devolution of the universe

Trimūrti   god as seen in three forms—Vishnu, Brahmā, and Shiva

Umā   "Peace-of-the-Night," a consort of Shiva

upādesha   instruction or advice, in this case a ceremony of giving advice to one's son on an auspicious occasion; instruction concerning the worship of Shiva

upākarma   domestic ceremony of recognition of one's blessings by benefactors both divine and human

upanāyana   ceremony of investiture with the sacred thread of the upper castes; when one is given the name of god and the proper mantra

Upanishads   the fourth and last class of proper Vedic literature (shruti), generally reflective and philosophic

Vaikuṇtha   the Land of Vishnu, His heaven; the Land of No Hindrance, where there is no fear, represented by the parasol above Vishnu

Vaishnavite   a member of one of the sects of worshippers of Vishnu as the principal god

Vāishya   the folk or third caste; a man of the folk; agriculturalists and merchants

Vālmīki   poet and author of the Rāmāyaṇa

Vāmana   the name of Vishnu in the form of the Dwarf avatāra

vānaprastha   a wood-dweller, a hermit; one in the third stage of life

Vanas   forest dwellers; the allies of Rāma in the battle with Rāvana; monkeys, apes

Varāha   the name of Vishnu in the Boar avatāra

varṇa   caste, originally color or complexion

Vāruṇī   Goddess of Liquor, wine, intoxication; wife of Vāruṇa; produced from the Ocean of Milk

Vāsuki   one of the three great kings of the snakes (nāgas); rules the "City of Pleasures"; was used as the churn-rope in the churning of the Ocean of Milk

Vedán   a southern hill-tribe; rustic people (Tamil)

Vindhyā Mountains   a moutain range in North Central India, which in Aryan literature marked the boundary of the wilderness

Vishvakarma   the architect and engineer of the universe; designer of the weapons of the gods; builder of cities

Vraja   the pastoral district or village in which Shrī Krishna grew up

Vyāsa   "The Compiler," divided the traditional branches of knowledge into Vedas, Purāṇas and Epics; compiled the Mahābhārata

Yadava   the clan of which Krishna was a member

yajña   sacrifice; rituals of sacrifice from the whole of Vedic tradition, contrasted with individual, personal worship (pūjā)

Yaksha   heavenly-human being, geni, spirit of the earth, the speedy one; a class of devas

Yama   "The Binder," the god of death; sovereign of the dead, King of Justice; a Vedic deity, also called Death, Lord of Ancestors

yoga   a technique of introspection and intuitive perception; by derivation a path or discipline or method of religious experience

yogi   one who accepts the discipline of a path; a seeker of liberation; often a sage

yoni   the vagina; the female sex symbol, normally worshipped as embracing the liṅga in the sanctum of the temple